Heaven on Earth

A Treatise on
Christian Assurance

THOMAS BROOKS

THE BANNER OF TRUTH TRUST

THE BANNER OF TRUTH TRUST
3 Murrayfield Road, Edinburgh EH12 6EL
P.O. Box 621, Carlisle, Pennsylvania 17013, USA

★

First published 1654
First Banner of Truth edition 1961
Reprinted 1982
ISBN 0 85151 356 5

★

Reproduced, printed and bound in Great Britain by
Hazell Watson & Viney Ltd, Aylesbury, Bucks

CONTENTS

3

4

The things that accompany salvation: PRAYER.

The things that accompany salvation: PERSE-
VERANCE.

The things that accompany salvation: HOPE.

7

EPISTLE TO THE SAINTS

To all saints that hold to Christ the head, and that walk according to the laws of the new creature, grace, mercy, and peace be multiplied from God the Father, through our Lord Jesus Christ.

BELOVED IN OUR DEAREST LORD,

You are those worthies "of whom this world is not worthy," Heb. 11. 38. You are the princes "that prevail with God," Gen. 32. 28. You are those "excellent ones" in whom is all Christ's delight, Ps. 16. 3. You are his glory. You are his picked, culled, prime instruments which he will make use of to carry on his best and greatest work against his worst and greatest enemies in these latter days. You are "a seal" upon Christ's heart, you are "engraven on the palms of his hand"; your names are written upon his breast, as the names of the children of Israel were upon Aaron's breastplate; you are the "epistle of Christ"; you are the "anointed" of Christ; you have "the spirit of discerning"; you have "the mind of Christ." You have the greatest advantages and the choicest privileges to enable you to try truth, to taste truth, to apply truth, to defend truth, to strengthen truth, to uphold truth, and to improve truth. And therefore to whom should I dedicate this following discourse, but to yourselves? You have the next place to Christ in my heart; your good, your gain, your glory, your edification, your satisfaction, your confirmation, your consolation, your salvation, hath put me upon casting in my little, little mite into your treasure.

Beloved, you know that in the time of the law, God did as kindly accept of goats' hair and badgers' skins, of turtle-doves and young pigeons—they being the best things that some of his children had then to offer—as he did accept of gold, jewels, silk, and purple from others. I hope you will shew the same God-like disposition towards me, in a kind accepting of what is offered in this treatise to your wise and serious consideration. I could wish it better for your sakes, yet such as it is I do in all love and humility present you with, desiring the Lord to make it an internal and eternal advantage to you.

I shall briefly acquaint you with the reasons that have moved unworthy me,—who am the least of all saints, who am not worthy to be reckoned among the saints,—to present this following discourse to public view:

First, To answer the desires, and gratify the earnest and pious requests, of several precious souls, who long to have these things printed upon their hearts by the hand of the Spirit, that are printed in this book. God speaks aloud through the serious and affectionate desires of the saints; and this hath made me willing to echo to their desires. If great men's desires are to be looked upon as commands, why should good men's desires be looked upon with a squint eye? Seneca, a heathen, could say that *ipse aspectus boni viri delectat,* the very looks of a good man delight one. How much more then should the desires of a good man overcome one?

Secondly, The good acceptance, the fair quarter that my labours of the like nature have found among those that fear the Lord, especially that treatise called " Precious Remedies against Satan's Devices," hath encouraged me to present this to public view, not doubting but that the Lord will bless it to the good of many, as I know he hath done the former. Which that he may, I shall not cease to pray, that my weak service may be accepted of the saints, and that their "love may abound yet more and more in knowledge and in all sense," Philip. 1. 9-11. That they may approve things that are excellent; that they may be sincere, and without offence till the day of Christ; being filled with the fruits of righteousness, which are by Jesus Christ, unto the glory and praise of God.

Thirdly, It is exceeding useful to the saints at all times, but especially in changing times, in times wherein every one calls out, "Watchman, what of the night? watchman, what of the night? and the watchman answereth, The morning cometh, and also the night," Isa. 21. 11, 12. Ah!

Christians, the Lord is a-shaking heaven and earth; he is a-staining the pride of all glory; he is a-staining his garments with the blood of his enemies, he is renting and tearing, he is burning and breaking, he is pulling up and throwing down, Jer. 45. 4, 5. Now in the midst of all these turmoils and revolutions, thrice happy are those souls that have gained a well-grounded assurance of celestial things, Heb. 10. 34. Such souls will not faint, sink, nor shrink in an hour of temptation. Such souls will keep their garments pure and white, and will follow the Lamb wheresoever he goes, Rev. 3. 4, and 14. 4. Assurance is a believer's ark, where he sits, Noah-like, quiet and still in the midst of all distractions and destructions, commotions and confusions. They are doubly miserable that have neither heaven nor earth, temporals nor eternals, made sure to them in changing times, Ps. 23, 3, 4, Rev. 6. 12.

The *fourth* ground of my presenting this treatise to public view is, that little well-grounded assurance that is to be found among most Christians. Most Christians live between fears and hopes, and hang, as it were, between heaven and hell, sometimes they hope that their state is good, at other times they fear that their state is bad: now they hope that all is well, and that it shall go well with them for ever; anon they fear that they shall perish by the hand of such a corruption, or by the prevalency of such or such a temptation; and so they are like a ship in a storm, tossed here and there. Now that these weak souls may be strengthened, that these unstable souls may be established, that these disconsolate souls may be comforted, I have presented this tract to the world, not doubting but that if the Lord shall draw out their spirits to a serious perusal of it, they shall find, through the blessing of Jehovah, that it will contribute very much to their attaining a full assurance of their everlasting happiness and blessedness, as also to the keeping and maintaining of that full and blessed assurance; which that it may, I shall follow it with my prayers.

Fifthly, I have published this following discourse, remembering that my life is but a vanishing vapour, James 4. 14, and that the time of my sojourn in this world will be but short, Ps. 39. 12. Man's life is so short, that Austin doubteth whether to call it a dying life, or a living death. Man's life is but the shadow of smoke, the dream of a shadow. This present life is not *vita, sed ad vitam,* life, but a motion, a journey towards life (*Bernard*). The life of a Christian is rather *via* (journey) than *vita* (life), a step towards life rather than life. Yet do I believe that that is not a death, but life, that joins the dying man to Christ; and that is not a life, but death, that separates the living man from Christ.

I know I shall not speak long to friends, saints, or sinners; therefore I was the more willing to take the opportunity of preaching to you when I am dead. As Abel by his faith, he being dead, yet speaketh, Heb. 11. 4, so this treatise may speak and live, when I shall return to my long home, and fall asleep in the bosom of Christ. Christ's prophets and apostles, though they are now in heaven, yet by their doctrines, examples, and writings, they still preach to the saints on earth.

Zisca desired his skin might serve the Bohemians in their wars, when his body could no more do it. Oh that poor I, that have been but a little serviceable to the saints in my life, might by this, and my former weak labours, be much serviceable to them after my death! Books may preach when the author cannot, when the author may not, when the author dares not, yea, and which is more, when the author is not.

Sixthly, To testify my cordial love and affection to all the true lovers of Christ, and to let them know that they are all, though under different forms, precious in my eyes, and very near and dear unto my heart. I bless God I am, and I desire more and more to be, one with every one that is one with Christ, Philip. 4. 21; Col. 1. 4; 2 Thess. 1. 3. I would fain have as free, as large, and as sweet a heart towards saints, as Christ hath. For a wolf to worry a lamb is usual, but for a lamb to worry a lamb is unnatural; for Christ's lilies to be among thorns, is ordinary, but for these lilies to become thorns, to tear and fetch blood of one another, is monstrous and strange. Ah, Christians! can

12

Turks and Pagans agree? can Herod and Pilate agree? can Moab and Ammon agree? can bears and lions, can wolves and tigers agree? yea, which is more, can a legion of devils agree in one body? and shall not the saints, whom heaven must hold at last, agree?

Pancirolus tells us, that the most precious pearl the Romans had was called *unio* (unity). Oh, the union of saints is an invaluable pearl! The heathen man, by the light of nature, could say, " That the thickest wall of a city in peace, and the safest rampire in war, is unity." Verily all saints are one in Christ, all saints partake of the same spirit, promises, graces, and privileges. All saints are fellow-members, fellow-soldiers, fellow-travellers, fellow-heirs, fellow-sufferers, and fellow-citizens; and therefore I cannot, dare not, but love them all, and prize them all; and to evidence it, I have dedicated this treatise to the service of their souls.

Seventhly and lastly, To fence and fortify the souls of real, serious Christians against those brain-sick notions, and those airy speculations, and imaginary revelations, and enthusiastical fancies, by which many are sadly deluded and deceived, even, I would have almost said, to their eternal overthrow.

Thus have I given you a brief account of the reasons that have prevailed with me to publish this treatise to the world, and to dedicate it to yourselves. Let your hearts dwell on truth as the bee doth upon the flower; every truth being a flower of paradise that is more worth than a world.

Now the God of all grace fill your hearts and souls with all the fruits of righteousness and holiness, that you may attain unto a full assurance of your everlasting happiness and blessedness; which that you may is the sincere, earnest, and constant desire of him who is your soul's servant,

THOMAS BROOKS.

THE PREFACE

TOUCHING THE NATURE OF ASSURANCE

To be in a state of true grace is to be miserable no more;
it is to be happy for ever. A soul in this state is a soul near
and dear to God. It is a soul much beloved, and very highly
valued of God. It is a soul housed in God. It is a soul safe
in everlasting arms. It is a soul fully and eminently interested in all the highest and noblest privileges. The being
in a state of grace makes a man's condition happy, safe, and
sure; but the seeing, the knowing of himself to be in such
a state, is that which renders his life sweet and comfortable.
The being in a state of grace will yield a man a heaven
hereafter, but the seeing of himself in this state will yield
him both a heaven here and a heaven hereafter; it will
render him doubly blest, blest in heaven, and blest in his
own conscience.

Now assurance is a reflex act of a gracious soul, whereby
he clearly and evidently sees himself in a gracious, blessed,
and happy state; it is a sensible feeling, and an experimental
discerning of a man's being in a state of grace, and of his
having a right to a crown of glory; and this rises from the
seeing in himself the special, peculiar, and distinguishing
graces of Christ, in the light of the Spirit of Christ, or from
the testimony and report of the Spirit of God, "the Spirit
bearing witness with his spirit, that he is a son, and an heir-
apparent to glory," Rom. 8. 16, 17.

It is one thing for me to have grace, it is another thing
for me to see my grace; it is one thing for me to believe, and
another thing for me to believe that I do believe; it is one
thing for me to have faith, and another thing for me to
know that I have faith. Now assurance flows from a clear,
certain, evident knowledge that I have grace, and that I do
believe, &c.

Now this assurance is the beauty and top of a Christian's

glory in this life. It is usually attended with the strongest joy, with the sweetest comforts, and with the greatest peace. It is a pearl that most want, a crown that few wear. His state is safe and happy whose soul is adorned with grace, though he sees it not, though he knows it not.

Assurance is not of the essence of a Christian. It is required to the *bene esse* (the well-being), to the comfortable and joyful being of a Christian; but it is not required to the *esse,* to the being of a Christian. A man may be a true believer, and yet would give all the world, were it in his power, to know that he is a believer. To have grace, and to be sure that we have grace, is glory upon the throne, it is heaven on this side heaven. But more of these things you will find in the following discourse, to which I refer you.

CHAPTER I

Proofs that believers may in this life attain unto a well-grounded assurance of their everlasting happiness and blessedness.

The basis of assurance

The ground on which the apostle Paul builds his assurance is not any special revelation, but such a foundation as is common to all believers, as clearly appears from

Rom. 8. 32-34, *He that spared not his own Son, but delivered him up for us all, how shall he not with him also freely give us all things? Who shall lay anything to the charge of God's elect? It is God that justifieth; who is he that condemneth? It is Christ that died, yea rather, that is risen again, who is even at the right hand of God, who also maketh intercession for us.*

It is clear from these words, that this blessed apostle had not that glorious assurance that he speaks of in the last two verses of this chapter by immediate revelation, for he concludes it from such arguments as are general or common to all the godly; and therefore it roundly follows,

First, That believers may in this life attain unto a well-grounded assurance of their everlasting happiness and blessedness. So Hezekiah's assurance did spring from a principle that is common to all believers, 2 Kings 20. 3. Therefore,—

The purpose of Scripture is to help believers to obtain assurance

Secondly, It is the very scope and end of the Scripture to help believers to a well-grounded assurance of their everlasting happiness and blessedness. "These things," saith John, "have I written unto you that believe on the name of the Son of God, that ye may *know* that ye have eternal life," 1 John 5. 13. These precious souls did believe, and they had eternal life, in respect of the promise of eternal life, Titus 1. 2, and in respect of Christ their head, who had prepared their places beforehand in heaven, and who as a public person doth represent all his people, Eph. 2. 6; and they had eternal life in respect of the beginnings of it; for what is grace but glory begun? and what is glory but grace perfected? Grace is glory in the bud, and glory is grace at the full. Now, though they had eternal life in all these respects, yet they did not know it; though they did believe, yet they did not believe that they did believe; therefore the apostle, in those previous epistles of his, doth make it his business, by variety and plenty of arguments, to help all, but especially such as are weak in the faith, to a well-grounded assurance of their eternal welfare.

It is the very drift and design of the whole Scripture, to bring souls first to an acquaintance with Christ, and then to an acceptance of Christ, and then to build them up in a sweet assurance of their actual interest in Christ: which made Luther to say, " That he would not live in paradise, if he might, without the Word, but with the Word he could live in hell itself." No histories are comparable to the histories of the Scripture for,

1, Antiquity; 2, rarity; 3, variety; 4, brevity; 5, perspicuity; 6, harmony; 7, verity.

The word evidences truth, it evinces falsehood; it fights against folly, it opens the bowels of mercy, and it assures believing souls of eternal felicity. That is a precious word in Heb. 6. 18. God hath given us his word, his oath, his seal, that our consolation may be strong, and that our salvation may be sure. Now, what comfort can a believer have without assurance? It is the assurance of my interest in the land of Canaan, in gospel-cordials, in precious promises, and in a precious Christ, that comforts and delights my soul. It is not enough to raise strong consolation in my soul, barely to know that there are mines of gold, mountains of pearl, heaps of treasures, a land flowing with milk and honey, but it is the knowledge of my interest in these that raises joy in my soul. To know that there are such things, and that I have no interest in them, is rather a vexation than a consolation to me; to know that there is a feast of choicest delicacies, but not a taste for me; that there are pleasant fountains and streams, but I must perish for thirst in a wilderness; to know that there are royal robes for others, but I must die in my rags; to know that there is a pardon for others, but I must be turned off the ladder of life; to know that there is preferment for others, but I must still lie with Lazarus at Dives' door; such knowledge as this may well add to my vexation, but it will not add to my consolation.

It was rather matter of sorrow than joy to the men of the old world, to know that there was an ark, when they were shut out; and to the Israelites, to know that there was a brazen serpent set up, whereby others were cured, when they died with the stinging of the fiery serpents. So how can it comfort me to know that there is peace in Christ, and pardon in Christ, and righteousness in Christ, and riches in Christ, and happiness in Christ, for others, but none for me! Ah, this knowledge will rather be a hell to torment me than a ground of joy and comfort to me. But now God hath in the Scripture revealed who they are that shall be eternally happy, and how they may reach to an assurance of their felicity and glory; which made one [Luther] to say, "That he would not take all the world for one leaf of the Bible." The Bible is a Christian's *magna charta*, his chief evidence for heaven. Men highly prize, and carefully keep their charters, privileges, conveyances, and title-deeds of their lands; and shall not the saints much more highly prize, and carefully keep in the closet of their hearts, the precious Word of God, which is to them instead of all assurances for their maintenance, deliverance, protection, confirmation, consolation, and eternal salvation.

Many believers have obtained assurance

Thirdly, Other believers have in an ordinary way attained to a sweet assurance of their everlasting happiness and blessedness. "We know," saith the apostle, in the name of the saints, "that, if our earthly house of this tabernacle were dissolved, we have a building of God, an house not made with hands, eternal in the heavens. For in this we groan, earnestly desiring to be clothed upon with our house which is from heaven," 2 Cor. 5. 1, 2. Their assurance sets them in triumph upon the throne. We have a house, a house above, a house in heaven, a house not made with hands, eternal in the heavens. We have a house, a heavenly house, a house made by the greatest wisdom and the highest love; a house, that for honour, pleasures, riches, safety, stability, glory, and perpetuity, transcends all the royal palaces in the world. It is a house "not made with hands, but eternal in the heavens."

So the church: Solomon's Song 2. 16, "My beloved is mine, and I am his." I know, says the spouse, that Jesus Christ is mine. I can with the greatest confidence and boldness affirm it: he is my head, my husband, my Lord, my Redeemer, my Justifier, my Saviour; "and I am his. I am as sure that I am his, as I am sure that I live. I am his by purchase, and I am his by conquest; I am his by donation, and I am his by election; I am his by covenant, and I am his by marriage. I am wholly his; I am peculiarly his; I am universally his; I am eternally his. This I well know, and the knowledge thereof is my joy in life, and my strength and crown in death. So the church: Isa. 63. 16, "Doubtless thou art our father, though Abraham be ignorant of us, and Israel acknowledge us not. Thou, O Lord, art our Father, and our Redeemer, thy name is from everlasting." David could say, "The Lord is my portion for ever." Ps. 73. 25, 26; and at another time he could sweetly sing it out, "I am thine, save me"! Ps. 119. 94. Job could look through the darkest cloud, and see that his Redeemer lives, Job 19. 25. Thomas cries out, "My Lord, and my God". John 20. 28. And Paul trumpets it out, "That nothing should separate him from the love of Christ," Rom. 8. 38. 39; and that he had "fought a good fight, and finished his course; and that there was laid up for him a crown of righteousness," 2 Tim. 4. 7, 8.

By what hath been said, it clearly appears that other believers have obtained assurance in an ordinary way, and therefore believers now may attain to a sweet assurance of their everlasting happiness and blessedness. Certainly, God is as loving, and his compassions are as strong towards believers now, as ever they were to believers of old; and it makes as much for the honour of God, the lifting up of Christ, the stopping of the mouths of the wicked, and the rejoicing of the hearts of the righteous, for God to give assurance now, as it did for God to give it then.

God has promised assurance to his people

Fourthly, God hath by promise engaged himself to assure his people of their happiness and blessedness. "The Lord will give grace and glory, and no good thing will he withhold from them that walk uprightly," Ps. 84. 11. If he will withhold no good thing, then certainly he will not always withhold assurance, which is the great good thing, the only thing, the chiefest thing, the peculiar thing that believers seek after. So Ezek. 34. 30, 31, "Thus shall they know that I the Lord their God am with them, and that they, even the house of Israel, are my people, saith the Lord God. And ye my flock, the flock of my pasture, are men, and I am your God, saith the Lord God." So John 14. 21, 23, "He that hath my commandments, and keepeth them, he it is that loveth me; and he that loveth me shall be loved of my Father, and I will love him, and will manifest myself to him." "If any man love me," saith Christ, "he will keep my words: and my Father will love him, and we will come unto him, and make our abode with him." Now hath the Lord spoken it, and shall it not come to pass? Men say and unsay, they eat their words as soon as they have spoken them, but will God do so? Surely no, he is faithful that hath promised, "All the promises of God in him are yea, and in him amen," 2 Cor. 1. 20; that is, they are stable and firm, and shall really be made good. The promises are a precious book, every leaf drops myrrh and mercy, therefore sit down and suck at these breasts, warm thyself at this fire. God hath been always as good as his Word, yea, he hath sometimes been better than his Word; he hath ever performed, and he hath over performed. He promised the children of Israel only the land of Canaan, but he gave them, besides the whole land of Canaan, two other kingdoms which he never promised. Ah, how often hath God gone before us with his blessings, and given us such mercies as have been as far beyond our hopes as our deserts. How hath God, in these days of darkness and blood, gone beyond the prayers, desires, hopes, and confidences of his people in this land, and beyond what we could read in the book of the promises. Satan promises the best, but pays with the worst: he promises honour and pays with disgrace, he promises pleasure and pays with pain, he promises profit and pays with loss, he promises life and pays with death; but God pays as he promises, all his payments are made in pure gold; therefore take these promises wherein God hath engaged hi iself to assure thee of his love, and spread them before the Lord, and tell him that it makes as well for his honour as thy comfort, for his glory as for thy peace, that he should assure thee of thy everlasting happiness and blessedness.

The springs of assurance are in the saints

Fifthly, There is in all the saints the springs of assurance, and therefore they may attain to assurance.

Precious faith is one spring of assurance, and this is in all the saints, though in different degrees, 2 Peter 1. 1. " Simon Peter, a servant and an apostle of Jesus Christ, to them that have obtained like precious faith with us, through the righteousness of God, and our Saviour Jesus Christ." Faith, in time, will of its own accord raise and advance itself to assurance. Faith is an appropriating grace; it looks upon God, and saith with David, " This God is my God for ever and ever, and he shall be my guide unto the death," Ps. 48. 14. It looks upon Christ, and saith with the spouse, " I am my beloved's, and his desire is towards me," Solomon's Song 7. 10. It looks upon an immortal crown, and saith with Paul, " Henceforth is laid up for me a crown of glory," 2 Tim. 4. 8. It looks upon the righteousness of Christ, and saith, " This righteousness is mine to cover me." It looks upon the mercy of Christ, and saith, " This mercy is mine to pardon me." It looks upon the power of Christ, and saith, " This power is mine to support me." It looks upon the wisdom of Christ, and saith, " This wisdom is mine to direct me." It looks upon the blood of Christ, and says, "This blood is mine to save me."

As faith, so hope is another spring of assurance. Col. 1. 27, "Christ in you," saith Paul, "the hope of glory." So Heb. 6. 19, "Which hope we have as an anchor of the soul, both sure and steadfast, and which entereth into that within the veil." Hope taketh fast hold upon heaven itself, upon the *sanctum sanctorum*, the holy of holies. A Christian's hope is not like that of Pandora, which may fly out of the box, and bid the soul farewell, as the hope of hypocrites do; no, it is like the morning light, the least beam of it shall lead to a complete sunshine; it shall shine brighter and brighter till perfect day.

When Alexander went upon a hopeful expedition, he gave away his gold; and when he was asked what he kept for himself, he answered, *Spem majorum et meliorum,* the hope of greater and better things. So a Christian will part with anything rather than with his hope; he knows that hope will keep the heart both from aching and breaking, from fainting and sinking; he knows that hope is a beam of God, a spark of glory, and that nothing shall extinguish it till the soul be filled with glory. Souls that are big in hope, will not be long without sweet assurance. God loves not to see the hoping soul go always up and down sighing and mourning for want of a good word from heaven, for want of possessing what it hopes in time to enjoy. Hold out hope and patience "a little longer, and he that hath promised to come, will come, and will not tarry," Heb. 10. 37.

Again, A good conscience is another spring of assurance: 2 Cor. 1. 12, "For our rejoicing is this, the testimony of our conscience, that in simplicity and godly sincerity, not with fleshly wisdom, but by the grace of God, we have had our conversation in the world, and more abundantly to youward." So 1 John 3. 21, "Beloved, if our heart condemn us not, then have we confidence towards God." A good conscience hath sure confidence; he that hath it sits, Noahlike, in the midst of all commotions and distractions, in sincerity and serenity, uprightness and boldness. A good conscience and a good confidence go together.

What the probationer-disciple said to our Saviour, Mat. 8. 19, "Master, I will follow thee whithersoever thou goest," that a good conscience says to the believing soul. I will follow thee from duty to duty, from ordinance to ordinance; I will stand by thee, I will strengthen thee, I will uphold thee, I will be a comfort to thee in life, and a friend to thee in death; "though all should leave thee, yet I will never forsake thee," Mat. 26. 35. A good conscience will look through the blackest clouds, and see a smiling God. Look, as an evil conscience is attended with the greatest fears and doubts, so a good conscience is attended with the greatest clearness and sweetness. And as there is no hell in this world to an evil conscience, so there is no heaven in this world to a good conscience. He that hath a good conscience hath one of the choicest springs of assurance, and it will not be long before God will whisper to such a man in the ear, and say unto him, "Son, be of good cheer, thy sins be forgiven thee," Mat. 9. 2.

Again, real love to the saints is another spring of assurance, and this spring is a never-failing spring. This spring is in the weakest as well as in the strongest saints: 1 John 3. 14, "We know that we have passed from death unto life, because we love the brethren. He that loveth not his brother abideth in death." The apostle doth not say, We think, we hope, &c., that we are translated from death to life, but, "we *know*" that we are translated from death to life, because we love the brethren. Love to the brethren is not the cause of our passing from death to life, that is, from a natural state to a spiritual state, from hell to heaven, but an evidence thereof. I confess it is very sad to consider how this precious stream of love is even dried up in many.

It was wont to be a proverb, *Homo homini deus,* one man is a god to another; but now it may be truly said, *Homo homini dæmon,* one man is a devil to another. He that wants love to his brethren, wants one of the sweetest springs from whence assurance flows. A greater hell I would not wish any man, than to live and not to love the beloved of God.

Now is it not as easy a thing as it is pleasant, for a man that hath several sweet springs in his garden, to sit down, draw water, and drink? John 4. 14. O believing souls! there are springs, there are wells of living water not only near you, but in you; why, then, do you, with Hagar, sit down sorrowing and weeping, Gen. 21. 15-19, when you should be a-tasting or a-drinking not only of the springs above you, but also of the springs within you? A man that hath fruit in his garden may both delight his eye and refresh his spirit with tasting of it, Gal. 5. 22, 23. Certainly we may both eye and taste the fruits of the Spirit in us, they being the first-fruits of eternal life. I think none but mad souls will say that grace is that forbidden fruit that God would have us neither see nor taste. We ought not so to mind a Christ in heaven, as not to find "Christ in us the hope of glory," Col. 1. 27. Christ would not have his spouse so to mind her own blackness, as to forget that she is all fair and glorious within, Solomon's Song 1. 5; 4. 7, and Ps. 45. 11.

The Spirit of God exhorts to assurance

Sixthly, The Holy Ghost exhorts us " to give all diligence to make our calling and election sure," 2 Pet. 1. 10, and presses us to look to the obtaining of a "full assurance." Therefore believers may attain unto an assurance of their everlasting happiness and blessedness: "Wherefore the rather, brethren," saith the apostle, "give diligence to make your calling and election sure; for if you do these things, you shall never fall." The Greek word translated "give diligence" signifieth two things: (1.) All possible haste and speed; (2.) All manner of seriousness and intention in doing. Make it your main business, your chief study, your greatest care, to "make your calling and election sure," saith the apostle. When this is done, your all is done. Till this be done, there is nothing done. And to shew the necessity, utility, excellency, and possibility of it, the apostle puts a "rather" upon it: "Wherefore the rather give all diligence to make your calling and election sure"; or, as it is in the original, "firm or stable." It is the one thing necessary; it is of an internal and eternal importance to make firm and sure work for your souls. Assurance is a jewel of that worth, a pearl of that price, that he that will have it must work, and sweat, and weep, and wait to obtain it. He must not only use diligence, but he must use all diligence; not only dig, but he must dig deep, before he can come to the golden mine. Assurance is that " white stone," that " new name," that "hidden manna," that none can obtain but such as labour for it as for life. Assurance is such precious gold, that a man must win it before he can wear it. Win gold, and wear gold, is the language both of heaven and earth.

The riches, honours, languages, and favours of this world cannot be obtained without much trouble and travel, without rising early and going to bed late, and do you think that assurance, which is more worth than heaven and earth, can be obtained by cold, lazy, heartless services? If you do, you do but deceive your own souls. There are five things that God will never sell at a cheap rate,—Christ, truth, his honour, heaven, and assurance. He that will have these must pay a good price for them, or go for ever without them.

And as Peter exhorts you to " give all diligence to make your calling and election sure," so Paul presseth you to look to the obtaining of full assurance, which does clearly evidence that there is a possibility of attaining unto a full assurance of our happiness and blessedness in this life. And " we desire," saith the apostle, " that every one of you do shew the same diligence, to the full assurance of hope unto the end, that ye be not slothful, but followers of them who through faith and patience inherit the promises." Heb. 6. 11, 12. We must not only strive after assurance, but we must strive and shew all diligence to the attaining of that rich and full assurance which will scatter all fears and doubts, which will make a soul patient in waiting, courageous in doing, and cheerful in suffering, and which will make a heaven in a man's heart on this side heaven, and make him go singing into paradise, in despite of all calamities and miseries. And certainly it can never stand with the holiness, righteousness, faithfulness, and goodness of God, to put his people upon making their calling and election sure, and upon obtaining full assurance, if there were not a possibility of obtaining a full and well-grounded assurance of their happiness and blessedness in this life; and therefore it doth undeniably follow that they may attain unto a blessed assurance of their felicity and glory whilst they are in this vale of misery. The contrary opinion will make a man's life a hell here, though he should escape a hell hereafter.

Means to be used to obtain assurance

Seventhly, The Lord hath, in much mercy and love, propounded in his Word the ways and means whereby believers may obtain a well-grounded assurance of their everlasting happiness and blessedness; and therefore it may be obtained. Take three scriptures to evidence this.

The first is in 2 Peter 1. 13. If you turn to the words, you shall find that the Lord does not only press them to "give all diligence to make their calling and election sure"; but he shews them plainly the way and means whereby this may be done, namely, by adding "to your faith virtue, and to virtue knowledge," &c.

The second scripture is that 1 Cor. 11. 28, "But let a man examine himself; and so let him eat of that bread, and drink of that cup." By examination the soul comes to see what right it hath to Christ and all the precious things of his house; and believingly to eat so of that bread of life, that heavenly manna, as that it may live for ever.

The third scripture is that 2 Cor. 13. 5, "Examine yourselves whether ye be in the faith; prove yourselves; know ye not your own selves how that Christ is in you, except ye be reprobates?" or unapproved, or rejected. By a serious examination of a man's own estate, he may know whether he hath faith or not, whether he be Christ's spouse or the devil's strumpet, whether there be a work of grace upon his heart or not. And certainly it cannot stand with the glorious wisdom, unspotted righteousness, and transcendent holiness of God, to put men upon the use of such and such means in order to the obtaining of such and such an end, if that end could not be obtained by the use of the means prescribed, Exodus 15. 11. Man, that hath but a spark of that wisdom, righteousness, and holiness that is in God, will not put any upon the use of such or such means for the obtaining of health, wealth, or the like, unless there be a proper tendency in the use of those means prescribed to reach such ends. And will God, who is wisdom, righteousness, and holiness in the abstract? Surely no. God is one infinite perfection in himself, which is eminently and virtually all perfections of the creatures; and therefore it is impossible that God should act below the creature, which he would do if he should put the creature upon the use of those means that would not reach the ends for which the means were used.

Thus you see clearly by this seventh argument that believers may in this life attain to a well-grounded assurance of their everlasting happiness and blessedness.

The Lord's Supper as related to assurance

Eighthly, It was the principal end of Christ's institution of the sacrament of the supper that he might assure them of his love, and that he might seal up to them the forgiveness of their sins, the acceptation of their persons, and the salvation of their souls, Mat. 26. 27, 28. The nature of a seal is to make things sure and firm among men; so the supper of the Lord is Christ's broad seal, it is Christ's privy-seal, whereby he seals and assures his people that they are happy here, that they shall be more happy hereafter, that they are everlastingly beloved of God, that his heart is set upon them, that their names are written in the book of life, that there is laid up for them a crown of righteousness, and that nothing shall be able to separate them from him who is their light, their life, their crown, their all in all.

In this sacrament Christ comes forth and shews his love, his heart, his bowels, his blood, that his children may no longer say, Doth the Lord Jesus love us? doth he delight in us? &c.; but that they may say with the spouse, " I am my beloved's, and his desire is towards me," Solomon's Song 7. 10. Many precious Christians there are that have lain long under fears and doubts, sighing and mourning; that have run from minister to minister, and from one duty to another, &c., and yet could never be persuaded of the love

27

of Christ to their poor souls; but still their fears and doubts have followed them, till they have waited upon the Lord in this glorious ordinance, by which the Lord hath assured them of the remission of their sins, and the salvation of their souls. In this ordinance God hath given them manna to eat, and a white stone, and new name, which no man knoweth but he that receiveth it, Rev. 2. 17. Tell me, ye precious, believing souls, whether you have not found God in this ordinance often whispering to you in the ear, saying, "Sons and daughters, be of good cheer, your sins are forgiven you"? Mat. 9. 2. I know you have.

The relation of assurance to rejoicing in the Lord

Ninthly, Those scriptures that do expressly require saints to be abundant and constant in rejoicing and in praising of God, to have always harps in their hands and hallelujahs in their mouths, do clearly evidence that believers may attain to a well-grounded assurance in this life. How can they rejoice and glory in God, that do not know whether he will be an everlasting friend or an everlasting enemy to them, whether he will always breathe out love or wrath upon them? How can they but hang their harps on the willows, that do not know but that they may live in a strange land, Ps. 137. 2; yea, in a land of darkness all their days? How can they be cheerful or thankful, that do not know but that they may at last hear that heart-breaking, that conscience-wounding, that soul-slaying word, "Depart from me, ye cursed, into everlasting fire, prepared for the devil and his angels," Mat. 25. 41. Now, there is no duty in the whole book of God that is more frequently and abundantly pressed upon believers than this of joy and rejoicing, of praise and thanksgiving, as all know that know anything of the Scripture: 1 Thes. 5. 16, "Rejoice evermore." God would not have his children always a-putting finger in the eye. Ah, Christians! remember what Christ hath done for you, and what he is still a-doing for you in heaven, and what he will do for you to all eternity, and spend your days in whining and mourning if you can. Ps. 32. 11, "Be glad in the Lord, and rejoice, ye righteous; and shout for joy, all ye that are upright in heart." Ps. 33. 1, "Rejoice in the Lord, O ye righteous; for praise is comely for the upright." Christians, are not your mercies greater than your miseries? Yes. Are your greatest sufferings comparable to the least spark of grace or beam of glory revealed in you or to you? No. Will not one hour's being in the bosom of Christ recompense you for all your trouble and travail? Yes. Why, then, do you spend more time in sighing than in rejoicing; and why do you, by your not rejoicing, sadden those precious hearts that God would not have saddened, and gladden those graceless hearts that God would not have gladdened?

A beautiful face is at all times pleasing to the eye, but then especially when there is joy manifested in the countenance. Joy in the face puts a new beauty, and makes that which before was beautiful to be exceeding beautiful. It puts a lustre and glory upon beauty; so does joy in the face, heart, and life of a Christian, cast a general splendour and glory upon him, and the ways of God wherein he walks. The joy of the Lord is not only the strength, but also the beauty and glory of Christians, Neh. 8. 10.

Joy and rejoicing is a consequent and effect of assurance, as many believers by experience find; and therefore, without all peradventure, believers may attain unto a well-grounded assurance of their everlasting happiness, else it is impossible that they should "rejoice evermore."; so that by this argument, as by the former, it clearly appears that believers may in this life be assured of their eternal well-being.

The clarity of Scripture on the differences between the righteous and the wicked

Tenthly, The *tenth* and last argument, to prove that believers may in this life attain to a well-grounded assurance, is this, *That God would never have made such a broad difference in the Scripture between the seed of the woman and the seed of the serpent, between the righteous and the wicked, between saints and sinners, between sons and slaves, sheep and goats, between lions and lambs, between wheat and chaff, light and darkness, &c., if it were impossible for men to know which of these two estates they are in.* Therefore they may know whether they are in a state of life or in a state of death, in a state of misery or in a state of felicity, in a state of wrath or in a state of love, Mat. 13. 1, *seq*. Oh! it is much below the grace of God, it is repugnant to the wisdom of God, to make such a wide difference between his own children and Satan's, John 8. 44, if it were not possible for every child to know his own father. "Thou art my father." Ps. 89. 26. "Doubtless thou art our Father, though Abraham be ignorant of us, and Israel acknowledge us not: thou, O Lord, art our Father and Redeemer; thy name is from everlasting." Isa. 63. 16. The weakest saint can say, "Abba, Father," Rom. 8. 15. The Lord will not leave his children comfortless, or as orphans and fatherless children, as it is in the Greek. Though the salvation of believers does not depend upon their knowledge of God to be their father, yet their consolation does; therefore the Lord will not be only a father to Israel, but he will make Israel know that he is his father: Jer. 3. 4, "Wilt thou not from this time cry unto me, My Father, thou art the guide of my youth?"

By these ten arguments it doth evidently appear that believers may in this life attain a well-grounded assurance of their everlasting happiness and blessedness. I shall apply this a little, and then close up this chapter.

Assurance is not for Arminians

Use. This precious truth thus proved, looks sourly and wishly upon all those that affirm that believers cannot in this life attain unto a certain well-grounded assurance of their everlasting happiness and blessedness,—as papists and Arminians: all know that know their writings and teachings, that they are in arms against this Christ-exalting, and soul-cheering doctrine of assurance. "I know no such thing as assurance of heaven in this life," saith Grevinchovius the Arminian. Assurance is a pearl that they trample under feet; it is a beam of heaven that hath so much light, brightness, and shining glory in it, that their blear-eyes cannot behold it. Assurance is glory in the bud, it is the suburbs of paradise, it is a cluster of the land of promise, it is a spark of God, it is the joy and crown of a Christian; the greater is their impiety and folly that deny assurance, that cry down assurance under any names or notions whatsoever. They are rather tormenters than comforters that say, poor souls may know that there is a crown of righteousness, but they must not presume to know that they shall have the honour to wear that crown; and that make God like King Xerxes, who crowned his steersman in the morning, and beheaded him in the evening of the same day.

Arminians are not ashamed to say, that God may crown a man one hour, and uncrown him in the next; they blush not to say that a man may be happy and miserable, under love and under wrath, an heir of heaven and a firebrand of hell, a child of light and a child of darkness, and all in an hour. Oh what miserable comforters are these! What is this but to torment the weary soul? to dispirit the wounded spirit, and to make them most sad whom God would have most glad? Ah! how sad is it for men to affirm that wounded spirits may know " that the Sun of righteousness hath healing in his wings," Mal. 4. 2; but they cannot be assured that they shall be healed. The hungry soul may know that there is bread enough in his Father's house but cannot know that he shall taste of that bread, Luke 15. 17. The naked soul may know that Christ hath robes of righteousness to cover all spots, sores, defects, and deformities of it, but may not presume to know that Christ will put these royal robes upon it, Rev. 3. 18. The impoverished soul may know that there be unsearchable riches in Christ, but cannot be assured that ever it shall partake of those riches, Eph. 3. 8. All that these men allow poor souls, is guesses and conjectures that it may be well with them. They will not allow souls to say with Thomas, " My Lord, and my God," John 20. 18; nor with Job to say, " My Redeemer lives," Job 19. 25; nor with the church, " I am my beloved's, and his desire is towards me," Solomon's Song 7. 10. And so they leave souls in a cloudy, questioning, doubting, hovering condition, hanging, like Mahomet's tomb at Mecca, between two loadstones; or like Erasmus, as the papists paint him, hanging betwixt heaven and hell. They make the poor soul a *Magor-missabib* (Jer. 20. 3), a terror to itself.

What more uncomfortable doctrine than this? What more soul-disquieting, and soul-unsettling doctrine than this? Thou art this moment in a state of life, thou mayest the next moment be in a state of death; thou art now gracious, thou mayest the next hour be graceless; thou art now in the promised land, yet thou mayest die in the wilderness; thou art to-day a habitation for God, thou mayest to-morrow be a synagogue of Satan; thou hast to-day received the white stone of absolution, thou mayest to-morrow receive the black stone of condemnation; thou art now in thy Saviour's arms, thou mayest to-morrow be in Satan's paws; thou art now Christ's freeman, thou mayest to-morrow be Satan's bondman; thou art now a vessel of honour, thou mayest suddenly become a vessel of wrath; thou art now greatly beloved, thou mayest soon be as greatly loathed; this day thy name is fairly written in the book of life, to-morrow the book may be crossed, and thy name blotted out for ever. This is the Arminians' doctrine, and if this be not to keep souls in a doubting, trembling and shivering condition, what is it? Well, Christians, remember this is your happiness and blessedness, that " none can pluck you out of your Father's hand," John 10. 29; that you are " kept," as in a garrison, or as with a guard, " by the power of God through faith unto salvation," 1 Peter 1. 5. " That the mountains shall depart, and the hills be removed; but the kindness of the Lord shall not depart from you, neither shall the covenant of peace be removed, saith the Lord that hath mercy on you," Isa. 54. 10. " That Christ ever lives to make intercession for you," Heb. 7. 25; and that men and devils are as able, and shall as soon, make a world, dethrone God, pluck the sun out of the firmament, and Christ out of the bosom of the Father, as they shall pluck a believer out of the everlasting arms of Christ, or rob him of one of his precious jewels, Deut. 33. 26, 27. I shall close up this chapter with an excellent saying of Luther: " The whole Scripture," saith he, " doth principally aim at this thing, that we should not doubt, but that we should hope, that we should trust, that we should believe, that God is a merciful, a bountiful, a gracious, and a patient God to his people."

CHAPTER II

Weighty propositions concerning assurance.

Seven reasons why God denies assurance for a time to some believers

The first proposition that I shall lay down concerning assurance is this, *That God denies assurance for a time to his dearest and choicest ones, and that upon many considerable grounds.*

(1) As, first, *for the exercise of their grace.* A gracious soul would always be upon mount Tabor, looking into Canaan; he would always be in his Father's arms, and under his Father's smiles; he would always be in the sunshine of divine favour; he would always have the heavens open, that he might always see his Christ and his crown; he would with Peter be always upon the mount; he is loth to walk through the valley of darkness, through the valley of Baca. As the king of Sodom said once to Abraham, " Give me the persons, and take the goods to thyself," Gen. 14. 21; so gracious souls are apt to say, Give me joy, give me peace, give me assurance, and do you take trials, afflictions, and temptations to yourselves. But pray, what use would there be of the stars, if the sun did always shine? Why, none. Why, no more use would there be of your graces, if assurance should be always continued; therefore the Lord, for the exercise of his children's faith, hope, patience, &c., is pleased, at least for a time, to deny them assurance, though they seek it by earnest prayer, and with a flood of penitent tears.

(2) The Lord denies assurance to his dearest ones, *that he may keep them in the exercise of those religious duties that are most costly and contrary to flesh and blood,* as to mourning, repenting, self-judging, self-loathing, self-abhorring, and self-searching; as Lam. 1. 16, "For these things I weep: mine eye, mine eye runneth down with water, because the comforter that should relieve my soul is far from me";

33

chap. 3. 2, 3, "He hath led me, and brought me into darkness, not into light. Surely against me he is turned; he turneth his hand against me all the day"; ver. 17, "And thou hast removed my soul far off from peace: I forgat prosperity." Now, the effect of God's dealings with the church may be seen in ver. 40. "Let us search and try our ways, and turn again to the Lord." And if you look throughout the book, you shall find the church much in self-examining, self-judging, self-loathing, &c., upon this ground, that God had hid his face, and drawn a curtain between him and them, and stood at a distance from them, and would not speak comfortably and friendly to them.

Now, if you ask me why God will put his children upon those duties of religion that are most costly and contrary to flesh and blood? I answer,

1. That his strength and power may appear in their weakness, 2 Cor. 12. 7-9.

2. To discover not only the truth, but also the strength of their graces. A little grace will put a man upon those religious duties that are easy and pleasing to flesh and blood, and not costly, but rather profitable and pleasurable; but it must be strength of grace that puts man upon those services that are costly and contrary to the old man.

3. That they may be more fully and eminently conformable to Christ their head, who, from first to last, who, even from the cradle to the cross, was most exercised in those duties and services that were most costly and contrary to flesh and blood, as is most evident to all that study the writings of the Holy Ghost more than the writings of men.

4. Because in the performance of such duties they do in a more singular way bear up the name and credit, the honour and glory of God, Christ, and the gospel in the world; the very world will cry out, Ah, these are Christians indeed!

5. Because the more they are in the exercise of such duties, the greater at last will be their reward, Heb. 11. 7.

6. That Satan's plots and designs may be the better prevented, and the wicked world more justly condemned, who do not only despise the hardest duties of religion, but also neglect the easiest, Mat. 25. 4-6.

(3) The third reason why God denies assurance to his most precious ones, is that *they may be the more clearly and fully convinced of that exceeding sinfulness and bitterness that is in sin,* Jer. 2. 19. Ah, Lord, says the soul that is sighing and mourning under the want of assurance, I see now that sin is not only evil, but the greatest evil in the world, in that it keeps me from an assurance of my interest in thee, who art the greatest good in the world, and from an assurance of that favour of thine that is better than life, and from the light of thy sweet countenance, that is better than corn, and wine, and oil; and from those joys and comforts that can alone make a paradise in my soul, Ps. 4. 7; 63. 3, 4. Ah, Lord! now I find sin not only to be bitter, but to be the very quintessence of bitterness. Ah! no bitterness so bitter as sin, that keeps my soul from that sweet assurance, that is not only the top and crown of mercy, but also the sweetener of all mercy, misery, and glory. Oh what unspeakable evil do I now see in that evil that keeps me from the most desirable good! Oh what bitterness do I now find in that which Satan, the world, and my own deluded heart told me I should find sweetness in! Ah, now I find by experience, that to be true, which long since the faithful messengers of the Lord have told me; viz., that sin debaseth the soul of man, that it defiles and pollutes the soul of man, that it renders the soul most unlike to God, who is *optimum maximum,* the best and greatest, who is *omnia super omnia,* all and above all, and renders it most like to Satan, who is a very sea and sink of sin. That it hath robbed the soul of the image of God, the holiness of God, the beauty of God, the glory of God, the righteousness of God, and that keeps the soul from wearing this golden chain of assurance.

(4) A fourth reason why God denies assurance to his dearest ones, is, *because they seek assurance more for themselves, than they do for his honour and glory*; more that they may have joy without sorrow, comfort without torment, peace without trouble, sweet without bitter, light without darkness, and day without night, than that he may be exalted and admired, and his name alone made great and glorious in the world.

35

Many Christians are like the bee that flies into the field to seek honey to eat, but brings it not into the master's hive. So they seek for assurance, that they may feed upon the sweet honeycomb, more than to fill their Lord and master's hive with thanks and praise.

That servant that minds his wages more than his work, must not wonder if his master be slack in paying; no more should he that minds comfort more than obedience, that minds assurance more than divine honour, wonder that God delays the giving of assurance, though it be sought with many prayers and tears. He that is most tender of God's honour, shall find by experience that God is most mindful of his comfort. God will not see that soul sit long in sackcloth and ashes, that makes it his business to set him up upon his throne. He that minds God's glory more than his own good, shall quickly find that God will even obscure his own glory to do him good. If we are not wanting to God's glory, he will not long be wanting to our joy.

(5) A fifth reason why God denies assurance to his children, is, *That when they have it, they may the more highly prize it, the more carefully keep it, the more wisely improve it, and the more affectionately and effectually bless God for it.* None sets such a price upon light, as he that hath lain long in a dungeon of darkness; so none sets such a price upon assurance, as those children of light that have walked most in spiritual darkness. Ah! how sweet was the light to Jonah, that had been in the belly of hell, Jonah 2. 2; so is assurance to those that, through slavish fears and unbelief, " have made their beds in hell," as the psalmist speaks, Ps. 139. 8. Gold that is far fetched, and dearly bought, is most esteemed; so that assurance that costs the soul most pains and patience, most waiting and weeping, most striving and wrestling, is most highly valued, and most wisely improved. As, by the want of temporals, God teaches his people the better to prize them, and improve them when they enjoy them; so by the want of spirituals, God teaches his people the better to prize them, and improve them when they enjoy them. Ah! how sweet was Canaan to those that had been long in the wilderness! How precious was the gold and

ear-rings to Israel, that had been long in Egypt, and the gifts and jewels to the Jews that had been long in Babylon! So is assurance to those precious souls that have been long without it, but at last come to enjoy it, Num. 14. 33, 34; Exod. 11; Ezra 1.

After the Trojans had been wandering a long time in the Mediterranean Sea, as soon as they espied land, they cried out with exulting joy, "Italy, Italy"; so when poor souls shall come to enjoy assurance, who have been long tossed up and down in a sea of sorrow and trouble, how will they with joy cry out, "Assurance, assurance, assurance!"

(6) The sixth reason why God denies assurance to his dearest ones, at least for a time, is, *That they be kept humble and low in their own eyes; as the enjoyment of mercy gladdens us, so the want of mercy humbles us.* David's heart was never more low than when he had a crown only in hope but not in hand. No sooner was the crown set upon his head, but his blood rises with his outward good, and in the pride of his heart he says, "I shall never be moved," Ps. 30. 6.

Hezekiah was a holy man, yet he swells big under mercy. 2 Chron. 32. No sooner doth God lift up his house higher than others, but he lifts up his heart in pride higher than others. When God had made him high in honours, riches, victories, ay, and in spiritual experiences, then his heart flies high, and he forgets God, and forgets himself, and forgets that all his mercies were from free mercy, that all his mercies were but borrowed mercies. Surely, it is better to lack any mercy than an humble heart, it is better to have no mercy than lack an humble heart! A little, little mercy, with an humble heart, is far better than the greatest mercies with a proud heart. I had rather have Paul's coat with his humble heart, than Hezekiah's lifted-up heart with his treasures and royal robes. Well, Christians, remember this, God hath two strings to his bow; if your hearts will not lie humble and low under the sense of sin and misery, he will make them lie low under the lack of some desired mercy. The want of assurance tends to bow and humble the soul, as the enjoyment of assurance doth to raise and rejoice the soul;

37

and therefore do not wonder why precious souls are so long without assurance, why Christ's chariot, assurance, is so long a-coming, Judges 5. 28.

(7) The seventh and last reason why God denies assurance, for a time, even to his dearest ones, is, *That they may live clearly and fully upon Jesus Christ, that Jesus Christ may be seen to be all in all.* It is natural to the soul to rest upon everything below Christ; to rest upon creatures, to rest upon graces, to rest upon duties, to rest upon divine manifestations, to rest upon celestial consolations, to rest upon gracious evidences, and to rest upon sweet assurances. Now the Lord, to cure his people of this weakness, and to bring them to live wholly and solely upon Jesus Christ, denies comfort, and denies assurance, &c., and for a time leaves his children of light to walk in darkness. Christians, this you are always to remember, that though the enjoyment of assurance makes most for your consolation, yet the living purely upon Christ in the absence of assurance, makes most for Christ's exaltation. He is happy that believes upon seeing, upon feeling, but thrice happy are those souls that believe when they do not see; that love when they do not know that they are beloved; and that in the want of all comfort and assurance, can live upon Christ as their only all. He that hath learned this holy art, cannot be miserable; he that is ignorant of this art cannot be happy.

Words used in Scripture to express assurance

The second proposition is this, *That the Scripture hath many sweet significant words to express that well-grounded assurance by, which believers may attain to in this life.*

Sometimes it is called a persuasion. Rom. 8. 38, " I am *persuaded* that neither death, nor life, &c., shall be able to separate us from the love of God which is in Christ Jesus our Lord." It is rendered a perspicuous and peculiar manifestation of Christ to the soul, John 14. 21-24. It is often rendered, *to know,* as 1 John 3. 14, 19, 24, and 5. 13, 19, &c. But the word that the Scripture doth most fully express this by is one that denotes full assurance, that is, when the soul, by the Spirit and word, is so fully persuaded of its eternal happiness and blessedness, that it is carried, like Noah's ark, above all waves, doubts, and fears, and, Noah-like, sits still and quiet, and can, with the apostle Paul, triumph over sin, hell, wrath, death, and the devil.

This is sometimes called "full assurance of understanding"; sometimes it is called "full assurance of hope"; and sometimes it is called "full assurance of faith"; because these are the choice and pleasant springs from whence assurance flows, Col. 2. 2; Heb. 6. 11, 18, 19; 10. 22.

Now though this full assurance is earnestly desired, and highly prized, and the want of it much lamented, and the enjoyment of it much endeavoured after by all saints, yet it is only obtained by a few. It is a mercy too good for most men's hearts, it is a crown too weighty for most men's heads. Full assurance is *optimum maximum,* the best and greatest mercy; and therefore God will only give it to his best and dearest friends.

Augustus in his solemn feasts, gave trifles to some, but gold to others. Honours and riches, &c., are trifles that God gives to the worst of men; but assurance is that "tried gold," Rev. 3. 18, that God only gives to tried friends. Among those few that have a share or portion in the special love and favour of God, there are but a very few that have an assurance of his love.

It is one mercy for God to love the soul, and another mercy for God to assure the soul of his love. God writes many a man's name in the book of life, and yet will not let him know it till his hour of death, as the experience of many precious souls doth clearly evidence. Assurance is a flower of paradise that God sticks but in a few men's bosoms. It is one thing to be an heir of heaven, and another thing for a man to know or see himself an heir of heaven. The child in the arms may be heir to a crown, a kingdom, and yet not understand it; so many a saint may be heir to a crown, a kingdom of glory, and yet not know it. As the babes that pass the pangs of the first-birth do not immediately cry, "Father, father"; so the new-born babes in Christ, that have passed the pangs of the second-birth, do not at once cry "Abba, Father"; they do not immediately cry out, Heaven,

heaven is ours; glory, glory is ours, Rom. 8. 16, 17; 1 Peter 2. 2.

True believers are saved even though they lack assurance

The third proposition is this, *That a man may have true grace, that hath not assurance of the love and favour of God, or of the remission of his sins and salvation of his soul.*

A man may be truly holy, and yet not have assurance that he shall be eternally happy. A man may be God's, and yet not know it; his estate may be good, and yet he may not see it; he may be in a safe condition, when he is not in a comfortable condition. All may be well with him in the court of glory, when he would give a thousand worlds that all were but well in the court of conscience.

The Canaanite woman shewed much love, wisdom, zeal, humility, and faith, yea, such strength of faith as makes Christ admire her, and yield to her, grace her, and gratify her, and yet she had no assurance that we read of, Mat. 15. 22, 29. So Paul, speaking of the believing Ephesians, saith, " In whom ye also trusted, after that ye heard the word of truth, the gospel of your salvation : in whom also, after that ye believed, ye were sealed with that Holy Spirit of promise." Eph. 1. 13. First, they heard the word; and then secondly, they believed; and then thirdly, they were sealed; that is, fully assured of a heavenly inheritance, of a purchased possession. So 1 John 5. 13, " These things have I written unto you that believe on the name of the Son of God, that ye may know that ye have eternal life, and that ye may believe on the Son of God." So Isa. 50. 10, " Who is among you that feareth the Lord, that obeyeth the voice of his servant, that walketh in darkness, and hath no light? let him trust in the name of the Lord, and stay himself upon his God." So Micah 7. 8, 9, " Rejoice not against me, O mine enemy: when I fall, I shall arise; when I sit in darkness, the Lord shall be a light unto me. I will bear the indignation of the Lord, because I have sinned against him, until he plead my cause, and execute judgment for me; he will bring me forth to the light, and I shall behold his righteousness." Asaph was a very holy man, a man eminent in grace, and yet without assurance, as may be seen at large, Ps. 77. Heman, doubtless, was a very precious soul, and yet from his youth up, he was even distracted with terrors, Ps. 88. There are thousands of Christians that are in a state of grace, and shall be saved, that want assurance and the proper effects of it, as high joy, pure comfort, glorious peace, and vehement longings after the coming of Christ.

Assurance is requisite to the well-being of a Christian, but not to the being; it is requisite to the consolation of a Christian, but not to the salvation of a Christian; it is requisite to the well-being of grace, but not to the mere being of grace. Though a man cannot be saved without faith, yet he may be saved without assurance. God hath in many places of the Scripture declared, that without faith there is no salvation, but God hath not in any one place of the Scripture declared, that without assurance there is no salvation. A man must first be saved before he can be assured of his salvation, for he cannot be assured of that which is not; and a man must have saving grace before he can be saved, for he cannot be saved by that which he hath not. Again, a man must be ingrafted into Christ, before he can be assured of remission or salvation, but this he cannot be before he hath faith, therefore there may be grace where there is no assurance. Christ went to heaven in a cloud, and the angel went up to heaven in the smoke and flame of the sacrifice; and so I doubt not but many precious souls do ascend to heaven in clouds and darkness, Acts 1. 9; Judges 13, 20.

Six reasons why some do not attain assurance

Now a man may have grace, and yet lack assurance, and that may arise from these causes.

(1) First, *From his cavilling spirit,* and from his siding with the old man against the new, with the flesh against the spirit, with corruption against grace, with the house of Saul against the house of David, with the work of Satan against the work of God. Sin is Satan's work; grace, holiness is God's; yet such is the weakness, yea, madness of many poor souls, that they will fall in and side with Satan's work, rather than with God's, against their own souls. Ah! Chris-

tians, will you condemn that judge for injustice and un-righteousness, that shall open his ears to the complaints of the plaintiff, but stops his ears against the answers of the defendant; and will you not condemn yourselves for that you do with both ears hear what sin and Satan hath to say against the soul, but have not one ear open to hear what the Spirit, what grace, what the new man, what the noble part of man, what the regenerate man, can say for the justification, satisfaction, and consolation of the soul. Let me tell thee, O thou cavilling soul! that it is thy wisdom and thy duty to remember that command of God, that doth prohibit thee from bearing false witness against thy neighbour. That same command doth enjoin thee not to bear false witness against the work of grace upon thy own heart, against the precious and glorious things that God hath done for thy soul. And thou shouldst make as much conscience of bearing false witness against anything the Lord hath wrought in thee, and for thee, as thou dost make conscience of bearing false witness against thy neighbour. It cannot but be sad with the soul, but be night with the soul, when it makes much conscience of the one, and no conscience of the other. Many heathens have been so loving and faithful one to another, that they would rather die, than they would bear false witness one against another. How dare you cavilling souls bear false witness against your own souls, and the gracious work of the Lord upon them! If this be not the way to keep off assurance, and keep the soul in darkness, yea, in a hell, I know nothing.

(2) Again, a man may have grace, and yet lack assurance, and that may arise in the second place from *the exceeding littleness and weakness of his grace.* A little candle yields but a little light, and a little grace yields but a little evidence. Great measures of grace carry with them great and clear evidences, but little measures carry with them but little evidence. Some stars are so small that they are scarce discernible; so some saints' graces are so small, that they can hardly see their graces to be graces. A little fire will yield but a little heat; a little grace will yield but a little comfort, a little evidence; a little grace will yield a man a heaven

hereafter, but it is a great deal of grace that must yield us a heaven here; a little stock will bring in but a little profit; a little grace will bring in but a little peace; a little jewel yields but a little lustre, a little glory; no more doth a little grace, and therefore it is that Christians that have but a little grace, have but a little of the shine and lustre of assurance, they have but little joy and comfort in this world. Yet that the spirits of weak Christians may not utterly faint, let me give them this hint, viz., that the weakest Christian is as much justified, as much pardoned, as much adopted, and as much united to Christ as the strongest, and hath as much interest and propriety in Christ as the highest and noblest Christian that breathes, though he cannot make so much advantage and improvement of his interest and propriety as the strong Christian, who hath a greater degree of grace.

Hierom [Jerome] observes upon the beatitudes, that there are many of the promises made to weak grace: Mat. 5. 3, 4, 6. "Blessed are the poor in spirit: blessed are they that mourn: blessed are they that hunger and thirst." Weak saints, remember this: the promise is a ring of gold, and Christ is the precious tried stone in that ring; and upon that stone must you rest, as you would have grace to thrive, and your souls to be safe and happy. Weak souls, remember this: as Joseph sent chariots to bring his father and his brethren to him, Gen. 45, so God would have your weak graces to be as chariots to bring you to himself, who is the cherisher, strengthener, and increaser of grace. He that makes his graces to be servants and handmaids to convey him to Christ, the fountain of grace, he shall find the greatest sweetness in grace, and the greatest increase of grace.

(3) Thirdly, A man may have true grace, and yet want assurance, and this may arise from *the resurrection of old sins.* Ah! when those sins which were long since committed, and long since lamented, and long since loathed, and long since crucified; when those old sins, which hath cost a soul many prayers and many tears, and many sighs, and many groans, and many complaints, when those sins that have been long buried shall be again revived, and meet the soul, and stare upon the soul, and say to the soul, We are thine,

and we will follow thee; we are thine, and we will haunt thee; ah, how will this cause a man's countenance to be changed, his thoughts to be troubled, his joints to be loosed, and his heart to be amazed. David and Job meeting with the sins of their youth, long after they were lamented and pardoned, makes their hearts startle and tremble, Ps. 25. 7; Job 13. 26. Upon the new risings of old sins, the soul begins to question all, and thus to expostulate the case: Surely my estate is not good, my pardon is not sealed; if it be, how comes these sins to be revived, to be remembered? Hath not God engaged himself in the promises of grace, that those sins that are pardoned shall never be remembered? Isa. 43. 25; Jer. 31. 34; and surely if these sins be not pardoned, I have reason to fear that others be not pardoned; and if my sins be not pardoned, how shall I escape being destroyed? Surely my repentance was not sound, my sorrow was not sincere; the blow, the wound I gave sin, was not mortal; if it had, how comes it to pass that it now meets me like an armed enemy? Thus, these new risings of old sins keeps many a man's soul and assurance asunder.

(4) Fourthly, A man may have grace and yet want assurance, and this may arise from *his falling short of that perfection that the Word requires, and that other saints have attained to.* Ah! says such a soul, surely I have no grace! Oh how short do I fall of such and such righteous rules, and of such and such precious Christians! Ah! how clear are they in their light! How strong are they in their love! How high are they in their attainments! How are their hearts filled with grace, and their lives with holiness! All their motions towards God, and towards man, speak out grace, grace; they pray indeed like saints, and live indeed like angels. Now many poor souls, comparing themselves with the perfect rule of righteousness, and with those that are in the highest forms in Christ's school, and that are the noblest and choicest patterns for purity and sanctity, and finding such a vast disproportion between their hearts and the rule, between their actions and lives, and the actions and lives of others, they are apt to sit down saddened and discouraged.

Suetonius reports of Julius Cæsar, that seeing Alexander's statue, he fetched a deep sigh, because he at that age had done so little. So many precious souls sit down sighing and weeping, that they have lived so long, and done so little for God, and for their own internal and eternal good. This wounds and sinks their spirits, that they are so unlike to those in grace, that they desire to be like unto in glory; and that they are so far below such and such in spirituals, whom they are so far above in temporals.

(5) Fifthly, A man may have true grace and yet want assurance, and this may arise from *that smoke and clouds, those fears and doubts that corruption raises in the soul; so that the soul cannot see those excellent graces that otherwise might be discerned.* Though there may be many precious gems and jewels in the house, yet the smoke may hinder a man from seeing them sparkle and shine. So though there may be many precious graces in the souls of saints, yet corruption may raise such a dust, such a smoke in the soul, that the soul is not able to see them in their beauty and glory. The well of water was near Hagar, but she saw it not till her eyes were opened by the Lord, Gen. 21. 19, 20. So grace is near the soul, yea, in the soul sometimes, and yet the soul doth not see it, till God opens the eye and shews it. "The Lord was in this place," saith Jacob, "and I knew it not," Gen. 28. 16. So many a precious soul may say, grace was in my heart, and I knew it not, I saw it not.

Blessed John Bradford in one of his epistles saith thus, "O Lord, methinks I feel it so with me, sometimes as if there were no difference between my heart, and the heart of the wicked; my mind is as blind as theirs, my spirit as stout, stubborn and rebellious as theirs, and my thoughts as confused as theirs, and my affections as disordered as theirs, and my services as formal as theirs," &c. Ah, Christians! have not many of your souls found it so? Surely yes! No wonder then, that though you have grace, yet you have not seen it sparkling and shining in your souls; as some have thought that their fields have had no corn, because they have been so full of weeds; and that their heap hath no wheat, because nothing hath appeared but chaff; and

45

that their pile hath no gold, because it hath been covered with much dross. So some have thought that their hearts have been void of grace, because they have been so full of fears and doubts. Peter at one time believes and walks, at another time he doubts and sinks, Mat. 14. 30. Abraham believes and offers up Isaac at one time, he fears and falls at another time. "Say thou art my sister, lest they kill me," Gen. 20. 2. So David and Job, they had their shufflings, tremblings, faintings, shakings, and questionings, Ps. 116. 11; Ps. 31. 22. It is not always high water with saints, sometimes they are reduced to a very low ebb. The best of saints are like the ark, tossed up and down with waves, with fears and doubts; and so it will be till they are quite in the bosom of Christ.

(6) *Lastly*, A man may have grace, and yet not see it, yet not know it; and this may arise from *his non-searching, his non-examining, his non-ransacking, of his own soul*. There is gold in the mine, and men might find it, if they would but dig and search diligently after it. There is grace in the heart, and you might see it, if you would but take the candle of the Lord and look narrowly after it. Look, as many a man upon a diligent search may find his temporal estate to be better than he apprehends it, so many choice souls upon a diligent search may find their spiritual estate to be far better than they conceived or judged it to be. Therefore souls, cease from complaining, cease from rash judging and dooming of yourselves to hell, and be diligent in inquiring what the Lord hath done, and what the Lord is a-doing, in you and for you. Compare the books together, compare his working upon you and others together. What! is there no light, no love, no longings, no hungerings, no thirstings after God? What! is there no sighing, no complaining, no mourning, under the sense of sin, and under the want of divine favour? Surely if you search, you will find some of these things; and if you do, prize them as jewels that are more worth than a world. God will not despise "the day of small things," and will you? Will you, dare you, say that that is little that is more worth than heaven? The least spark of grace shall at last be turned

into a crown of glory. Well! remember this, that as the least grace, if true and sincere, is sufficient to salvation, so the sense of the least grace should be sufficient to your consolation.

God requires some believers to wait long for assurance

The fourth proposition is this, viz., *That God may deny assurance long, and yet give it in to his children at last, after patient waiting.* God appears to David, and brings him out of " an horrible pit " (or out of a " pit of noise "), " and sets his feet upon a rock, and puts a new song into his mouth," Ps. 40. 1-4.

After the church in the Canticles had run through many hazards and hardships, many difficulties and dangers, she finds " him whom her soul loved," chap. 3. 5.

The prophet sits down and bewails his sad condition thus: Ps. 69. 3, 20, " I am weary of my crying; my throat is dried: mine eyes fail while I wait on my God. . . And I am full of heaviness; and I looked for some to take pity, but there was none; and for comforters, but I found none." Ay, but at last God appears, and then says he: " I will praise the name of God with a song, and will magnify him with thanksgiving," ver. 30.

Job sighs it out: " Behold I go forward, but he is not there; and backward, but I cannot perceive him: on the left hand, where he doth work, but I cannot behold him: he hideth himself on the right hand, that I cannot see him," Job 8. 9. But after this sighing, he sings it out: " Till I die, I will not remove my integrity from me. My righteousness I hold fast, and will not let it go: my heart shall not reproach me so long as I live," chap. 27. 5, 6.

Mr. Frogmorton was as holy and as choice a preacher as most was in England in those days, and he lived seven and thirty years without assurance, and then died, having assurance but an hour before he died. He went to die at Mr. Dod's, who is now with the Lord, and did die there in full assurance of the justification of his person, the remission of his sins, and the salvation of his soul. God denied assurance a great while to Mr. Glover, the martyr, though he sought it with many prayers and tears; and yet when he was in sight of the fire, the Lord shined forth in his favour so sweetly upon him, that he cries out to his friend, "He is come, he is come!" So Mrs. Katherine Bretterge, after many bitter conflicts with Satan the day before she died, she had sweet assurance of that kingdom that shakes not, of those riches that corrupt not, and of that crown of righteousness that fades not away.

I have read of three martyrs that were bound and brought to the stake. One of them, Mr. Hudson, gets from under his stake to supplication, and falls down upon the ground, and wrestles earnestly with God for the sense of his love, and God gave it him then at that instant, and so he came and embraced the stake, and died cheerfully and resolutely a glorious martyr. God delayed till he was bound, and then lets out himself sweetly and gloriously to him.

Now God doth delay the giving of assurance to his dearest ones, and that partly to let them know that he will be waited on, and that assurance is a jewel worth waiting for.

The least smile from God when our glass is running, will make our souls amends for all their waiting. And partly that we may know that he is free in his workings, and that he is not tied to any preparations or qualifications in the creature, but is free to come when he will, and go when he will, and stay as long as he will, though the soul doth sigh it out, "How long, Lord, how long will it be before my mourning be turned into rejoicing?"

Again, God delays the giving in of assurance, not because he delights to keep his children in fears and doubts, nor because he thinks that assurance is too rare, too great, too choice a jewel to bestow upon them; but it is either because he thinks their souls do not stand at a sufficient distance from sin, or because their souls are so taken up and filled with creature enjoyments as that Christ is put to lodge in an out-house, or else it is because they pursue not after assurance with all their might; they give not all diligence to make their calling and election sure; or else it is because their hearts are not prepared, are not low enough, for so high a favour.

Now God's delaying assurance upon these weighty grounds should rather work us to admire him, to justify him, and quietly to wait for him, than to have any hard thoughts of him, or to carry it unkindly to him, or impatiently to say, " Why is his chariot so long a-coming? " Judges 5. 28.

Assurance may be possessed and afterwards lost

The fifth proposition is this, *That those choice souls that have assurance may lose it, they may forfeit it.* The freshness and greenness, the beauty, lustre, and glory of assurance may be lost.

It is true, believers cannot lose the habits, the seeds, the root of grace; yet they may lose assurance, which is the beauty and fragrancy, the crown and glory of grace, 1 John 3. 9; 1 Peter 1. 5. These two lovers, grace and assurance, are not by God so nearly joined together but that they may by sin on our side, and justice on God's, be put asunder. The keeping of these two lovers, grace and assurance, together, will yield the soul two heavens, a heaven of joy and peace here, and a heaven of happiness and blessedness hereafter; but the putting these two lovers asunder will put the soul into a hell here, though it escape a hell hereafter. This Chrysostom knew well, when he professed that the want of the enjoyment of God would be a far greater hell to him than the feeling of any punishment.

As you would keep your Christ, as you would keep your comfort, as you would keep your crown, keep grace and assurance together, and neither by lip nor life, by word nor works, let these be put asunder. It is possible for the best of men so to blot and blur their evidences for felicity and glory, as that they may not be able to read them nor understand them. They may so vex and grieve the Spirit either by gross enormities, or by refusing his comforts and cordials, or by neglecting or slighting his gracious actings in themselves and others, or by misjudging his work, as calling faith fancy, or sincerity hypocrisy, &c., or by fathering those brats upon him that are the children of their own distempered hearts, that he may refuse to witness to their interest in him, though he be a witnessing Spirit, and refuse to comfort them, though he be the only Comforter.

The best believer that breathes may have his summer-day turned into a winter-night, his rejoicing into sighing, his singing into weeping, his wedding-robes into mourning weeds, his wine into water, his sweet into bitter, his manna, his angels' food, into husks, his pleasant grapes into the grapes of Sodom, his fruitful Canaan, his delightful paradise, into a barren and unlovely wilderness. Look, as faith is often attended with unbelief, and sincerity with hypocrisy, and humility with vain-glory, so is assurance with fears and doubts.

Blessed Hooker lived near thirty years in close communion with God, without any considerable withdrawings of God all that while; and yet, upon his dying bed, he went away without any sense of assurance, or discoveries of the smiles of God, to the wonder and deceiving of the expectation of many precious souls, and without doubt in judgment to wicked men.

Look, as many a man loses the sight of the city when he comes near to it, so many a choice soul loses the sight of heaven, even then when he is nearest to heaven. Abraham, you know, had assurance in an extraordinary way concerning his protection from God; and yet says Abraham, "Say thou art my sister; for otherwise they will kill me," Gen. 12. 13, and 20. 2. Ah! how was the freshness, the greenness, the beauty and glory of his assurance worn off, that he should, out of slavish fears, expose his wife to other men's pleasure, and himself and his neighbour to God's displeasure; that he should wound four at once, the honour of God, his wife's chastity, his own conscience, and Pharaoh's soul.

David, you know, sometimes sings it out sweetly: "The Lord is my portion, and the lot of mine inheritance; he is my salvation: of whom shall I be afraid? He is my rock and fortress, and my deliverer, my God, my strength, my trust, my buckler, and my high tower," Ps. 18. 2. At other times you have him sighing it out: "Why art thou cast down, O my soul? why art thou disquieted in me? why hast thou forgotten me?" Ps. 42. 5. "O God, my rock! why go

I mourning?" "Thine arrows stick fast in me, and thy hand presseth me sore. There is no soundness in my flesh because of thine anger; neither is there any rest in my bones because of my sin. For mine iniquities are gone over my head; as an heavy burden they are too heavy for me. I am troubled; I am bowed down greatly; I go mourning all the day long," Ps. 38. 2-6. "Thou didst hide thy face, and I was troubled," Ps. 30. 7. "Restore to me the joy of thy salvation, that the bones that thou hast broken may rejoice," Ps. 51. 12. His heart was more often out of tune than his harp. He begins many of his psalms sighing, and ends them singing; and others he begins in joy, and ends in sorrow; "So that one would think," says Peter du Moulin, "that those psalms had been composed by two men of a contrary humour." Yea, it is very observable, that though David had assurance in an extraordinary way that he should be king, being anointed by the great prophet Samuel, yet the lustre and glory of this assurance wears off; and he, overcome by slavish fears, cries out that "All men are liars" (even Samuel as well as others), and that "he shall one day perish by the hand of Saul." It is true, says David, I have a crown, a kingdom in promise; but I must swim to the crown through blood, I must win the crown before I wear it; and the truth is, I am like to die before I attain it. Yea, and after he was king, when king Jesus did but hide his face, he was sorely troubled; so that neither his glorious throne, nor his royal robes, nor his golden crown, nor his glistering courtiers, nor his large revenues, nor his cheerful temper, nor his former experiences, could quiet him or satisfy him when God had turned his back upon him. Look, as all lights cannot make up the want of the light of the sun, so all temporal comforts cannot make up the want of one spiritual comfort.

So Job sometimes sings it out, "My witness is in heaven, and my record is on high; and my Redeemer lives," &c., Job 16. 19, and 19. 25. At other times you have him complaining, "The arrows of the Almighty stick fast in me, and their poison drinketh up my spirit," Job. 6. 4; "The terrors of God do set themselves in array against me." And chap. 29. 2-5, you have him sighing it out thus: "Oh that I were as in months past, as in the days when God preserved me; when his candle shined upon my head, and when by his light I walked through darkness; as I was in the days of my youth, when the secret of God was upon my tabernacle; when the Almighty was yet with me!" &c.

Now, by all these clear instances, and by many other saints' experiences, it is evident that the choicest saints may lose their assurance, and the lustre and glory of it may decay and wither. What the soul should do in such a case, and how it should be recovered out of this sad state, I shall shew you towards the close of this discourse.

Assurance is a personal matter

The sixth proposition is this, *That the certainty and infallibility of a Christian's assurance cannot be made known to any but his own heart.* He can say as the blind man once said, "This I know, that once I was blind, but now I see," John 9. 25. Once I was a slave, but now I am a son; once I was dead, but now I am alive; once I was darkness, but now I am light in the Lord; once I was a child of wrath, an heir of hell, but now I am an heir of heaven; once I was Satan's bondman, but now I am God's freeman; once I was under the spirit of bondage, but now I am under the spirit of adoption, that seals up to me the remission of my sins, the justification of my person, and the salvation of my soul. All this I know, says the assured saint; but I cannot make you know it certainly and infallibly if you would give me a thousand worlds. What I have found and felt, and what I do find and feel, is wonderfully beyond what I am able to express. I am as well able to tell the stars of heaven, and to number the sand of the sea, as I am able to declare to you the joy, the joy, the unconceivable joy, the assurance, the glorious assurance, that God hath given me.

Severinus, the Indian saint, under the power of assurance, was heard to say, O my God! do not for pity so over-joy me; if I must still live, and have such consolations, take me to heaven, &c. So say souls under the power of assurance: Lord! we are so filled with joy and comfort, with delight and content, that we are not able to express it here on earth;

and therefore take us to heaven, that we may have that glory put upon us, that may enable us to declare and manifest those glorious things that thou hast wrought in us. 1 Peter 1. 8.

Parents do by experience feel such soundings, such meltings, such sweet workings of their affections and bowels towards their children, that for their lives they cannot describe to others what it is to be a father, to be a mother; what it is to have such compassions towards children. Assurance is that white stone that none knoweth but he that hath it: Rev. 2. 17, "To him that overcometh will I give to eat of the hidden manna, and give him a white stone, and in the stone a new name written, which no man knoweth saving he that receiveth it." White stones were in great use among the Romans.

(1) In white stones they used to write the names of such as were victorious and conquerors; so in that text, "To him that overcometh, will I give a white stone."

(2) They used to acquit the innocent in courts of justice, by giving them a white stone; and so here the white stone points out absolution and remission.

(3) They used to give a white stone to those that were chosen to any places of honour; so the white stone of assurance is an evidence of our election, of our being chosen to a kingdom that shakes not, to riches that corrupt not, and to a crown of glory that fades not. And thus much for this sixth proposition, viz., that the certainty and infallibility of a Christian's assurance cannot be made known to any but his own heart, Heb. 12. 28; Mat. 6. 20; 1 Pet. 1. 4.

Nine special seasons when assurance is enjoyed:

The seventh proposition is this, That there are some special seasons and times, wherein the Lord is graciously pleased to give to his children a sweet assurance of his favour and love, and they are these that follow.

(1) AT CONVERSION

1. First, *Sometimes, I say not always, at first conversion, the Lord is pleased to make out sweet manifestations of his*

53

love to the penitent soul. When the soul hath been long under guilt and wrath, when the soul hath been long under the frowns and displeasure of God, and hath long seen the gates of heaven barred against him, and the mouth of hell open to receive him; when the soul hath said, Surely there is no hope, there is no help, surely I shall lose God, Christ and heaven for ever, then God comes in and speaks peace to the soul, then he says, " I will blot out thy iniquities for my name's sake, and will remember thy sins no more," Isa. 43. 25. Hark, soul, hark, says Christ, " My thoughts are not as your thoughts, nor my ways as your ways." Isa. 55. 8, 9. My thoughts towards you are thoughts of peace and thoughts of love. Hark, soul! here is mercy to pardon thee, and here is grace to adorn thee; here is righteousness to justify thee; here is eye-salve to enlighten thee, and gold to enrich thee, and raiment to clothe thee, and balm to heal thee, and bread to nourish thee, and wine upon the lees to cheer thee, and happiness to crown thee, and myself to satisfy thee. Ah, souls! have not some of you found it so? surely you have.

God deals sometimes with rebellious sinners as princes do with those that are in arms, that are in open rebellion against them. You know princes will put such persons hard to it: they shall fare hard, and lie hard; chains, and racks, and what not, shall attend them; and yet after the sentence is passed upon them, and they are upon the last step of the ladder of life, ready to be turned off, and all hope of escape is gone, then the prince's pardon is put into their hand. So the Lord brings many poor souls to the last steps of the ladder, to a hopeless condition, and then he puts their pardon into their bosoms; then he says, " Be of good cheer, I have received you into favour, I have set my love upon you, I am reconciled to you, and will never be separated from you."

You know how God dealt with Paul: after he had awakened and convinced him, after he had unhorsed him and overthrown him, after he had amazed and astonished him, then he shewed himself graciously and favourably to him, taking him up into the third heaven, and making such manifestations of his love and favour, of his beauty and glory, of his mercy and majesty, as Paul was not able to utter. Acts 9. 3.

So upon the prodigal's return, the fatted calf is killed, and the best robe is put upon his back, and the ring is put on his hand, and shoes on his feet, Luke 15. 22, 23.

Some understand by the robe, the royalty of Adam, others, the righteousness of Christ; and by the ring, some understand the pledges of God's love, rings being given as pledges of love; some the seal of God's Spirit, men using to seal with their rings.

Among the Romans, the ring was an ensign of virtue, honour, and nobility, whereby they that wore them were distinguished from the common people. I think the main thing intended by all these passages, is to shew us, that God sometimes upon the sinner's first conversion and returning to him, is graciously pleased to give him some choice and signal manifestations of his love and favour, of his good-will and pleasure, and that upon these following grounds:

(1) *The first ground, That they may not be swallowed up of sorrow, nor give up the ghost under the pangs and throes of the new birth.* Ah! did not the Lord let in some beams of love upon the soul, when it is *Magor-missabib*, a terror to itself; when the heart is a hell of horror, the conscience an *Aceldama*, a field of black blood; when the soul is neither quiet at home nor abroad, neither at bed nor board, neither in company nor out of company, neither in the use of ordinances nor in the neglect of ordinances; how would the soul faint, sink, and despair for ever! But now when it is thus night with the soul, the Lord sweetly comes in and tells the soul that all is well, that he hath found a ransom for the soul, that the books are crossed, that all debts are discharged, and that his favour and love upon the soul is fixed, Job 33. 24. And so God by his sweet and still voice, speaking thus to the soul, quiets and satisfies it, and keeps it from sinking and despairing.

(2) *The second ground.* God gives assurance sometimes at first conversion, *that he may the more raise and inflame their love and affections to him.* Ah! how does a pardon given when a man is ready to be turned off, draw out his

55

love, and raise his affections to that prince that shews bowels of mercy, when he is upon the brink of misery! So when a poor sinner is upon the last step of the ladder, upon the very brink of hell and misery, now for God to come in and speak peace and pardon to the soul, ah! how does it inflame the soul, and works the soul to a holy admiration of God, and to a spiritual delighting in God!

The pulling of a sheep, by King Antigonus, with his own hands out of a dirty ditch, as he was passing by, drew his subjects exceedingly to commend him and love him. So King Jesus's pulling of poor souls out of their sins, and as it were out of hell, cannot but draw them to be much in the commendations of Christ. and strong in their love to Christ. Christ hath nothing more in his eye, nor upon his heart, than to act towards his people in such ways and at such seasons as may most win upon their affections. And therefore it is, that sometimes he gives the strongest consolation at first conversion.

(3) *The third ground.* Christ sometimes at first conversion grants to his people the sweetest manifestations of his love, *that they may be the more active, fervent, abundant, and constant in ways of grace and holiness.* He knows that divine manifestations of love will most awaken, quicken, and engage the soul to ways of piety and sanctity.

Look, what wings are to the bird, oil to the wheels, weights to the clock, a reward to the coward, and the lodestone to the needle, that are the smiles and discoveries of God to a poor soul at his conversion. The manifestations of divine love puts heat and life into the soul, it makes the soul very serious and studious how to act for God, and live to God, and walk with God. Ah! says a soul under the beams of divine love, it is my meat and drink, it is my joy and crown to do all I can for that God that hath done so much for me, as to know me in darkness, and to speak love to me when I was most unlovely; to turn my mourning into rejoicing, and my hell into a heaven.

(4) *The fourth ground.* Christ sometimes at first conversion gives his people the sweetest manifestations of his love, *to fence and fortify them against Satan's fiery temptations.*

Before Christ shall be led into the wilderness to be tempted by the devil, the Spirit of the Lord shall descend upon him like a dove, and he shall hear a voice from heaven, saying, "This is my beloved Son, in whom I am well pleased," Mat. 3. 16, 17, that so he may be strong in resisting, and glorious in triumphing over all the assaults and temptations of Satan, Eph. 6. 16. So, many times at first conversion, the Lord makes sweet manifestations of his love to the soul, so that the soul may stand fast, and not give ground, and in the sense of divine love may so manage the shield of faith as to quench all the fiery darts of the devil.

The Lord knows that when he sets upon the delivering of a poor soul from the kingdom of darkness. and translating it into the kingdom of his dear Son, Satan will roar and rage, rend and tear, as he did him, Mark 9. 25, 26, "When Jesus saw that the people came running together, he rebuked the foul spirit, saying unto him, Thou dumb and deaf spirit, I charge thee to come out of him. And the spirit cried, and rent him sore, and came out of him: and he was as one dead; insomuch that many said, He is dead." No sooner did Jesus Christ look with an eye of love, pity, and compassion upon the boy, but the devil in his rage and wrath falls a-rending and tearing of him, as mad dogs do things they fasten upon. This poor child had never so sore a fit as now he was nearest the cure. When rich mercy and glorious power is nearest the soul, then Satan most storms and rages against the soul, Col. 1. 13. The more the bowels of Christ do work towards a sinner, the more furiously will Satan assault that sinner. Therefore divine wisdom and goodness does the more eminently shine in giving the poor soul some sights of Canaan, and some bunches and clusters of that land, upon its first coming out of the wilderness of sin and sorrow.

But that no soul may mistake this last proposition, give me leave to premise these two cautions.

[1] *The first caution. That God does manifest his love only to some at their first conversion, not to all.* Though he dearly loves every penitent soul, yet he does not manifest his love at first conversion to every penitent soul. God is a free agent, to work where he will, and when he will, and

to reveal his love how he will, and when he will, and to whom he will. It is one thing for God to work a work of grace upon the soul, and another thing for God to shew the soul that work.

God oftentimes works grace in a silent and secret way, and takes sometimes five, sometimes ten, sometimes fifteen, sometimes twenty years; yea, sometimes more, before he will make a clear and satisfying report of his own work upon the soul. Though our graces be our best jewels, yet they are sometimes, at first conversion, so weak and imperfect, that we are not able to see their lustre. The being of grace makes our estates safe and sure, the seeing of grace makes our lives sweet and comfortable.

[2] *The second caution. A man may at first conversion have such a clear glorious manifestation of God's love to him, and of his interest in God, and his right to glory, that he may not have the like all his days after.* The fatted calf is not every day slain, the robe of kings is not every day put on, every day must not be a festival day, a marriage day; the wife is not every day in the bosom, the child is not every day in the arms, the friend is not every day at the table, nor the soul every day under the manifestations of divine love; Jacob did not every day see the angels ascending and descending; Stephen did not every day see the heavens open, and Christ standing on the right hand of God; Paul was not every day caught up to heaven, nor was John every day rapt up in the Spirit. No saint can every day cry out, I have my Christ, I have my comfort, I have my assurance, as the Persian king cried out in his dream, " I have Themistocles, I have Themistocles." Job had his harp turned into mourning, and his organ into the voice of them that weep, Job 30. 31. The best of saints are sometimes put to hang their harps upon the willows, and cry out, " Hath God forgotten to be gracious, and will he be favourable no more? " Ps. 137. 2; 77. 7-9.

(2) BEFORE ENGAGING IN HARD OR DANGEROUS SERVICE

II. There is a second special season or time wherein the Lord is pleased to give to his children a sweet assurance of his favour and love, and that is, *when he intends to put them upon some high and hard, some difficult and dangerous service.* Oh then he gives them some sweet taste of heaven beforehand; now he smiles, now he kisses, now he embraces the soul, now he takes a saint by the hand, now he causes his goodness and glory to pass before the soul, now he opens his bosom to the soul, now the soul shall be of his court and counsel, now the clouds shall be scattered, now it shall be no longer night with the soul, now the soul shall sit no longer mourning in the valley of darkness, now Christ will carry the soul up into the mount, and there reveal his glory to it, that it may act high and brave, noble and glorious in the face of difficulties and discouragements. Christ did intend to put Peter, James, and John upon hard and difficult service, and therefore brings them up into an high mountain, and there gives them a vision of his beauty and glory; there they see him transfigured, metamorphosed, or transformed; there they see his face shining as the sun, and his raiment glistering, Mat. 17. 1-6. In the mount he shews them such beams of his deity, such sparkling glory, as did altogether amaze them, transport them, and astonish them; and all this grace and glory, this goodness and sweetness Christ shews them, to hearten and encourage them to own him and his truth, to stand by him and truth, to make him and his truth known to the world, though hatred, bonds, and contempt did attend them in so doing.

Thus God dealt with Paul before he put him upon that hard and dangerous service that he had cut out for him, Acts 9. 1-23. He takes him up into heaven, and sheds abroad his love in his heart, and tells him that he is a chosen vessel; he appears to him in the way, and fills him with the Holy Ghost, that is, with the gifts, graces, and comforts of the Holy Ghost, and straightway Paul falls upon preaching of Christ, exalting of Christ, to the amazement and astonishment of all that heard him. And as he had more clear, full, and glorious manifestations of God's love and favour than others, so he was more frequent, more abundant, and more constant in the work and service of Christ than others, 2 Cor. 11. 21-33.

And this hath been the constant dealing of God with the patriarchs, as with Abraham, Isaac, and Jacob, &c., and with the prophets, as with Moses, Isaiah, Jeremiah, Ezekiel, &c. When he hath put them upon weighty services, he hath shed abroad his love into their hearts, he hath set his seal upon their spirits, and made them to know that he hath set them as a seal upon his hand; he hath assured them of his countenance, and of his presence, and of his assistance; he hath told them, though others should desert them, yet he will stand by them, and strengthen them, and support them, and uphold them with the right hand of his righteousness; he hath told them that his power should be theirs to defend them, and his wisdom should be theirs to direct them, and his goodness should be theirs to supply them, and his grace should be theirs to heal them, and his mercy should be theirs to pardon them, and his joy should be theirs to strengthen them, and his promise should be theirs to cheer them, and his Spirit should be theirs to lead them; and this hath made them as bold as lions, this hath made them stedfast, and able to stand close to the work of God in the face of all dangers and difficulties; this hath made them, with stout Nehemiah, scorn to desist or fly from the work of the Lord; this hath made their bows to abide in strength, though the archers have shot sore at them. Now there are considerable reasons why God is pleased to give his children some sweet tastes of his love, some assurance of his favour, when he puts them upon some hard and difficult service, and they are these that follow.

(1) *The first reason, That they may not faint nor falter in his service, but go through it resolutely and bravely, in the face of all difficulties and oppositions.* When God put Joshua upon that hard service of leading and governing his people Israel, he assures him of his love and of his presence: "Fear not, be of good courage, I am with thee," Joshua 1. 6. And this makes him hold on and hold out in the service of the Lord bravely and resolutely, in the face of all discouragements: "Choose you whom you will serve, whether your fathers' gods or the gods of the Amorites; but as for me and my house, we will serve the Lord," Joshua 24. 15. So

when the Lord put Paul upon such service that occasioned bonds and afflictions to abide him in every city, Acts 20. 23, he gives him a taste of heaven beforehand, and lifts up the light of his countenance upon him, and this makes him resolute and bold in the work of the Lord. Now Paul will not consult with flesh and blood, Gal. 1. 15-17; now it is not reproaches, nor stripes, nor prisons, nor whips, nor perils, nor deaths, that can make him look back, having put his hand to the Lord's plough. Oh! the beamings forth of divine love upon his soul filled him with such courage and resolution that, with Shammah, one of David's worthies, he stands and defends the field, when others fall, and fly, and quit the field, 2 Tim. 4. 16, 17.

(2) *The second reason:* God gives his people some tastes of his love, some sense of his favour, when he puts them upon hard and difficult services, *because else he should not only act below himself, as he is a wise God, a faithful God, a powerful God, a merciful God, a righteous God, &c., but also act below his poor weak creatures.* For what husband will put his wife, what father will put his child, what master will put his servant, what captain will put his soldier, what prince will put his ambassadors, upon hard and difficult services, but they will smile upon them, and speak kindly to them, and make large promises to honour their persons, and kindly to accept, and nobly to reward their services, &c. Surely none. And will God? Will God, who will not give his glory to those that have the most glorious beings, suffer his glory to be clouded and eclipsed by the prudent actings of weak worms? Surely no. Isa. 42. 8, and 48. 11.

(3) *The third reason:* God lifts up the light of his countenance upon his people when he puts them upon hard and difficult services, *that they may never repent of listing themselves in his service.* Ah! if the Lord did not warm the hearts of his people with the glorious beams of his love, when he puts them upon hard work, they would be ready, when they meet with oppositions and hazards, to throw up all, and to sit down lamenting and repenting that ever they were engaged in his service. They would be as peevish and froward as Jonah, and with him venture a drowning, to avoid

God's service. Ah! but now the Lord, by letting his goodness drop upon their hearts, and by putting an earnest-penny into their hands, he causes them to go cheerfully on in his work, without sighing or repenting. The kisses and embraces of God do put such life, such spirit, such mettle into their souls, as makes them bid defiance to the greatest dangers, and as crowns them conquerors of the greatest difficulties. Ah! says a soul that hath walked some turns in paradise, What is dross to gold! what is darkness to light! what is hell to heaven! No more are all difficulties and oppositions to me, who have found the sweetness of divine grace, and have had the happiness to lie in the bosom of God.

Diocletian, the worst and last persecutor in all the ten persecutions, observed, " that the more he sought to blot out the name of Christ, the more it became legible; and to block up the way of Christ, the more it became passable; and whatever of Christ he thought to root out, it rooted the deeper, and rose the higher in the hearts and lives of the saints, among whom he had scattered the beams of his love and the rich pearls of his grace." Such souls as have once been in the arms of God, in the midst of all oppositions, they are as men made all of fire walking in stubble; they consume and overcome all oppositions; all difficulties are but as whetstones to their fortitude. The moon will run her course, though the dogs bark at it; so will all those choice souls that have found warmth under Christ's wings run their Christian race in spite of all difficulties and dangers. The horse neighs at the trumpet, the leviathan laughs at the spear; so does a saint, under the power of assurance, laugh at all hazards and dangers that he meets with in the Lord's service. The sense of God's love and goodness makes him to triumph over the greatest difficulties.

(4) *The fourth reason*, and lastly: God gives his people some tastes of his love when he puts them upon hard and difficult services, that *the mouths of the wicked may be stopped*. Should God lay heavy burdens upon his people's shoulders, and not put under his fingers to give some ease; should God double their tale of brick, and yet deny them

straw; should God engage them against a potent enemy, and then desert them; should God send them upon some weighty embassage, and not give proportionable encouragements to them, what would the world say? Exod. 32. 12; Num. 14. 12-16. Would they not say that he is a hard master, and that his ways are not equal? Would they not say, Verily they are liars that say he is glorious in power, and wonderful in counsel, and infinite in mercy, and admirable in goodness and rich in grace, and unsearchable in his understanding? For surely were he, he could not, he would not, put his children upon such hard and dangerous services, but he would own them, and stand by them; he would assist them, and smile upon them; he would be as careful to bring them bravely off, as he hath been ready to bring them freely on. Oh! he could not see them in garments rolled in blood, but his bowels would yearn towards them, and he would arise, and have mercy on them.

(3) DURING TIMES OF WAITING

III. Then, thirdly, *Waiting times are times wherein God is pleased to give his people some secret tastes of his love, and to lift up the light of his countenance upon them:* " I waited patiently for the Lord," saith David, "and he inclined unto me, and heard my cry. He brought me up also out of an horrible pit" (or out of a pit of noise), "out of the miry clay, and set my feet upon a rock, and established my goings. And he hath put a new song in my mouth, even praise unto our God," Ps. 40. 1-3. After God had exercised David's patience in waiting, he sweetly breaks in upon him, and knocks off his bolts, and opens the prison doors, and takes him by the hand, and leads him out of the pit of noise and confusion, in which he was, and causes his love and goodness so to beam forth upon him as causes his heart to rejoice, and his tongue to sing. So after devout Simeon had waited for the consolation of Israel, that is, for Christ's coming, the Holy Ghost falls upon him, and leads him to a sight of Christ in the temple, and this makes the good old man sing, *Nunc dimittis,* Now, let thy servant depart in peace, Luke 2. 25-33. Ah, says Simeon, I have lived long enough!

now I have got Christ in my heart, and Christ in my arms, who is my light, my life, my love, my joy, my crown, let me depart, according to thy word. Ah! saints, I appeal to you, have not many of you found by experience the sweet breathings of Christ upon you, even whilst you have been waiting at the door of mercy? while you have been weeping and waiting, hath not the Lord Jesus come in and said, "Peace be to you"; "Waiting souls, be of good cheer, it is I; be of good cheer, your sins are pardoned"? Surely you have. Hath not God made that word good unto you, "Wait on the Lord, be of good courage, and he shall strengthen thine heart: wait, I say, on the Lord"? Ps. 27. 24; yes. And hath he not made that good to you, "They shall not be ashamed that wait for me"? Isa. 49. 23; that is, they shall not be deceived, or disappointed of their hopes and expectations, that wait for me. Yes. And have you not found that word made sweet to your souls, "Therefore will the Lord wait, that he may be gracious: blessed are all they that wait for him"? Yes. And hath not the Lord made that word good to you, "The Lord is good unto them that wait for him, to the soul that seeketh him"? Lam. 3. 25. Yes. Waiting souls, remember this assurance is yours, but the time of giving it is the Lord's; the jewel is yours, but the season in which he will give it is in his own hand; the gold chain is yours, but he only knows the hour wherein he will put it about your necks. Well! wait patiently and quietly, wait expectingly, wait believingly, wait affectionately, and wait diligently, and you shall find that scripture made good in power upon your souls, "Yet a little while, and he that shall come will come, and will not tarry," Heb. 10. 37, Hab. 2. 3. He will certainly come, he will seasonably come, he will suddenly come, as the prophet Malachi speaks: "Behold, I will send my messenger, and he shall prepare the way before me: and the Lord, whom ye seek, shall suddenly come to his temple, even the messenger of the covenant whom ye delight in: behold, he shall come, saith the Lord of hosts," Mal. 3. 1. Well! I will say but this, if assurance of God's love be not a jewel worth waiting for, it is worth nothing.

IV. Fourthly, *Suffering times are times wherein the Lord is pleased to give his people some sense of his favour.* When they are in sufferings for righteousness' sake, for the gospel's sake, then usually God causes his face to shine upon them. Now they shall hear best news from heaven when they hear worst from earth. God loves to smile most upon his people when the world frowns most. When the world puts its iron chains upon their legs, then God puts his golden chains about their necks; when the world puts a bitter cup into their hands, then God drops some of his honey, some of his goodness and sweetness into it. When the world is ready to stone them, then God gives them the white stone; and when the world is a-tearing their good names, then he gives them a new name, that none knows but he that hath it, a name that is better than that of sons and daughters. When the world cries out, " Crucify them, crucify them," then they hear that sweet voice from heaven, " These are my beloved ones, in whom I am well pleased." When the world clothes them with rags, then the Lord puts on his royal robes, and makes a secret proclamation to their spirits, " Thus shall it be done to the men whom the King is pleased to honour." When the world gives into one hand a cup of water, God gives into the other a cup of nectar, a cup of ambrosia. When the world gnasheth upon them, and presents all imaginary tortures before them, then the Lord opens paradise to them, as he did to Stephen. When Paul and Silas were in prison for the gospel's sake, then God fills them with such unspeakable joy, that they cannot but be singing when others are sleeping, Acts 16. 23, 24. God turns their prison into a palace, a paradise, and they turn his mercies into praises. Paul and Silas found more pleasure than pain, more joy than sorrow, more sweet than bitter, more day than night, in the prison.

God will make some beams of his goodness and glory to break through stone walls, to warm and gladden the hearts of his suffering ones. When John was banished into the isle of Patmos, " for the word of God and the testimony of Jesus," Rev. 1. 9, 10, then he is filled with the Spirit, and hath the choicest manifestations, and the most glorious revelations that ever he had all his days. Now God makes him one of his court and counsel, and tells him what glorious and mighty things shall be in the latter days. Now he is in a spiritual rapture and ecstasy, and carried above himself, and above all outward things, to attend those glorious visions that God would make known to him.

It was God's lifting up the light of his countenance that made the martyrs to sing in the fire, to clap their hands in the flames, and to tread upon hot burning coals as upon beds of roses. This made Vincentius say, when he felt the flame come to his beard, "What a small pain is this, compared to the glory to come? What is a drop of vinegar put into an ocean of wine? What is it for one to have a rainy day, that is going to take possession of a kingdom?" The smiles of God made Sanctus to sing under dreadful sufferings, *Christianus sum,* "I am a Christian"; and this made the Christians to sing, in Tertullian's time, *Crudelitas vestra gloria nostra,* "your cruelty is our glory."

This made a French martyr to say, when the rope was about his fellow's neck, "Give me that golden chain, and dub me a knight of that noble order." This made another to desire, when he was to die, the favour of having his chains buried with him, as the ensigns of his honour.

This made Basil say, "Fire, sword, prison, famine, are all a pleasure, a delight unto me." This made Paul to rattle his iron chains, and to glory in it, more than worldly men glory in all their outward glory.

This made Theodoret to complain, that his persecutors did him wrong, when they took him off the rack, and ceased tormenting of him; for, said he, "All the while I was on the rack, I found methought there was a young man in white, an angel stood by me, which wiped off the sweat; and I found a great deal of sweetness in it, which now I have lost."

To conclude, the smiles of God upon the prisoners of hope, is that which makes them more cheerful and delightful in their sufferings than Jesus Christ was in his.

When Faninus, an Italian martyr, was asked by one, why he was so merry at his death, since Christ himself was so sorrowful: "Christ," said he, "sustained in his soul all the sorrows and conflicts with hell and death, due to us, by whose sufferings we are delivered from sorrow and fear of them all; and therefore we have cause of rejoicing in the greatest sufferings."

Now there are these special reasons to be given, why the Lord is pleased in suffering times to visit his people with his loving-kindness, and to lift up the light of his countenance upon them.

(1) *The first reason. That their patience and constancy under the cross may be invincible.* God knows right well, that if his left hand in suffering times be not under his people, and his right hand over them, if he does not give them some sips of sweetness, some relishes of goodness, they would quickly grow impatient and inconstant. Oh, but now the smiles of God, the gracious discoveries of God, makes their patience and constancy invincible, as it did Vincentius, who by his patience and constancy madded his tormentors; wherefore they stripped him stark naked, whipped his body all over to a gore blood, sprinkled salt and vinegar over all his wounds, set his feet on burning coals, then cast him naked into a loathsome dungeon, the pavement whereof was sharp shells, and his bed to lie on, a bundle of thorns. All which this blessed martyr received, without so much as a groan, breathing out his spirit in these words, "Vincentius is my name, and by the grace of God I will be still Vincentius, in spite of all your torments." Persecution brings death in one hand and life in the other; for while it kills the body it crowns the soul.

The most cruel martyrdom is but a crafty trick to escape death, to pass from life to life, from the prison to paradise, from the cross to the crown.

Justin Martyr says, that when the Romans did immortalise their emperors, as they called it, they brought one to swear that he saw him go to heaven out of the fire. But we may see, by an eye of faith, the blessed souls of suffering saints fly to heaven, like Elias in his fiery chariot, like the angel that appeared to Manoah in the flames, Judges 13. 20.

John Huss, martyr, had such choice discoveries of God,

67

and such sweet fillings of the Spirit, as made his patience and constancy invincible. When he was brought forth to be burned, they put on his head a triple crown of paper, painted over with ugly devils; but when he saw it, he said, " My Lord Jesus Christ, for my sake, did wear a crown of thorns; why should not I then for his sake wear this light crown, be it never so ignominious? Truly I will do it, and that willingly." And as they tied his neck with a chain to the stake, smiling, he said, " That he would willingly receive the same chain for Jesus Christ's sake, who he knew was bound with a far worse chain for his sake." Well! remember this, that their names who by a patient suffering are written in red letters of blood in the church's calendar, are written in golden letters in Christ's register, in the book of life.

(2) *The second reason.* A second reason why the Lord lifts up the light of his countenance upon his people in times of suffering is, *for the confirmation of some, for the conversion of others, and for the greater conviction and confusion of their adversaries, who wonder, and are like men amazed, when they see the comfort and the courage of the saints in times of suffering.* Paul's choice carriage in his bonds was the confirmation of many. "And many of the brethren in the Lord, waxing confident by my bonds, are much more bold to speak the word without fear," Philip 1. 14. And as the sufferings of the saints do contribute to the confirmation of some, so by the blessing of God they contribute to the conversion of others. "I beseech thee," says Paul, "for my son Onesimus, whom I have begotten in my bonds," Philemon 10. It was a notable saying of Luther, *Ecclesia totum mundum convertit sanguine et oratione,* The church converteth the whole world by blood and prayer. Basil affirms that the primitive saints shewed so much heroic zeal and constancy, that many of the heathens turned Christians; so that the choice spirit which the saints have shewn in their sufferings, when Christ hath overshadowed them with his love, and "stayed them with flagons, and comforted them, with apples," Solomon's Song 2. 5, hath maddened, grieved, vexed, and extremely tormented their tormentors.

Lactantius boasts of the braveness of the martyrs in his time: "Our children and women, not to speak of men, do in silence overcome their tormentors, and the fire cannot so much as fetch a sigh from them."

Hegesippus reports an observation of Antoninus the emperor, viz., "That the Christians were most courageous and confident always in earthquakes, whilst his own heathen soldiers were at such accidents most fearful and dispirited." Certainly no earthquakes can make any heartquakes among the suffering saints, so long as the countenance of God shines upon their face, and his love lies warm upon their hearts. The suffering saint may be assaulted, but not vanquished; he may be troubled, but can never be conquered; he may lose his head, but he cannot lose his crown, which the righteous Lord hath prepared and laid up for him, 2 Tim. 4. 7, 8. The suffering saint shall still be master of the day; though they kill him, they cannot hurt him; he may suffer death, but never conquest. "And they overcame him by the blood of the Lamb, and by the word of their testimony; and they loved not their lives unto the death," Rev. 12. 11. They love not their lives that love Christ and his truth more than their lives; they that slight, contemn, and despise their lives, when they stand in competition with Christ, may be truly said not to love their lives. In these words you see that the saints by dying do overcome: "They may kill me," said Socrates of his enemies, "but they cannot hurt me." A saint may say this and more. The herb *heliotropium* doth turn about and open itself according to the motion of the sun; so do the saints in their sufferings, according to the internal motions of the Sun of righteousness upon them.

(3) *The third reason.* A third reason why the Lord causes his goodness to pass before his people, and his face to shine upon his people in times of suffering, and that is, *for the praise of his own grace, and for the glory of his own name.* God would lose much of his own glory, if he did not stand by his people, and comfort them and strengthen them, in the day of their sorrows. Ah the dirt, the scorn, the contempt, that vain men would cast upon God! Exod. 32. 12; Num. 14. 13. Look, as our greatest good comes through the

sufferings of Christ, so God's greatest glory that he hath from his saints comes through their sufferings: "If ye be reproached for the name of Christ, happy are ye; for the Spirit of glory and of God resteth upon you: on their part he is evil spoken of, but on your part he is glorified," 1 Pet. 4. 14. It makes much for the glory of God, that his people are cheered and comforted, quickened, and raised, spiritualised and elevated in the day of their sufferings. Oh, the sight of so noble a spirit in the saints, causes others to admire God, to lift up God, to fall in love with God, and to glorify God, for owning his people, and for being a light to them in darkness, a joy to them in sorrow, and a palace to them in prison, Dan. 3. 28-30; Dan. 6. 25-27. God is very sensible of the many praises and prayers that he should lose, did he not cause his love and his glory to rest upon his people in suffering times. There is nothing that God is so tender of, as he is of his glory, and that his heart is so much set upon as his glory; and therefore he will visit them in a prison, and feast them in a dungeon, and walk with them in a fiery furnace, and shew kindness to them in a lions' den, that every one may shout and cry, Grace, grace! Isa. 48. 11; Gen. 39. 20; Dan. 6. 10; Zech. 4. 7. God loves to act in such ways of grace towards his suffering ones, as may stop the mouths of their enemies, and cause the hearts of his friends to rejoice.

(4) *The fourth reason. Believing times are times wherein the Lord is graciously pleased* to lift up the light of his countenance upon his people. When his children are in the exercise of faith, then the Lord is pleased to make known his goodness, and to seal up to them everlasting happiness and blessedness: Eph. 1. 13, "In whom ye also trusted, after that ye heard the word of truth, the gospel of your salvation: in whom also, after that ye believed, ye were sealed with the Holy Spirit of promise"; or "in whom believing ye were sealed," that is, as you were in the very exercise and actings of faith upon the Lord Jesus Christ, the Spirit of the Lord made sure, and sealed up to you your adoption, your reconciliation, your pardon, and everlasting inheritance.

Him that honours Christ by believing, by fresh and frequent acts of faith upon him, him will Christ certainly honour and secure by setting his seal and mark upon him, and by assuring him of a kingdom that shakes not, of riches that corrupt not, and of glory that fades not. Ah, Christians, you wrong two at once, Christ and your own souls, whilst you thus reason: Lord, give me first assurance, and then I will believe in thee and rest upon thee; whereas your great work is to believe, and to hold on believing and acting of faith on the Lord Jesus, till you come to be assured and sealed up to the day of redemption. This is the surest and shortest way to assurance.

That is a remarkable passage of the apostle in Rom. 15. 13, " Now the God of hope fill you with all joy and peace in believing, that ye may abound in hope, through the power of the Holy Ghost." "The God of hope," saith the apostle, " shall fill you with all joy and peace in believing." That is, whilst you are in the exercise and actings of faith, the God of hope shall fill you with that joy that is " unspeakable and full of glory," and with that " peace that passes understanding."

Faith is the key that unlocks paradise, and lets in a flood of joy into the soul. Faith is an appropriating grace, it appropriates all to itself; it looks upon God, and says with the psalmist, " This God is my God for ever and ever," Ps. 63. 1, and 48. 14. It looks upon Christ and says, " My beloved is mine, and his desires are towards me," Song of Solomon 7. 10. It looks upon the precious promises and says, These " precious promises " are mine, 2 Pet. 1. 4. It looks upon heaven and says, " Henceforth is laid up for me a crown of righteousness," 2 Tim. 4. 8; and this fills the soul with joy and peace. Faith hath an influence upon other graces; it is like a silver thread that runs through a chain of pearl, it puts strength and vivacity into all other virtues. It made Abraham to rejoice, and it made Noah sit still and quiet in the midst of a deluge.

Faith is the first pin that moveth the soul; it is the spring in the watch that sets all the golden wheels of love, joy, comfort and peace a-going. Faith is a root-grace, from whence springs all the sweet flowers of joy and peace. Faith is like the bee, it will suck sweetness out of every flower; it will extract light out of darkness, comforts out of distresses, mercies out of miseries, wine out of water, honey out of the rock, and meat out of the eater, Judges 14. 14. 1 Pet. 1. 8, "Whom having not seen, ye love; in whom, though now ye see him not, yet believing, ye rejoice with joy unspeakable, and full of glory." Upon the exercise of faith, their hearts are filled with joy, with unspeakable joy, with glorious joy. Faith sees in Christ *plenitudo abundantiæ* and *plenitudo redundantiæ,* a fulness of abundance and a fulness of redundancy; and this fills the heart with glorious joy.

Ah, Christians! believing, believing is the ready way, the safest way, the sweetest way, the shortest way, the only way to a well-grounded assurance, and to that unspeakable joy and peace that flows from it, as the effect from the cause, the fruit from the root, the stream from the fountain. There is such assurance, and such joy that springs from the fresh and frequent actings of faith, that cannot be expressed, that cannot be painted. No man can paint the sweetness of the honeycomb, the sweetness of a cluster of Canaan, the sweetness of paradise, the fragrancy of the rose of Sharon. As the being of things cannot be painted, and as the sweetness of things cannot be painted, no more can that assurance and joy that flows from believing be painted or expressed; it is too great and too glorious for weak man to paint or set forth.

When Abraham believed in hope against hope, Rom. 4. 18, and when in the face of all dangers and difficulties, he put forth such noble and glorious acts of faith, as to conclude that "the Lord would provide himself a lamb for a burnt-offering," Gen. 22. 8, and that "in the mount he would be seen," Gen. 22. 14; God is so taken with the actings of his faith and the effects of it, that he swears by himself, that "in blessing he would bless him"; that is, I will certainly bless him, and will bless his blessing to him; "and in multiplying, he would multiply his seed as the stars of heaven, and as the sand which is upon the sea shore," Gen. 22. 17. Now the angel of the Lord, viz., the Lord Jesus, as his own words shew, verses 12, 15, 16, calls unto Abraham out of heaven, not once but twice; and now he shews his admirable love in countermanding of Abraham, and in providing a ram, even to a miracle, for a burnt-offering.

And thus you see that believing times are times wherein the Lord is graciously pleased to reveal his love, and make known his favour to his people, and to look from heaven upon them, and to speak again and again in love and sweetness to them.

(5) DURING "HEARING AND RECEIVING" TIMES

V. *Fifthly, Hearing and receiving times are times wherein the Lord is graciously pleased to cause his face to shine upon his people.* When they are a-hearing the word of life and a-breaking the bread of life, then God comes in upon them, and declares to them that love that is better than life: Acts 10. 44, "While Peter yet spake these words, the Holy Ghost fell on all them which heard the word." As Peter was speaking, the Holy Ghost, that is, the graces of the Holy Ghost, viz., the joy, the comfort, the love, the peace, &c., of the Holy Ghost, fell upon them. So in Gal. 3. 2, "This only would I learn of you, received ye the Spirit by the works of the law, or by the hearing of faith?"

By the Spirit here, Calvin and Bullinger and other expositors do understand the joy, the peace, the assurance that is wrought in the heart by the hearing of faith, that is, by the doctrine of the gospel; for in these words of the apostle, hearing is put for the thing heard, and faith for the doctrine of the gospel, because the gospel is the ordinary means of working faith. "Faith comes by hearing," saith the apostle, Rom. 10. 17. So 1 Thes. 1. 5, 6, "For our gospel came not unto you in word only, but also in power, and in the Holy Ghost, and in much assurance; as ye know what manner of men we were among you for your sake. And ye became followers of us, and of the Lord, having received the word in much affliction, with joy of the Holy Ghost."

In these words you have a divine power attending Paul's ministry, a power convincing, enlightening, humbling, raising, delighting, reforming, renewing, and transforming of them that heard him. Also you have the sweet and blessed

73

testimony of the Spirit attending his ministry, and assuring those of their effectual calling and election, upon whom the word came in power, and raising up their spirits to joy in the midst of sorrow. Ah! you precious sons and daughters of Zion, that have sat waiting and trembling at Wisdom's door, tell me, tell me, hath not God rained down manna upon your souls whilst you have been hearing the word? Yes. Hath not God come in with power upon you, and by his Spirit sealed up to you your election, the remission of your sins, the justification of your persons, and the salvation of your souls? Yes, without controversy, many saints have found Christ's lips, in this ordinance, to drop honey and sweetness, marrow and fatness.

And as Christ in hearing times, when his people are a-hearing the word of life, does lift up the light of his countenance upon them; so when they are a-receiving the bread of life, he makes known his love to them, and their interest in him. In this feast of fat things, the master of the feast, the Lord Jesus, comes in the midst of his guests, saying, "Peace be here." Here the beams of his glory do so shine, as that they cause the hearts of children to burn within them, and as scatters all that thick darkness and cloud that are gathered about them. When saints are in this wine-cellar, Christ's banner over them is love; when they are in this Canaan, then he feeds them with milk and honey; when they are in this paradise, then they shall taste of angels' food; when they are at this gate of heaven, then they shall see Christ at the right hand of the Father; when they are before his mercy-seat, then they shall see the bowels of mercy rolling towards them. In this ordinance they see that, and taste that, and feel that of Christ, that they are not able to declare and manifest to others; in this ordinance saints shall see the truth of their graces, and feel the increase of their graces, and rejoice in the clearness of their evidences; in this ordinance Christ will seal up the promises, and seal up the covenant, and seal up his love, and seal up their pardon sensibly to their souls. Many precious souls there be that have found Christ in this ordinance, when they could not find him in other ordinances, though they have sought him sorrowingly. Many a cold soul hath been warmed in this ordinance, and many a hungry soul hath been fed with manna in this ordinance, and many a thirsty soul hath been refreshed with wine upon the lees in this ordinance, and many a dull soul hath been quickened in this ordinance. I do not say that ever a dead soul hath been enlivened in this ordinance, this being an ordinance appointed by Christ, not to beget spiritual life where there was none, but to increase it where the Spirit hath formerly begun it. In this ordinance, weak hands and feeble knees have been strengthened, and fainting hearts have been comforted, and questioning souls have been resolved, and staggering souls have been settled, and falling souls have been supported. Ah, Christians! if you will but stand up and speak out, you must say, that in this ordinance, there hath been between Christ and you such mutual kisses, such mutual embraces, such mutual opening and shutting of hands, such mutual opening and closing of hearts, as hath made such a heaven in your hearts as cannot be expressed, as cannot be declared. Christ in this ordinance opens such boxes of precious ointment, as fill the saints with a spiritual savour; he gives them a cluster of the grapes of Canaan, that makes them earnestly look and long to be in Canaan, Num. 13. 23-25. The Christians in the primitive times, upon receiving the sacrament, were wont to be filled with that zeal and fervour, with that joy and comfort, with that faith, fortitude, and assurance, that made them to appear before the tyrants with transcendent boldness and cheerfulness, as many writers do testify. Now there are these reasons why God is pleased to lift up the light of his countenance upon his people, when they are a-hearing the word of life, and a-breaking the bread of life.

(1) *The first reason. That they may highly prize the ordinances, the choice discoveries that God makes to their souls in them, works them to set a very high price upon them.* Oh! says our souls, we cannot but affect them for what of God we have enjoyed in them, Ps. 84. 10, 11. Many there are that are like old Barzillai, that had lost his taste and hearing, and so cared not for David's feasts and music, 2 Sam. 19. 32, *seq.* So many there are that can see nothing

75

of God, and taste nothing of God in ordinances: they care not for ordinances, they slight ordinances. Oh! but souls that have seen, and heard, and tasted of the goodness of the Lord in ordinances, they dearly love them, and highly prize them: "I have esteemed thy word," says Job, "above my necessary food," Job 23. 12. And David sings it out: "The law of thy mouth is better unto me than thousands of gold and silver" [Ps. 119. 72]. Luther prized the word at such a high rate that he saith he would not live in paradise, if he might, without the word: *At cum verbo etiam in inferno facile est vivere*, but with the word he could live in hell itself, Ps. 27. 4.

(2) *The second reason.* God lifts up the light of his countenance upon his people in ordinances, *that he may keep them close to ordinances and constant in ordinances.* The soul shall hear good news from heaven when it is waiting at wisdom's door, Prov. 8. 34, 35. God will acquaint the soul with spiritual mysteries, and feed it with the droppings of the honeycomb, that the soul may cleave to them as Ruth did to Naomi, and say of them as she said of her: "Where these go, I will go; where these lodge, I will lodge," Ruth 1. 15-17; and nothing but death shall make a separation between ordinances and my soul. After Joshua had had a choice presence of God with his spirit in the service he was put upon, he makes a proclamation, "Choose you whom you will serve, I and my household will serve the Lord," Josh. 24. 15. Let the issue be what it will, I will cleave to the service of my God; I will set myself in God's way, I will wait for him in his temple, Malachi 3. 1; I will look for him in the midst of the seven golden candlesticks, Rev. 2. 1; I have found him a good master; I will live and die in his service; I have found his work to be better than wages; I have found a reward, not only for keeping, but also "*in* keeping his commandments," as the psalmist speaks, Ps. 19. 11. The good works, the sweet aspects, the choice hints, the heavenly intercourse that hath been between the Lord Jesus and my soul, in his service, hath put such great and glorious engagements upon my soul that I cannot but say with the servant in the law, "I love my master, and I will

not quit his service, because it is well with me; my ear is bored, and I will be his servant for ever," Exod. 21. 5; Deut. 15. 16, 17.

(3) *The third reason* why the Lord causes the beams of his love, and the brightness of his glory to shine forth upon his people in ordinances is, *To fence and strengthen their souls against all those temptations that they may meet with from Satan and his instruments, that lie in wait to deceive, and by their cunning craftiness endeavour with all their might* to work men first to have low thoughts of ordinances, and then to neglect them, and then to despise them. Now the Lord by the sweet discoveries of himself, by the kisses and love-tokens that he gives to his people in ordinances, does so endear and engage their hearts to them, that they are able not only to withstand temptations, but also to triumph over temptations, through him that hath loved them, and in ordinances manifested his presence, and the riches of his grace and goodness, to them. The sweet converse, the blessed turns and walks that the saints have with God in ordinances, makes them strong in resisting, and happy in conquering of those temptations that tend to lead them from the ordinances; which are Christ's banqueting-house, where he sets before his people all the dainties and sweet-meats of heaven, and bids them eat and drink abundantly, there being no danger of surfeiting in eating or drinking of Christ's delicacies. Truly, many a soul hath had a surfeit of the world's dainties, and died for ever; but there is not a soul that hath had the honour and happiness to be brought into Christ's banqueting-house, and to eat and drink of his dainties, but they have lived for ever. Solomon's Song 2. 4.

(4) *The fourth reason* why the Lord is pleased to give his people some sense of his love, and some taste of heaven in ordinances, is, *That he may fit and ripen them for heaven, and make them look and long more after a perfect, complete, and full enjoyment of God.* Souls at first conversion are but rough-cast, but God, by visiting of them, and manifesting of himself to them in his ways, doth more and more fit those vessels of mercy for glory, Isa. 64. 5. Ah! Christians, tell me, do not those holy influences, those spiritual breath-

77

ings, those divine in-comes, that you meet with in ordin-ances, make your souls cry out with David, "As the hart panteth after the water brooks, so panteth my soul after thee, O God. My soul thirsteth for God, even for the living God: When shall I come and appear before the presence of God?" Ps. 42. 1, 2. So in Ps. 63. 1. 2, "O God, thou art my God, early will I seek thee! my soul thirsteth for thee, my flesh longeth for thee in a dry and thirsty land, where no water is: to see thy power and thy glory, so as I have seen thee in the sanctuary." In these words you have David's strong, earnest, and vehement desires; here you have desire upon desire; here you have the very flower, and vigour of his spirit, the strength and sinews of his soul, the prime and top of his inflamed affections, all strongly working after a fuller enjoyment of God. Look, as the espoused maid longs for the marriage day, the apprentice for his freedom, the cap-tive for his ransom, the condemned man for his pardon, the traveller for his inn, and the mariner for his haven; so doth a soul, that hath met with God in his ordinances, long to meet with God in heaven. It is not a drop, it is not a lap and away, a sip and away, that will suffice such a soul. No. This soul will never be quiet, till it sees God face to face, till it be quiet in the bosom of God. The more a saint tastes of God in an ordinance, the more are his desires raised and whetted, and the more are his teeth set on edge for more and more of God. Plutarch saith, that when "once the Gauls had tasted of the sweet wine that was made of the grapes of Italy, nothing would satisfy them but Italy, Italy." So a soul that hath tasted of the sweetness and goodness of God in ordinances, nothing will satisfy it, but more of that goodness and sweetness. A little mercy may save the soul, but it must be a great deal of mercy that must satisfy the soul. The least glimpse of God's countenance may be a staff to support the soul, and an ark to secure the soul, and a cloud by day and a pillar of fire by night to guide the soul; but it must be much, very much of God, that must be enough to satisfy the soul.

(5) *The fifth reason.* The fifth and last reason why the Lord is graciously pleased to give his people some sense of

his love, and some assurance of his favour in ordinances, is, *That they may have wherewithal to silence and stop the mouths of wicked and ungodly men, whose words are stout against the Lord;* who say, it is in vain to serve God, and what profit is there in keeping his statutes and ordinances, and in walking mournfully before the Lord of hosts? Mal. 3. 13, 14. Now the Lord causes his face to shine upon his people in ordinances, that they may stand up, and bear him witness before the wicked world, that he is no hard master, that he reaps not where he sows not. In ordinances he kisses them, and there he gives them his love, and makes known his goodness and glory, that his children may, from their own experiences, be able to confute all the lies and clamours of wicked men against God and his ways. And blessed be God, that hath not left himself without witness, but hath many thousands that can stand up before all the world and declare that they have seen " the beauty and glory of God in his sanctuary," that they have met with those joys and comforts in the ways of God, that do as far surpass all other joys and comforts, as light does darkness, as heaven does hell, that they have met with such heart-meltings, such heart-humblings, such heart-revivings, such heart-cheerings, as they have never met with before, in all their days.

Ah, say these souls, " One day in his courts is better than a thousand " years elsewhere, Ps. 84. 10. Oh, we had rather with Moses lose all, and be whipped and stripped of all, than lose the sweet enjoyments of God in ordinances. Oh, in them God hath been light and life, a joy and a crown to our souls. God is tender of his own glory, and of his children's comfort; and therefore he gives them such choice views of Himself, and such sweet visits in ordinances, that they may have arguments at hand to stop the mouths of sinners, and to declare from their own experience that all the ways of God are ways of pleasantness, and that all his paths drop fatness, Prov. 3. 17; Ps. 65. 11. And thus much for the reasons why God lifts up the light of his countenance upon his people in ordinances. Before I pass to the next particular, it will be necessary that I lay down these cautions, to prevent weak saints from stumbling and doubting, who have not yet found the Lord giving out his favours, and making known his grace and love, in such a sensible way to their souls, in breaking the bread of life, as others have found.

(1) *The first caution.* Now, the first caution I shall lay down is this, *That even believers may sometimes come and go from this ordinance, without that comfort, that assurance, that joy, that refreshment that others have, and may meet with.* And this may arise, partly from their unpreparedness and unfitness to meet with God in the ordinance, 2 Chron. 30. 19, 20; 1 Cor. 11. 20-34; and partly from their playing and dallying with some bosom sin; or else it may arise from their not stirring up themselves to lay hold on God, as the prophet Isaiah complains, " There is none that calleth upon thy name, that stirreth up himself to take hold of thee," Isa. 64. 7; or else it may arise from the Spirit's standing at a distance from the soul. It may be, O soul, that thou hast set the Comforter, the Spirit, a-mourning; and therefore it is, that he refuses to comfort thee, and to be a sealing and witnessing Spirit unto thee. Thou hast grieved him with thy sins, and he will now vex thee by his silence; thou hast thrown the cordials against the wall; thou hast trampled his manna under thy feet; and therefore it is that he hath veiled his face, and changed his countenance and carriage towards thee; thou hast been unkind to the Spirit; and therefore he carries it towards thee as an enemy, and not as a friend, Ps. 77. 2; Gen. 31. 5.

(2) *The second caution* is this, *That though God doth in this ordinance withhold comfort and assurance from thee, yet thou must hold on in the duty, thou must wait at hope's hospital.* At this heavenly pool, thou must lie till the angel of the covenant, the Lord Jesus, comes and breathes upon thee; at these waters of the sanctuary thou must lie, till the Spirit moves upon thy soul; thou must not neglect thy work, though God delays thy comfort; thou must be as obedient in the want of assurance, as thou art thankful under the enjoyment of assurance. Laban often changed Jacob's wages, yet Jacob never changed nor neglected his work. Though

God should change thy wages, thy comforts into discomforts, thy spring into an autumn, &c., yet thou must never change nor neglect thy work, which is obeying, believing, and waiting, till God, in his ordinances, shall lift up the light of his countenance upon thee, and turn thy night into day, and thy mourning into rejoicing. God is the same, and the commands of the gospel are the same, and therefore thy work is the same, whether it be night or day with thy soul, whether thou art under frowns or smiles, in the arms or at the feet of God.

(3) *The third caution* is this, *Many of the precious sons and daughters of Sion have had and may have so much comfort and sweetness, so much life and heat, so much reviving and quickening, so much marrow and fatness in this ordinance, as may clearly evidence the special presence of God with their spirits, and as they would not exchange for all the world, and yet they would give a world, were it in their power, for those strong comforts and full assurance, that others enjoy in this ordinance.* In this ordinance, Christ looks upon one and kisses another; he gives a nod to one, and his hand to another. Some in this ordinance shall have but sips of mercy, others shall have large draughts of mercy; some in this ordinance shall see but the back-parts of Christ, others shall see him face to face, Lam. 1. 16; to one he gives silver, to another he gives gold; to one he gives but a glass of consolation, to another he gives flagons of consolation, Solomon's Song 2. 5; some shall have but drops, others shall swim in the ocean; some shall have a large harvest, others shall have but a few gleanings, and yet they, if rightly valued, are of more worth than a world. The Sun of righteousness is a free agent, and he will work and shine forth as he pleases, and on whom he pleases; and who art thou that darest say to Christ, Why doest thou so? Ah! Christians, you may not, you must not say, We have not met with Christ in the sacrament, because we have not met with joy and assurance in the sacrament; for you may enjoy very much of Christ in that ordinance, and yet not so much as may boil up to full assurance, and make you go away singing, " My beloved is mine, and I am his," Solomon's Song

2. 16. We may enjoy the warmth and heat of the sun, when we cannot see the sun; so souls may enjoy much of Christ, by holy influences, in the sacrament, when they cannot see Christ in the sacrament.

(6) DURING TIMES OF PERSONAL AFFLICTIONS

VI. *Sixthly, Times of personal afflictions are times wherein the Lord is graciously pleased to vouchsafe to his people sweet manifestations of his love and favour.* When his hand is heavy on them, then he lifts up the light of his countenance upon them: Ps. 71. 20, 21, " Thou which hast shewed me great and sore troubles, shalt quicken me again; and shalt bring me up again from the depths of the earth. Thou shalt increase my greatness, and comfort me on every side." So Ps. 94. 19, " In the multitude of my careful troubled thoughts, thy comforts delight my soul." Ah, Christians! hath not God by all afflictions lifted up your souls nearer heaven, as Noah's ark was lifted up nearer and nearer heaven by the rising of the waters higher and higher? So afflictions do but elevate and raise a saint's affections to heaven and heavenly things.

When Münster lay sick, and his friends asked him how he did, he pointed to his sores and ulcers, whereof he was full, and said, " These are God's gems and jewels, wherewith he decketh his best friends; and to me they are more precious than all the gold and silver in the world."

Afflictiones benedictiones, afflictions are blessings. God's corrections are our instructions, his lashes our lessons, his scourges our schoolmasters, his chastisements our admonitions! And to note this, the Hebrews and Greeks both do express chastening and teaching by one and the same word, because the latter is the true end of the former. Ah, you afflicted sons and daughters of Zion, have you not had such sweet discoveries of God, such sensible demonstrations of his love, such bowels of affections working in him towards you? Have you not had such gracious visits, and such glorious visions, that you would not exchange for all the world? Yes. Have you not had the precious presence of God with you, quieting and stilling your souls, supporting and upholding your souls, cheering and refreshing your souls? Yes. And have you not had the Lord applying precious promises, and suitable remedies, to all your maladies? Have you not found God a-bringing in unexpected mercy in the day of your adversity, suitable to that promise, Hosea 2. 14, "I will allure her, and bring her into the wilderness, and speak comfortably to her" (or, I will speak earnestly to her heart, as the Hebrew reads it)? Yes. Have you not found that God hath so sweetened and sanctified afflictions to you, as to make them a means to discover many sins that lay hid, and to purge you from many sins that cleaved close unto you, and to prevent you from falling into many sins that would have been the breaking of your bones, and the loss of your comfort? Yes. Have you not found that you have been like the walnut tree, the better for beating; and like the vine, the better for bleeding; and like the ingenuous child, the better for whipping? Yes. Have you not found afflictions to revive, quicken, and recover your decayed graces? Have they not inflamed that love that hath been cold, and put life into that faith that hath been dying, and quickened those hopes that have been withering, and put spirit into those joys and comforts that have been languishing? Yes. Oh, then, stand up and declare to all the world that times of affliction have been the times wherein you have seen the face of God, and heard the voice of God, and fed upon the delicacies of God, and drunk deep of the consolations of God, and have been most satisfied and delighted with the presence and in-comes of God.

When Hezekiah in his greatest affliction lamentingly said, Isa. 38. 9-20, "I shall go mourning to my grave, I shall not see the Lord in the land of the living. He will cut me off with pining sickness, he will break all my bones. Like a crane, or a swallow, so did I chatter; I did mourn as a dove; mine eyes fail with looking upward. O Lord, I am oppressed, undertake for me": so now God comes in a way of mercy to him, and prints his love upon his heart: ver. 17, "Thou hast in love to my soul delivered it from the pit of corruption"; or rather, as the Hebrew reads it, "Thou hast loved my soul from the grave, for thou hast cast all my sins behind thy back." Ah, says Hezekiah, I have now found that in my afflictions thy affections have been most strongly carried towards me, as towards one whom thou art exceedingly taken with. Oh, now thou hast warmed me with thy love, and visited me with thy grace; thou hast made my darkness to be light, and turned my sighing into singing, and my mourning into rejoicing. So when Habakkuk's belly trembled, and his lips quivered, and rottenness entered into his bones, and all creature comforts failed, yet then had he such a sweet presence of God with his spirit, as made him to rejoice in the midst of sorrows: "Yet," says he, "I will rejoice in the Lord, I will joy in the God of my salvation," chap. 3. 16-18. And thus you see it clear, that in times of affliction God makes sweet manifestations of his love and favour to his children's souls.

(7) DURING SEASONS OF PRAYER

VII. *Seventhly, Praying times are times wherein the Lord is graciously pleased to give his people some sweet and comfortable assurance of his love and favour towards them.* Prayer crowns God with the honour and glory that is due to his name; and God crowns prayer with assurance and comfort. Usually the most praying souls are the most assured souls. There is no service wherein souls have such a near, familiar, and friendly intercourse with God, as in this of prayer; neither is there any service wherein God doth more delight to make know his grace and goodness, his mercy and bounty, his beauty and glory, to poor souls, than this of prayer. The best and the sweetest flowers of paradise, God gives to his people when they are upon their knees. Prayer is *porta cœli*, the gate of heaven, *clavis paradisi*, a key to let us into paradise. When John was weeping, in prayer doubtless, the sealed book was opened to him. Many Christians have found by experience that prayer times are sealing times, times wherein God hath sealed up to them the remission of their sins, and the salvation of their souls. They have found prayer to be a shelter to their souls, a sacrifice to God, a sweet savour to Christ, a scourge to Satan, and an inlet to assurance. God loves to lade the wings of

84

prayer with the choicest and chief blessings. Ah! how often, Christians! hath God kissed you at the beginning of prayer, and spoken peace to you in the midst of prayer, and filled you with joy and assurance upon the close of prayer! That ninth of Daniel, from the seventeenth to the three and twentieth verse, is full to the point in hand; I shall only cite the words of the last four verses: Dan. 9. 20-23, "And whilst I was speaking, and praying, and confessing my sin, and the sin of my people Israel, and presenting my supplication before the Lord my God for the holy mountain of my God; yea, whilst I was speaking in prayer, even the man Gabriel, whom I had seen in the vision at the beginning, being caused to fly swiftly, touched me about the time of the evening oblation. And he informed me, and talked with me, and said, O Daniel, I am now come forth to give thee skill and understanding. At the beginning of thy supplications, the commandment came forth, and I am come to shew thee, for thou art greatly beloved; therefore understand the matter, and consider the vision." In these words you see, whilst Daniel was in prayer, the Lord appears to him and gives him a divine touch, and tells him that he is "a man greatly beloved," or as the Hebrew hath it, "a man of desires." So Acts 10. 1-4, "There was a certain man in Cæsarea, called Cornelius, a centurion of the band called the Italian band, a devout man, and one that feared God with all his house; which gave much alms to the people, and prayed to God alway; he saw in a vision evidently about the ninth hour of the day, an angel of God coming in to him, and saying unto him, Cornelius. And when he looked on him, he was afraid, and said, What is it, Lord? And he said unto him, Thy prayers and thine alms are come up for a memorial before God." Praying Cornelius, you see, is remembered by God, and visited sensibly and evidently by an angel, and assured that his prayers and good deeds are not only an odour, a sweet smell, a sacrifice acceptable and well pleasing to God, but also that they shall be gloriously rewarded by God. So when Peter was praying, he fell into a trance, and saw heaven opened, and had his mind elevated, and all the faculties of his soul filled with a divine revelation, Acts 10. 9-16; so when Paul was a-praying, he sees a vision, Acts 9. 11-16, Ananias a-coming and laying his hands on him, that he might receive his sight. Paul had not been long at prayer before it was revealed to him that he was a chosen vessel, before he was filled with the voice and comforts of the Holy Ghost; so our Saviour was transfigured as he was praying, Mat. 17. 1, 2. Thus you see, that praying times are times wherein the Lord is graciously pleased to lift up the light of his countenance upon his people, and to cause his grace and favour, his goodness and kindness, to rest on them, as the spirit of Elijah did rest on Elisha, 2 Kings 2. 15.

Obj. But some may object and say, We have been at the door of mercy, early and late, for assurance, and yet we have not obtained it; we have prayed and waited, and we have waited and prayed, we have prayed and mourned, and we have mourned and prayed, and yet we cannot get a good word from God, a smile from God; he hath covered himself with a cloud, and after all that we have done, it is still night with our souls; God seems not to be at home, he seems not to value our prayers; we call, and cry and shout out for assurance, and yet he shutteth out our prayer; we are sure that we have not found praying times to be times of assurance to our souls, &c., Lam. 3. 8.

Ans. 1. Now to this objection I shall give these answers:

(1) *First,* That it may be you have been more earnest and vehement for assurance, and the effects of it, viz., joy, comfort, and peace, than you have been for grace and holiness, for communion with God, and conformity to God. It may be your requests for assurance have been full of life and spirits, when your requests for grace and holiness, for communion with God, and conformity to God, have been lifeless and spiritless. If so, no wonder that assurance is denied you. Assurance makes most for your comfort, but holiness makes most for God's honour. Man's holiness is now his greatest happiness, and in heaven man's greatest happiness will be his perfect holiness. Assurance is the daughter of holiness; and he that shall more highly prize, and more earnestly press after the enjoyment of the daughter than the

86

mother, it is not a wonder if God shuts the door upon him, and crosses him in the thing he most desires. The surest and the shortest way to assurance is to wrestle and contend with God for holiness, as the angel contended with the devil about the body of Moses, Jude 9. When the stream and cream of a man's spirit runs after holiness, it will not long be night with that man; the Sun of righteousness will shine forth upon that man, and turn his winter into summer, and crown him with the diadem of assurance, Mal. 4. 2. The more holy any person is, the more excellent he is. All corruptions are diminutions of excellency. The more mixed anything is, the more it is abased, as if gold and tin be mixed; and the more pure it is as mere gold, the more glorious it is. Now the more divinely excellent any man is, the more fit he is to enjoy the choicest and highest favours. Assurance is a jewel of that value, that he will bestow it upon none but his excellent ones, Ps. 16. 3. Assurance is that tried gold, that none can wear but those that win it in a way of grace and holiness, Rev. 3. 18. It may be, if thou hadst minded, and endeavoured more after communion with God, and conformity to God, thou mightest before this time have looked upward, and seen God in Christ smiling upon thee, and have looked inward into thy own soul, and seen the Spirit of grace witnessing to thy spirit that thou wert a son, an heir, an heir of God, and a joint heir with Christ, Rom. 8. 15-17. But thou hast minded more thy own comfort than Christ's honour; thou hast minded the blossoms and the fruit, assurance and peace, more than Christ the root; thou hast minded the springs of comfort, more than Christ, the fountain of life; thou hast minded the beams of the sun, more than the Sun of righteousness; and therefore it is but a righteous thing with God to leave thee to walk in a valley of darkness, to hide his face from thee, and to seem to be as an enemy to thee.

Ans. 2. But secondly, I answer, *It may be thou art not yet fit for so choice a mercy, thou art not able to bear so great a favour.* Many heads are not able to bear strong waters. Why, the very quintessence of all the strong consolations of God is wrung out into this golden cup of assurance; and can you drink of this cup, and not stammer nor stagger? Believe it, assurance is meat for strong men; few babes, if any, are able to bear it, and digest it. The apostle saith, Heb. 5. 12, 14, that "strong meat belongeth to them that are of full age" (or that are comparatively perfect, or full-grown), "even those who, by reason of use" (Greek, by reason of habit, which is got by continual custom and long practice), "have their senses exercised to discern both good and evil." The Greek word properly signifies such an exercise as wrestlers, or such as contend for victory, do use, which is with all their might and strength, being trained up unto it by long exercise. It may be, O complaining Christian, that thou are but a scrub, a babe in grace, 1 Cor. 3. 1-3; haply thou art not yet got beyond the breast, or, if thou art, yet thou art not past the spoon. Ah! Christian, if it be thus with thee, cease complaining of want of assurance, and be up and growing; be more aged in grace and holiness, and thou shalt find assurance growing upon thee. Divine wisdom sparkles much in this, in giving milk to babes that are more carnal than spiritual, and meat, *i.e.* assurance, to strong men, that have more skill and will, that have a greater ability and choicer faculty to prize and improve this jewel of assurance than babes have. The Hebrew word *chabodh* signifies both weight and glory; and verily, glory is such a weight, that if the body were not upheld by that glorious power that raised Jesus Christ from the grave, if it were not borne up by everlasting arms, it were impossible it should bear it, Deut. 33. 27. Now assurance is the top of glory, it is the glory of glory. Then certainly they had need be very glorious within that shall be crowned with such a weight of glory as assurance is, Ps. 45. 13. Well! remember this, it is mercy to want mercy till we are fit for mercy, till we are able to bear the weight of mercy, and make a divine improvement of mercy.

Ans. 3. Thirdly, *You must distinguish between delays and denials.* God may delay us, when he does not deny us; he may defer the giving of a mercy, and yet, at last, give the very mercy begged. Barren Hannah prays, year after year, for a mercy. God delays her long, but at last gives her her desire; and the text says expressly, that her countenance was no more sad, 1 Sam. 1. 18. After many prayers and tears, the Lord comes in, and assures her, that she should have the desire of her soul; and now she mourns no more, but sits down satisfied, comforted, and cheered. After much praying, waiting, and weeping, God usually comes with his hands and heart full of mercy to his people. He loves not to come *vacuis manibus,* empty-handed, to those that have sat long with wet eyes at mercy's door. Christ tried the faith, patience, and constancy of the Canaanite woman, Mat. 15. 21-29; he deferred and delayed her, he reproached and repulsed her; and yet at last is overcome by her, as not being able any longer to withstand her importunate requests. "O woman, great is thy faith; be it unto thee, even as thou wilt." Christ puts her off at first, but closes with her at last; at first a good word, a good look is too good for her, but at last good words and good looks are too little for her: " Be it unto thee, even as thou wilt." At first Christ carries himself to her as a churlish stranger, but at last as an amorous lover. Though at first he had not an ear to hear her, yet at last he had a heart to grant her, not only her desires, but even what else she would desire over and above what she had desired. God heard Daniel at the beginning of his supplications, and his love was working strongly towards him, but the angel Gabriel doth not inform Daniel of this till afterwards, Dan. 9. 15-25. Praying souls, you say that you have prayed long for assurance, and yet you have not obtained it. Well, pray still. Oh pray and wait, wait and pray; " the vision is for an appointed time, but at the end it shall speak, and not lie: though it tarry, wait for it; because it will surely come, it will not tarry," Hab. 2. 3. God hath never failed, God will never fail, the praying soul; in the long run, thou shalt be sure to obtain that assurance that will richly recompense thee for all thy praying, waiting, and weeping; therefore hold up and hold on praying, though God doth delay thee, and my soul for thine, thou shalt reap in due season such a harvest of joy and comfort, as will sufficiently pay thee for all thy pains, Gal. 6. 9. Shall the husbandman wait patiently for the precious fruits of the earth, James 5. 7; and wilt not thou wait patiently for assurance, which is a jewel worth more than heaven and earth? Praying souls, remember this. It is but weakness to think that men shall reap as soon as they sow, that they shall reap in the evening when they have but sowed in the morning. The emperor Titus Vespasian never dismissed any petitioner with a tear in his eye, or with a heavy heart; and shall we think that the God of compassions will always dismiss the petitioners of heaven with tears in their eyes? Surely no.

(8) BEFORE CONFLICTS WITH SATAN

VIII. *Eighthly, Sometimes before the soul is deeply engaged in sore conflicts with Satan, the Lord is graciously pleased to visit his people with his loving-kindness, and to give them some sweet assurance, that though they are tempted, yet they shall not be worsted; though they are tried, yet they shall be crowned,* John 10. 28; *though Satan doth roar as a lion against the soul, yet he shall not make a prey of the soul; for the Lion of the tribe of Judah will hold it fast, and none shall pluck it out of his hand,* Rev. 5. 5. God first fed Israel with manna from heaven, and gave them water to drink out of the rock, before their sore fight with Amalek, Exod. 17. 8-16. Before Paul was buffeted by Satan, he was caught up into the third heaven, where he had very glorious visions and revelations of the Lord, even such as he was not able to utter, 2 Cor. 12. 1-8. Before Jesus Christ was led into the wilderness to be tempted by Satan, to question and doubt of his Sonship, he heard a voice from heaven, saying, "This is my beloved Son, in whom I am well pleased," Mat. 3. 17. The Spirit of the Lord did first descend upon him as a dove, before Satan fell upon him as a lion. God walks with his people some turns in paradise, and gives them some tastes of his right-hand pleasures, before Satan, by his tempting, shall do them a displeasure, Ps. 16. 11. But I must hasten to a close of this chapter; and therefore,

(9) AFTER CONFLICTS WITH SATAN

IX. *Ninthly, and lastly, After some sharp conflicts with Satan, God is graciously pleased to lift up the light of his countenance upon his people, and to warm and cheer their hearts with the beams of his love:* Mat. 4. 11, " Then the devil leaveth him, and behold, angels came and ministered unto him." When Christ had even spent himself in foiling and quelling, in resisting and scattering Satan's temptations, then the angels come and minister cordials and comforts unto him. So after Paul had been buffeted by Satan, he heard that sweet word from heaven, " My grace is sufficient for thee, for my strength is made perfect in weakness," 2 Cor. 12. 7-10, which filled his heart with joy and gladness. The hidden manna, the new name, and the white stone, is given to the conqueror, Rev. 7. 17; to him that hath fought " with principalities, and powers, and spiritual wickedness in high places," Eph. 6. 12, and is come off with his garments dipped in blood. After the Roman generals had gotten victory over their enemies, the senate did use not one way, but many ways, to express their loves to them. So after our faith hath gotten victory over Satan, God usually takes the soul in his arms, and courts it, and shews much kindness to it. Now the soul shall be carried in triumph, now the chariot of state attends the soul, now white raiment is put upon the soul, Rev. 3. 5, and 7. 9; now palms are put into the conqueror's hands, now the garland is set upon the conqueror's head, and now a royal feast is provided, where God will set the conqueror at the upper end of the table, and speak kindly, and carry it sweetly towards him, as one much affected and taken with his victory over the prince of darkness. Conflicts with Satan are usually the sharpest and the hottest; they spend and waste most the vital and noble spirits of the saints; and therefore the Lord, after such conflicts, doth ordinarily give his people his choicest and his strongest cordials.

And thus, by divine assistance, we have shewed you the special times and seasons wherein the Lord is graciously pleased to give his people some tastes of his love, some sweet assurance that they enjoy his favour, that all is well, and shall be for ever well between him and them; and that, though many things may trouble them, yet nothing shall separate them from their God, their Christ, their crown.

CHAPTER III

Hindrances and impediments that keep poor souls from assurance; with the means and helps to remove those impediments and hindrances.

To despair of mercy hinders assurance

(1) *The first impediment.* Now the first impediment and hindrance to assurance that we shall instance is, *Despairing thoughts of mercy.* Oh! these imprison the soul, and make it always dark with the soul; these shut the windows of the soul, that no light can come in to cheer it. Despairing thoughts make a man fight against God with his own weapons; they make a man cast all the cordials of the Spirit against the wall, as things of no value; they make a man suck poison out of the sweetest promises; they make a man eminent in nothing unless it be in having hard thoughts of God, and in arguing against his own soul and happiness, and in turning his greatest advantages into disadvantages, his greatest helps into his greatest hindrances. Despairing thoughts of mercy make a man below the beast that perisheth. Pliny speaks of the scorpion, that there is not one minute wherein it doth not put forth the sting, as being unwilling to lose any opportunity of doing mischief. Despairing souls are scorpions; they are still a-putting out their stings, a-wrangling with God or Christ or the Scripture or the saints or ordinances, or their own souls. A despairing soul is *Magor-missabib,* a terror to itself; it cannot rest, but, like Noah's ark, is always tossed here and there; it is troubled on every side, it is full of fears and fightings. A despairing soul is a burden to others, but the greatest burden to itself. It is still a-vexing, terrifying, tormenting, condemning, and perplexing itself. Despair makes every sweet bitter, and every bitter exceeding bitter; it puts gall and wormwood into the sweetest wine, and it puts a sting, a cross, into every cross. Now whilst the soul is under these

92

despairing thoughts of mercy, how is it possible that it should attain to a well-grounded assurance. Therefore for the helping of the soul out of this despairing condition, give me leave a little to expostulate with despairing souls. Tell me, O despairing souls, is not despair an exceeding vile and contemptible sin? Is it not a dishonour to God, a reproach to Christ, and a murderer of souls? Is it not a belying of God, a denying of Christ, and a crowning of Satan? It doth without doubt proclaim the devil a conqueror, and lifts him up above Christ himself. Despair is an evil that flows from the greatest evil in the world; it flows from unbelief, from ignorance, and misapprehensions of God and his grace, and from mistakes of Scripture, and from Satan, who, being for ever cast out of paradise, labours with all his art and might to work poor souls to despair of ever entering into paradise. O despairing souls, let the greatness of this sin effectually awaken you, and provoke you to labour as for life, to come out of this condition, which is as sinful as it is doleful, and as much to be hated as lamented.

Again, tell me, O despairing souls, hath not despairing Judas perished, whereas the murderers of Christ, believing on him, were saved? Did not Judas sin more heinously by despairing than by betraying of Christ? Despairing Francis Spira is damned, when repenting Manasseh is saved. O despairing souls, the arms of mercy are open to receive a Manasseh, a monster, a devil incarnate; he caused that gospel prophet Isaiah to be sawed in the midst with a saw, as some rabbins say; he turned aside from the Lord to commit idolatry, and caused his sons to pass through the fire, and dealt with familiar spirits, and made the streets of Jerusalem to overflow with innocent blood, 2 Chron. 33. 1-15. The soul of Mary Magdalene was full of devils; and yet Christ cast them out, and made her heart his house, his presence chamber, Luke 7. 47. Why dost thou then say there is no hope for thee, O despairing soul? Paul was full of rage against Christ and his people, and full of blasphemy and impiety, and yet behold, Paul is a chosen vessel, Paul is caught up into the heaven, and he is filled with the gifts and graces of the Holy Ghost, Acts 8. 1, 2; 9. 1; 26. 11; 1 Tim. 1. 13, 15,

16. Why shouldst thou then say there is for thee no help, O despairing soul! Though the prodigal had run from his father, and spent and wasted all his estate in ways of baseness and wickedness, yet upon his resolution to return, his father meets him, and instead of killing him, he kisses; instead of kicking him, he embraces him; instead of shutting the door upon him, he makes sumptuous provision for him, Luke 15. 13-23. And how then dost thou dare to say, O despairing soul, that God will never cast an eye of love upon thee, nor bestow a crumb of mercy on thee! The apostle tells you of some monstrous miscreants that were unrighteous, fornicators, idolaters, adulterers, effeminate, abusers of themselves with mankind, thieves, covetous, drunkards, revilers, extortioners; and yet these monsters of mankind, through the infinite goodness and free grace of God, are washed from the filth and guilt of their sins, and justified by the righteousness of Christ, and sanctified by the Spirit of Christ, and decked and adorned with the precious graces of Christ, 1 Cor. 6. 9-11. Therefore do not say, O despairing soul, that thou shalt die in thy sins, and lie down at last in everlasting sorrow. Did it make for the honour and glory of his free grace to pardon them, and will it be a reproach to his free grace to pardon thee? Could God be just in justifying such ungodly ones, and shall he be unjust in justifying of thee? Did their unworthiness and unfitness for mercy turn the stream of mercy from them? No. Why then, O despairing soul, shouldst thou fear that thy unworthiness and unfitness for mercy will so stop and turn the stream of mercy, as that thou must perish eternally for want of one drop of special grace and mercy?

Again, tell me, O despairing soul, is not the grace of God free grace, is not man's salvation of free grace? "By grace ye are saved," Ephes. 2. 8. Every link of this golden chain is grace. It is free grace that chose us, Rom. 11. 5. Even so then at this present time also there is "a remnant according to the election of grace." It is free grace that chooses some to be jewels from all eternity, that chooses some to life, when others are left in darkness.

The Lord Jesus Christ is a gift of free grace. Christ is the greatest, the sweetest, the choicest, the chiefest gift that ever God gave; and yet this gift is given by a hand of love. " God so loved the world that he gave his only begotten Son," &c., John 3. 16; Isa. 9; 6; John 4. 10. " God *so* loved the world "; so freely, so vehemently, so fully, so admirably, so unconceivably, " That he gave his only Son." His Son, not his servant, his begotten Son, not his adopted Son, yea, his only begotten Son.

I have read of one that had four sons; and in a famine, sore oppressed with hunger, the parents resolved to sell one for relief; but then they considered with themselves which of the four they should sell. They said the eldest was the first of their strength, therefore loath were they to sell him. The second was the picture of his father, and therefore loath were they to part with him. The third was like the mother, and therefore they were not willing to part with him. The fourth, and youngest, was the child of their old age, their Benjamin, the dearly beloved of them both; and therefore they were resolved not to part with any of them, and so would rather suffer themselves to perish than to part with any of their children.

Oh! but God's heart is so strongly set upon sinners, that he freely gives Jesus Christ, who is his first-born, who is his very picture, who is his beloved Benjamin, who is his chiefest joy, who is his greatest delight. As Solomon speaks: Prov. 8. 30, " Then I was by him as one brought up with him, and I was daily his delight " (in the Hebrew " his delights," that is, his greatest delight), "rejoicing always before him," or sporting greatly before him, as little ones do before their parents. Why, then, O despairing soul! dost thou sit down sighing, and walk up and down mourning, sadly concluding that there is no mercy for thee? Hold up thy head, O despairing soul! Jesus Christ himself is a gift of free grace. The consideration of his free, boundless, bottomless, and endless love, may afford thee much matter of admiration and consolation, but none of desperation.

And as Jesus Christ is a gift of free grace, or a free-grace gift, so the precious covenant of grace is a gift of grace: Gen. 17. 2, " I will make my covenant betwixt me and thee ";

but in the original it is, " I will give thee my covenant."
Here you see that the covenant of grace is a free gift of grace.

God gave the covenant of the priesthood unto Phinehas as
a gift, Num. 25. 12; so God gives the covenant of grace as a
gift of favour and grace to all that he takes into covenant
with himself. From first to last all is from free grace. God
loves freely: " I will heal their backsliding; I will love them
freely," &c., Hosea 14. 4.

So Moses: " The Lord," saith he, " set his love upon you
to take you into covenant with him: not because you were
more in number than other people, but because he loved
you, and chose your fathers," Deut. 7. 7, 8.

The only ground of God's love is his love. The ground
of God's love is only and wholly in himself. There is neither
portion nor proportion in us to draw his love. There is no
love nor loveliness in us that should cause a beam of his love
to shine upon us. There is that enmity, that filthiness, that
treacherousness, that unfaithfulness, to be found in every
man's bosom, as might justly put God upon glorifying himself in their eternal ruin, and to write their names in his
black book in characters of blood and wrath. And as God
loves freely, so God justifies us freely: Rom. 3. 24, " Being
justified freely by his grace through the redemption that is
in Jesus Christ." And as poor sinners are justified freely,
so they are pardoned freely: Acts 5. 31, " Him hath God
exalted," speaking of Christ, " with his right hand, to be a
Prince and a Saviour, for to give repentance to Israel, and
forgiveness of sins." And as they are pardoned freely, so
they shall be saved freely: Rom. 6. 23, " For the wages of
sin is death, but the gift of God is eternal life," &c. Thus
you see, O despairing souls! that all is of free grace; from
the lowest to the highest round of Jacob's ladder, all is of
grace. Christ is a gift, the covenant of grace is a gift, pardon
of sin is a gift, heaven and salvation is a gift. Why, then,
O despairing souls! should you sit down sighing under such
black, sad, and dismal apprehensions of God and of your
own state and condition?

Verily, seeing all happiness and blessedness comes in a
way of free grace, and not in a way of doing, not in a way of

works, you should arise, O despairing souls! and cast off all despairing thoughts, and drink of the waters of life freely, Rev. 21. 6; 22. 18. What though thy heart be dead, and hard, and sad; what though thy sins be many, and thy fears great; yet behold here is glorious grace, rich grace, wondrous grace, matchless and incomparable riches of free grace spread before thee. Oh! let this fire warm thee, let these waters refresh thee, let these cordials strengthen thee, that it may be day and no longer night with thee, that thy mourning may be turned into rejoicing, and that thy beautiful garments may be put on, that so the rest of thy days may be days of gladness and sweetness, and free grace may be an everlasting shade, shelter, and rest unto thee, Isa. 52. 1.

Again, tell me, O despairing souls! do you understand, and most seriously and frequently ponder upon those particular scriptures that do most clearly, sweetly, and fully discover the mercies of God, the bowels of God, the grace and favour of God to poor sinners, as that Ps. 86. 5, "For thou, Lord, art good, and ready to forgive, and plenteous in mercy, unto all them that call upon thee"? God's mercies are above all his works, and above all ours too. His mercy is without measures and rules. All the acts and attributes of God sit at the feet of mercy. The weapons of God's artillery are turned into the rainbow; a bow, indeed, but without an arrow, bent but without a string. The rainbow is an emblem of mercy; it is a sign of grace and favour, and an assurance that God will remember his covenant. It is fresh and green, Rev. 4. 3, to note to us that God's mercy and grace to poor sinners is always fresh and green.

Again, tell me, O despairing souls! have you seriously pondered upon Neh. 9. 16, 17, "But they and our fathers dealt proudly, and hardened their necks, and hearkened not to thy commandments, and refused to obey; neither were mindful of the wonders that thou didst among them, but hardened their necks, and in their rebellion appointed a captain to return to their bondage. But thou art a God ready to pardon, gracious and merciful, slow to anger, and of great kindness, and forsookest them not"? "Thou art a God," says he, "ready to pardon," or rather as it is in the original, " Thou art a God of pardons." There is a very great emphasis in this Hebraism, " a God of pardons." It shews us that mercy is essential unto God, and that he is incomparable in forgiving iniquity, transgression, and sin. Here Nehemiah sets him forth as one made up all of pardoning grace and mercy. As a circle begins everywhere, but ends nowhere, so do the mercies of God, Micah 7. 18.

When Alexander did sit down before a city, he did use to set up a light, to give those within notice that if they came forth to him whilst the light lasted, they might have quarter; if otherwise, no mercy was to be expected. Oh! but such is the mercy and patience of God to sinners, that he sets up light after light, and waits year after year upon them. When they have done their worst against him, yet then he comes with his heart full of love, and his hands full of pardons, and makes a proclamation of grace, that if now at last they will accept of mercy, they shall have it, Luke 13. 7; Jer. 3. 1-15. Why, then, O despairing soul! dost thou make thy life a hell by having such low and mean thoughts of God's mercy, and by measuring of the mercies of God by the poor measure of thy weak and dark understanding?

Again, tell me, O despairing souls! have you seriously pondered upon those words in Isa. 55. 7-9: " Let the wicked forsake his way, and the unrighteous man " (or rather as it is in the original, " the man of iniquity ") " his thoughts, and let him return unto the Lord, and he will have mercy upon him, and to our God, for he will abundantly pardon," or as it is in the original, " He will multiply to pardon." " For my thoughts are not your thoughts, neither are your ways my ways, saith the Lord. For as the heavens are higher than the earth, so are my ways higher than your ways, and my thoughts than your thoughts "? Turn, O despairing souls! to these scriptures: Num. 14. 19, 20; Exod. 34. 6, 7; Micah 7. 18, 19; Isa. 30. 18, 19; Ps. 78. 34-40; 103. 8-13; Jer. 3. 1-12; Luke 15. 20-24; 1 Tim. 1. 13-17; and tell me whether you have seriously and frequently pondered upon them!

Oh! how can you look so much grace and so much love and favour, and such tender bowels of compassion, in the face, as appears in these scriptures, and yet rack and tear your precious souls with despairing thoughts!

Oh! there is so much grace and goodness, so much love and favour, so much mercy and glory, sparkling and shining through these scriptures, as may allay the strongest fears, and scatter the thickest darkness, and cheer up the saddest spirits, &c.

Again, tell me, O despairing souls, do you not do infinite wrong to the precious blood of the Lord Jesus? Three things are called precious in the Scripture: the blood of Christ is called " precious blood," 1 Peter 1. 19; and faith is called " precious faith," 2 Peter 1. 1; and the promises are called " precious promises," 2 Peter 1. 4. Now, what a reproach it is to this precious blood, " that speaks better things than the blood of Abel," Heb. 12. 24, for you to faint and sink under the power of despair; what doth this speak out? Oh! doth it not proclaim to all the world that there is no such worth and virtue, no such power and efficacy in the blood of Christ, as indeed there is? Oh! how will you answer this to Christ in that day wherein his blood shall speak and plead, not only with the profane that have trodden it under their feet, but also with despairing souls that have undervalued the power, virtue, and merit of it? Heb. 10. 29. Hath not the blood of Jesus Christ washed away the sins of a world of notorious sinners, and is it not of virtue to wash away the sins of one sinner? Hath it had that power in it as to bring many thousands to glory already, and is there not so much virtue left in it as to bring thy soul to glory? 1 John 1. 7-9. Hath it actually delivered such a multitude from wrath to come as cannot be numbered, and is the virtue of it so far spent as that it cannot reach to thy deliverance? Are there not yet millions of thousands that shall hereafter be actually saved and justified by this blood? Why, then, shouldst thou despair of being justified and saved from wrath to come by the virtue and power of this precious blood? There were five monks that were studying what was the best means to mortify sin. One said, to meditate on death; the second, to meditate on judgment; the third, to meditate on the joys of heaven; the fourth, to meditate on the torments of hell; the fifth, to meditate on the blood and sufferings of Jesus Christ: and certainly, the last is the choicest and strongest motive of all to the mortifying of sin. O despairing souls, despairing souls! if ever you would cast off your despairing thoughts and get out of your present hell, then dwell much, muse much, and apply much this precious blood to your own souls. So shall " sorrow and mourning flee away, and everlasting joy shall rest upon you," and the Lord shall give you " an everlasting name," and be " everlasting light and glory to you," and " you shall be no more called Forsaken "; for " the Lord will rejoice over you," and be a well-spring of life unto you, and make his abode with you, and turn your sighing into singing, your trembling into rejoicing, and your prison into a paradise of pleasure; so that your souls shall be able to stand up and say, Oh, blessed be God for Jesus Christ; blessed be God for that precious blood that hath justified our persons, and quieted our consciences, and scattered our fears, and answered our doubts, and given us to triumph over sin, hell, and death. " Who is he that condemneth? it is Christ that died," Rom. 8. 33-38. The apostle, upon the account of Christ's death, of Christ's blood, cries out, Victory, victory; he looks upon all his enemies and sings it sweetly out, " Over all these we are more than conquerors," or " above conquerors." We do over-overcome.

O despairing souls, to all your former sins do not add this, of making light and slight of the blood of Christ. As there is no blood that saves souls like the blood of Christ, so there is no blood that sinks souls like the blood of Christ. A drop of this blood upon a man's head at last will make him miserable for ever; but a drop of it upon a man's heart at last will make him happy for ever. In the day of vengeance, the destroying angel will spare you if this blood be found upon the door-posts of your hearts, otherwise you are lost for ever, Exod. 12. 7.

Lastly, I can tell you, O despairing souls, that God hath brought some out of the very gulf of despair, out of the very belly of hell; and therefore thou mayest hope that thy sins, that are thy present burden, shall not be thy future ruin.

Doth not Asaph resemble the despairing soul to the life?
"My soul refused to be comforted. I remembered God, and
was troubled; I complained, and my spirit was overwhelmed.
Thou holdest mine eyes waking; I am so troubled that I cannot speak." "Will the Lord cast off for ever? and will he be
favourable no more? Is his mercy clean gone for ever? and
will his promise fail for evermore? Hath God forgotten to
be gracious? hath he in anger shut up his tender mercies?"
Ps. 77. 2-9. Now, out of this gulf God delivers him: ver. 10,
"And I said, This is my infirmity"; or "this maketh me
sick," as it is in the original. Here Asaph checks himself for
casting the cordials, the comforts of the Spirit, against the
wall, and for his having such hard, sad, and black thoughts
of God. And in the thirteenth verse he speaks like one
dropped out of heaven: "Thy way, O God, is in the sanctuary: who is so great a God as our God?" Formerly, the
thoughts of God troubled him and overwhelmed him; but
now, at last, the thoughts of the greatness of God, and of his
interest in God, is matter of admiration and consolation to
him. So Heman, the Ezrahite, sighs it out thus: "My soul
is full of troubles, and my life draweth nigh unto the grave."
"Thou has laid me in the lowest pit, in darkness, in the
deeps. Thy wrath lieth hard upon me, and thou hast
afflicted me with all thy waves." "Lord, why casteth thou
off my soul? why hidest thou thy face from me? I am
afflicted, and ready to die from my youth up; while I suffer
thy terrors, I am distracted. Thy fierce wrath goes over me;
thy terrors have cut me off," Ps. 88, 3, 6, 7, 14-16. And yet,
for all this, Heman's state was good; his soul was safe and
happy: he calls God in the same psalm "the God of his
salvation," ver. 1. So Jonah, when he was in the belly of
hell, concludes, "that he was cast out of the sight of God,"
Jonah 2. 4. The sense of his sin, and of God's anger and
wrath, was so eminent and transcendent upon him, that it
even distracts him, and makes him speak like a departing
soul: "I am cast out from the presence of the Lord; I am
expelled out of God's sight," as Moses was expelled from
Egypt. God hath cast me out as one in whom he can take
no pleasure nor delight, as a husband doth a wife that hath

been false and unfaithful to him; and yet God's heart and love is so set upon Jonah that he will save him by a miracle rather than he shall not be saved. Jonah was much in the heart of God, and God made his faith at last victorious. To these I shall add some other famous instances. In king James's time there was one Mistress Honiwood of Kent, an ancient and religious gentlewoman, who lived many years in much horror and terror of conscience, for want of assurance of the favour of God, and of her eternal well-being. She would very often cry out, "I am damned, I am damned." Several men of eminent piety and parts left no means unattempted whereby her doubts might be answered, her conscience pacified, and her soul satisfied and cheered; yet she being strongly under the power of despair, persisted in crying out, "Oh! I am damned, I am damned." When these gentlemen were about to depart, she called for a cup of wine for them, which being brought, she drank to one of them a glass of the wine, and as soon as she had done, in an extreme passion she threw the Venice glass against the ground, saying, "As sure as this glass will break, so surely am I damned." The glass rebounded from the ground without any harm, which one of the ministers suddenly caught in his hand, and said, "Behold, a miracle from heaven to confute your unbelief, Oh! tempt God no more, tempt God no more." Both the gentlewoman and all the company were mightily amazed at this strange incident, and all glorified God for what was done; and the gentlewoman, by the grace and mercy of God, was delivered out of her hell of despair, and was filled with much comfort and joy, and lived and died full of peace and assurance.

Take another instance. There lived lately at Tilbury, in Essex, a gentleman who was a long time under such an eminent degree of despair, that he rejected all comfort that was tendered to him by any hand, and would not suffer any to pray with him; nay, he sent to the ministers and Christians that lived near him, and desired them, that as they would not wish to increase his torments in hell, they would cease praying for him. He would not suffer any religious service to be performed in his family, though formerly himself was much in the use of them; yet God gave him at last such inward refreshings, and by degrees filled him with such abundance of heavenly comforts, as he told all that came to him that it was impossible for any tongue to utter, or heart to imagine, that did not feel them. At last God gave him "the new name, and the white stone, that none knows but he that hath it," Rev. 2. 17. He lived about three quarters of a year, enjoying heaven upon earth, and then breathed out his last in the bosom of Christ.

Poor I, that am but of yesterday, have known some that have been so deeply plunged in the gulf of despair, that they would throw all the spiritual cordials that have been tendered to them against the walls. They were strong in reasoning against their own souls, and resolved against everything that might be a comfort and support unto them. They have been much set against all ordinances and religious services; they have cast off holy duties themselves, and peremptorily refused to join with others in them; yea, they have, out of a sense of sin and wrath, which hath lain hard upon them, refused the necessary comforts of this life, even to the overthrow of natural life. And yet out of this horrible pit, this hell upon earth, hath God delivered their souls, and given them such manifestations of his grace and favour, that they would not exchange them for a thousand worlds.

O despairing souls, despairing souls, you see that others, whose conditions have been as bad, if not worse than yours, have obtained mercy. God hath turned their hell into a heaven; he hath remembered them in their low state; he hath pacified their raging consciences, and quieted their distracted souls; he hath wiped all tears from their eyes; and he hath been a well-spring of life unto their hearts. Therefore be not discouraged, O despairing souls, but look up to the mercy-seat; remember who is your rest, and kick no more, by despair, against the wooings of divine love.

To dispute about things too high for our thoughts hinders assurance

(2) *The second impediment* to assurance is, *men's entering*

103

into the lists of dispute with Satan about those things that are above their reach, as about the decrees and counsel of God. Oh by this Satan keeps many precious souls off from assurance. Since God hath cast him out of paradise, and bound him in chains of darkness, he will make use of all his skill, power, and experience to draw men into the same misery with himself; and if he cannot prevent their entering at last into paradise above, he will labour might and main to make their life a wilderness here below; and to this purpose he will busy their thoughts and hearts about the decrees of God, and about their particular elections; as, whether God hath decreed them to eternal happiness, or chosen them to everlasting blessedness, &c., that so by this means he may keep them from that desirable assurance that may yield believers two heavens, a heaven of joy and comfort here, and a heaven of felicity and glory hereafter.

It is said of Marcellus, the Roman general, that he could not be quiet, *nec victor, nec victus,* neither as conqueror nor as conquered. Such a one is Satan: if he be conquered by faith, yet he will continue striving; if he conquers, yet he will be roaring and triumphing. Satan's great design is eternally to ruin souls; and where he cannot do that, he will endeavour to distress souls by busying them about the secret decrees and counsels of God. If the soul break through his temptations, as David's worthies did break through the hosts of the Philistines, 1 Sam. 23. 16, and snap his snares in sunder, as Samson did his cords, Judges 15. 13, 14, then his next shift is to engage them in such debates and disputes that neither men nor angels can certainly and infallibly determine, that so he may spoil their comforts when he cannot take away their crown.

Now thy wisdom and thy work, O doubting soul, lieth not in disputing, but in believing, praying, and waiting on God. No way to heaven, no way to assurance, like this. Adam disputes with Satan, and falls, and loses paradise; Job believes, and resists Satan, and stands, and conquers upon the dunghill. When Satan, O trembling soul, would engage thee in disputes about this or that, say to him, " Satan, revealed things belong to me," but " secret things belong to the Lord," Deut. 29. 29. It is dangerous to be curious in prying into hidden matters, and careless and negligent in observing known laws; say to him, Satan, thou hast been "a liar and a murderer from the beginning," John 8. 44; thou art a professed enemy to the saints' confidence and assurance, to their consolation and salvation. If thou hast anything to say, say it to my Christ; he is my comfort and crown, my joy and strength, my redeemer and intercessor, and he shall plead for me. Ah, Christians! if you would but leave disputing, and be much in believing and obeying, assurance would attend you; and you should "lie down in peace, and take your rest, and none should make you afraid." Job. 11. 13-20.

The lack of self-examination may hinder assurance

(3) *The third impediment* that keeps poor souls from assurance is, *The lack of a thorough search and examination of their own souls, and of what God hath done and is a-doing in them.* Some there be that can read better in other men's books than in their own, and some there be that are more critical and curious in observing and studying other men's tempers, hearts, words, works, and ways, than their own. This is a sad evil, and causes many souls to sit down in darkness, even days without number. He that will not seriously and frequently observe the internal motions and actings of God, in and upon his noble part, his immortal soul, may talk of assurance, and complain of the want of assurance, but it will be long before he shall obtain assurance. O you staggering, wavering souls, you tossed and disquieted souls, know for a certain that you will never come to experience the sweetness of assurance, till your eyes be turned inward, till you live more at home than abroad, till you dig and search for the mines that be in your own hearts, till you come to discern between a work of nature and a work of grace, till you come to put a difference between the precious and the vile, between God's work and Satan's work. When this is done, you will find the clouds to scatter, and the Sun of righteousness to shine upon you, and the day-star of assurance to rise in you. Doubting, trembling souls, do

not deceive yourselves; it is not a careless, slight, slender searching into your own hearts, that will enable you to see the deep, the secret, the curious, the mysterious work of God upon you. If you do not "seek as for silver," and search for Christ and grace "as for hid treasures," you will not find them, Prov. 2. 3-5. Your richest metals lie lowest, your choicest gems are in the bowels of the earth, and they that will have them, must search diligently, and dig deep, or else they must go without them. Doubting souls, you must search, and dig again and again, and you must work and sweat, and sweat and work, if ever you will find those spiritual treasures, those pearls of price that are hid under the ashes of corruption, that lie low in the inmost recesses of your souls.

Tell me, O doubting souls, hath that sweet word of the apostle been ever made to stick in power upon you: 2 Cor. 13. 5, "Examine yourselves, whether you be in the faith"; or, whether faith be in you, "prove yourselves," &c. The precept is here doubled, to shew the necessity, excellency, and difficulty of the work; to shew that it is not a superficial, but a thorough, serious, substantial examination that must enable a man to know whether he hath precious faith or no; whether he be Christ's spouse or the devil's prostitute. All is not gold that glisters; all is not faith that men call faith; therefore, he that would not prove a cheater to his own soul, must take some pains to search and examine how all is within. Climacus reports that the ancients used to keep in a little book a memorial of what they did in the day against their night reckoning. But ah! how few there be in these days that keep a diary of God's mercies and their own infirmities, of spiritual experiences and the inward operations of heavenly graces! Seneca reports of a heathen man that every night asked himself these three questions: first, What evil hast thou healed this day? secondly, What vice has thou stood against this day? thirdly, In what part art thou bettered this day? And shall not Christians take pains with their own hearts, and search day and night to find out what God hath done, and is a-doing there? God hath his doing hand, his working hand in every man's heart; either he is a-working there in ways of mercy or of wrath; either he is building up or a-plucking down; either he is a-making all glorious within, or else he is a-turning all into a hell. Well! doubting souls, remember this, that the soundest joy, the strongest consolation, flow from a thorough examination of things within. This is the way to know how it is with you for the present, and how it is like to go with you for the future. This is the way to put an end to all the wranglings of your hearts, and to put you into a possession of heaven on this side heaven.

Mistaken views about God's work of grace hinder assurance

(4) *The fourth impediment* that keeps many precious souls from assurance is, *Their mistakes about the work of grace.* Look, as many hypocrites mistake a good nature for grace, and those common gifts and graces that may be in a Saul, a Jehu, a Judas, for a special distinguishing grace, &c., so the dear saints of God are very apt to mistake grace for a good nature, to take pearls of price for stones of no value, to take special grace for common grace. Many trembling souls are apt to call their faith unbelief, with the man in the Gospel, Mark 9. 24, and their confidence presumption, and their zeal passion, &c.; and by this means many are kept off from assurance. Now, the way to remove this impediment is, wisely and seriously to distinguish between renewing grace and restraining grace, betwixt common grace and special grace, betwixt temporary grace and sanctifying grace. Now, the difference betwixt the one and the other I have shewed in ten particulars in my treatise called "Precious Remedies against Satan's Devices," and to that I refer thee for full and complete satisfaction. If thou wilt cast thy eye upon the particulars, I doubt not but thou wilt find that profit and content that will recompense thee for thy pains. And this I thought more convenient to hint to thee, than to write over the same things that there thou wilt find to thy delight and settlement.

(5) *The fifth impediment* to assurance is, *Their grieving and vexing the Spirit of grace by not hearkening to his voice, by refusing his counsel, by stopping the ear, by throwing water upon that fire he kindles in their souls and by attributing that to the Spirit that is to be attributed to men's own passions and distempers, and to the prince of darkness and his associates.* By these and such like ways, they make sad that precious Spirit that alone can gladden them, they set him a-mourning that alone can set them a-rejoicing, they set him a-grieving that alone can set them a-singing; and therefore it is that they sigh it out with Jeremiah, Lam. 1. 16, " Behold, he that should comfort our souls, stands afar off." Ah, doubting souls! if ever you would have assurance, you must observe the motions of the Spirit, and give up yourselves to his guidance; you must live by his laws, and tread in his steps; you must live in the Spirit, and walk in the Spirit; you must let him be chief in your souls. This is the way to have him to be a sealing Spirit, a witnessing Spirit to your hearts. Believe it, souls, if this be not done, you will be far off from quietness and settlement. The word that in 1 John 3. 19 is rendered "assure," signifies to persuade : to note to us that our hearts are froward and peevish, and apt to wrangle and raise objections against God, against Christ, against the Scripture, against our own and others' experiences, and against the sweet hints and joyings of the Spirit; and this they will do, especially when we omit what the Spirit persuades us to. Omissions raise fears and doubts, and make work for hell, or for the Spirit and physician of souls. Or else, when we do that which the Spirit dissuades us from. If you be kind and obedient to the Spirit, it will not be long night with your souls; but if you rebel and vex him, he will make your life a hell, by withholding his ordinary influences, by refusing to seal you to the day of redemption, and by giving you up to conflict with horrors and terrors, &c., Isa. 63, 10. Therefore, be at the Spirit's beck and check, and assurance and joy will ere long attend you.

(6) *The sixth impediment* to assurance is, *Doubting souls making their sense, reason, and feeling the judges of their spiritual conditions.* Now so long as they take this course, they will never reach to assurance. Reason's arm is too short to reach this jewel of assurance. This pearl of price is put in no hand but that hand of faith that reaches from earth to heaven. What tongue can express or heart conceive the fears, the doubts, the clouds, the darkness, the perplexities that will arise from the soul's reasoning thus: —I find not that the countenance of God is towards me as before, Gen. 31. 5; therefore, surely my condition is bad; I feel not those quickenings, those cheerings, those meltings as before; I am not sensible of those secret stirrings and actings of the Spirit and grace in my soul as before; I do not hear such good news from heaven as before; therefore certainly God is not my God, I am not beloved, I am not in the state of grace, I have but deceived myself and others; and therefore the issue will be that I shall die in my sins. To make sense and feeling the judges of our spiritual conditions, what is it but to make ourselves happy and miserable, righteous and unrighteous, saved and damned in one day, ay, in one hour, when sense and reason sit as judges upon the bench? Hath God made sense and feeling the judges of your conditions? No. Why, then, will you? Is your reason Scripture? Is your sense Scripture? Is your feeling Scripture? No. Why, then, will you make them judges of your spiritual estate? Is not the Word the judge, by which all men and their actions shall be judged at last? "The word that I have spoken," says Christ, "shall judge you in the last day," John 12. 48. "To the law and to the testimony, if they speak not according to this word, it is because there is no light, or no morning in them," Isa. 8. 20. Why, then, O doubting souls, will you make your sense and feeling the judge, not only of your condition, but of the truth itself? What is this but to dethrone God, and to make a god of your sense and feeling? What is this, but to limit and bind up the Holy One of

Israel? What is this but to toss the soul to and fro, and to expose it to a labyrinth of fears and scruples? What is this but to cast a reproach upon Christ, to gratify Satan, and to keep yourselves upon the rack? Well! doubting souls, the counsel that I shall give you is this, be much in believing, and make only the Scripture the judge of your condition; maintain the judgment of the Word against the judgment of sense and feeling; and if upon a serious, sincere, and impartial comparing of thy heart and the Word together, of thy ways and the Word together, the Word speaks thee out to be sincere, to be a Nathanael, to be a new creature, to be born again, to have an immortal seed in thee, &c., cleave to the testimony of the Word, joy in it, rest upon it, and give no more way to fears and doubts. Let thy countenance be no more sad; for nothing can speak or make that soul miserable, that the Word speaks out to be happy, Ps. 119. 24.

Constantine would have all differences and disputes in the Nicene Council ended by the Bible. O doubting souls, look cheerfully to this, that all differences and controversies that arise in your hearts be ended by the Word. There is danger in looking away from the Scripture, or beyond the Scripture, or short of the Scripture, or upon sense and feeling, so much as upon the Scripture; therefore let the Word be always the man of thy counsel: no way to assurance and joy, to settlement and establishment, like this. If you are resolved to make sense and feeling the judge of your conditions, you must resolve to live in fears, and lie down in tears.

The indulging of laziness and carelessness hinders assurance

(7) *The seventh impediment* to assurance is, *Men's remissness, carelessness, laziness, and shallowness in religious services, and in the exercise of their graces.* Ah, how active and lively are men in pursuing after the world! but how lifeless and inactive in the ways of grace and holiness! Ah, doubting Christians! remember this, that the promise of assurance and comfort is made over, not to lazy but laborious Christians; not to idle but to active Christians; not to negli-

gent but to diligent Christians: John 14. 21-23, "He that hath my commandments, and keepeth them, he it is that loveth me; and he that loveth me shall be loved of my Father, and I will love him, and will manifest myself to him." Now "Judas saith unto him (not Iscariot), Lord! how is it that thou wilt manifest thyself unto us, and not unto the world? Jesus answered and said unto him, If any man love me, he will keep my words: and my Father will love him, and we will come unto him, and make our abode with him." So 2 Peter 1. 10, 11, "Wherefore the rather, brethren, give diligence to make your calling and election sure: for if you do these things, ye shall never fall: for so an entrance shall be ministered unto you abundantly into the everlasting kingdom of our Lord and Saviour Jesus Christ."

A lazy Christian will always lack four things, viz., comfort, content, confidence, and assurance. God hath made a separation between joy and idleness, between assurance and laziness; and therefore it is impossible for thee to bring these together that God hath put so far asunder. Assurance and joy are choice gifts that Christ gives only to laborious Christians. The lazy Christian hath his mouth full of complaints, when the active Christian hath his heart full of comforts. God would have the hearts of his children to be hot in religious services. "Be fervent" (or seething hot, as it is in the original) "in spirit, serving the Lord," Rom. 12. 11.

That service that hath not heavenly heat, that hath not divine fire in it, is no service, it is lost service. A lazy spirit is always a losing spirit. Oh! remember, lazy Christians, that God is a God of action, therefore he loves activeness in religious services. Remember the angels, those princes of glory, are full of life and activity, and they always behold the Father's face in glory, Matt. 18. 10. Remember, he that will find rich minerals must dig deep, he that will be rich must sweat for it, he that will taste the kernel must crack the shell, he that will have the marrow must break the bone, he that will wear the garland must run the race, he that will ride in triumph must get the victory; so he that will get assurance must be active and lively in duty, Prov. 2. 4-6. It is only fervent prayer that is effectual prayer, it is only the working prayer that works wonders in heaven, and that brings down wonderful assurance into the heart. Cold prayers shall never have any warm answers; God will suit his returns to our requests; lifeless services shall have lifeless answers; when men are dull, God will be dumb. Elias prayed earnestly, or as it is in the Greek, "He prayed in prayer," and God answered him. Many there be that pray, but they do not pray in prayer, they are not lively and earnest with God in prayer; and therefore justice shuts out their prayers. When one desired to know what kind of man Basil was, there was, saith the history, presented to him in a dream, a pillar of fire with this motto, *Talis est Basilus,* Basil is such a one, all on a-fire for God. Ah! lazy, doubting Christians, were you all on a-fire, in hearing, in praying, &c.; it would not be long before the windows of heaven would be open, before God would rain down manna, before he would drop down assurance into your bosoms.

My advice to you, lazy Christians, is this, cease complaining of the want of assurance, and be no more formal, slight, and superficial in religious services, but stir up yourselves, and put out all your might and strength in holy actions, and you shall experimentally find that it will not be long before you shall have such good news from heaven, as will fill you with joy unspeakable, and full of glory.

Neglect of duties hinders assurance

(8) *The eighth impediment* to assurance is, *Men's living in the neglect of some ordinance, or in the omission of some religious duties.* They seek Christ in some of his ways, but not in all; they wait upon him in this and that ordinance, but not in every ordinance. Are there not many doubting souls that wait upon God, in hearing the word of life, and yet neglect, and make light of waiting upon Christ, in breaking the bread of life? Are there not many that are very careful daily to perform family duties, and yet are very rarely found seeking God privately? Some there be that are all ear, all for hearing; and others there be that are all

112

tongue, all for speaking and praying; and others there be that are all eye, all for believing, all for searching, all for inquiring into this and that; and others there be that are all hand, all for receiving the Lord's supper, &c. And seriously, when I consider these things, I cease wondering that so many want assurance, and do rather wonder that any obtain assurance, considering how few there be that are conscientious and ingenuous in waiting upon God in every way and service wherein he is pleased to manifest his grace and favour to poor souls.

Well! doubting souls, remember this, God will give assurance in one ordinance, when he will deny it in another, that you may seek his face in all. God loves as well that you should wait on him as that you should wrestle with him. He that will not give God the honour of attending him in every duty, in every ordinance, may long enough complain of the want of assurance, before God will give him the white stone and the new name, that none knows but he that hath it, Rev. 2. 17. Many of the precious sons of Zion have found God giving assurance in one ordinance, others have found him giving assurance in another ordinance. God speaks peace to some in such and such services, and comfort to others in such and such duties. Therefore, as you would have assurance, O doubting souls, seek the Lord in every way and service, wherein he is pleased to make known his glory and goodness. In hearing, Christ opens his box of ointments to some, and in praying and breaking of bread, he lets his sweet myrrh fall upon the hearts of others. Some have seen the glory of the Lord in the sanctuary, that have been clouded in their private devotions; others have heard a sweet still voice in their private devotions, that have sat long trembling in the sanctuary. Remember, doubting souls, Moab and Ammon were banished the sanctuary to the tenth generation, for a mere omission, because they met not God's Israel in the wilderness with bread and water, Deut. 23. 3, 4. And I verily believe that God doth banish, as I may say, many from his favourable presence, as David did Absalom, for their sinful omissions, for their non-attendance upon him in all his ways. Therefore, if ever you would have assurance, seek the Lord, not only while he may be found, but also in every gracious dispensation where he may be found. "Then shall the joy of the Lord be your strength," and his "glory shall rest upon you." "The days of your mourning shall be ended," and "you shall lie down in peace, and none shall make you afraid." I would earnestly desire you, O doubting souls, seriously to consider, that all the ways of Christ are ways of pleasantness; as Solomon speaks, Prov. 3. 17, not only this way or that way, but every way of Christ is a way of pleasantness; every way is strewed with roses, every way is paved with gold, every way is attended with comfort and refreshing. So the psalmist, "Thy paths drop fatness," Ps. 65. 11, 12; not only this or that path, but all the paths of God drops fatness. Oh then, walk in every way, tread in every path of God, and you would have your souls filled with marrow and fatness, Ps. 63. 5; and never forget that choice saying of the prophet Isaiah, "Thou meetest him that rejoiceth, and worketh righteousness, those that remember thee in thy ways," Isa. 64. 5. They that would have God to meet with them in a way of peace and reconciliation, in a way of grace and favour, must remember God in all his ways; not only in this or that particular way, but in every way wherein he is pleased to cause his glory to shine. Therefore, doubting souls, cease complaining, and be more conscientious and ingenuous in waiting upon God in all his appointments, and it will not long be night with you.

Love of the world hinders assurance

(9) *The ninth impediment* that keeps Christians from assurance is *An immoderate love of the world.* Their thoughts and hearts are so busied about getting the world and keeping the world, that they neither seek assurance as they should, nor prize assurance as they should, nor lament the want of assurance as they should, nor study the worth and excellency of assurance as they should; and therefore it is no wonder, that such are without assurance. As it is very hard for a rich man to enter into heaven, Mat. 19. 23, 24, so it is very hard for a worldly Christian to get assurance

of heaven. The "thick clay," Hab. 2. 6, of this world doth so affect him, and take him, so satisfy him, and sink him, that he is not able to pursue after assurance, with that life and love, with that fervency and frequency, as those must do that will obtain it. It is said, Gen. 13. 2, "That Abraham was very rich in cattle, in silver, and in gold"; according to the Hebrew, Abraham was "very heavy"; to shew, saith one, that riches are a heavy burden, and a hindrance many times to a Christian's comfort and confidence, to his happiness and assurance. Solomon got more hurt by his wealth, than he got good by his wisdom. Such a fire rose out of his worldly enjoyments, as did even consume and burn up his choicest spirits and his noblest virtues; under all his royal robes, he had but a thread-bare soul. Sicily, saith one, is so full of sweet flowers, that dogs cannot hunt there, the scent of the sweet flowers diverteth their smell. And ah! what doth all the sweet delights and contents of this world, but make men lose the scent of heaven, but divert men from hunting after assurance, and from running after Christ, in the sweetness of his ointments.

The creature is all shadow, and vanity of vanities. Vanity is the very quintessence of the creature, and all that can possibly be extracted out of it. It is *filia noctis,* the daughter of a night, like Jonah's gourd. A man may sit under its shadow for a while, but it soon decays and dies. "Why shouldst thou set thy heart upon that which is not?" Prov. 23. 5. Were ever riches true to them that trusted them? As the bird hops from twig to twig, so do riches hop from man to man, &c. Worldly Christians, cease complaining of the want of assurance, and sincerely humble and abase your souls before the Lord; for that you have so eagerly pursued after lying vanities; for that you have in so great a measure forsaken the fountain of living water; for that with Martha you have been busied about many things, when Christ and assurance, the two things necessary, have been so much neglected and disregarded by you. Get this world, this moon, under your feet; take no rest till you have broken through this silken net, till you have got off these golden fetters. A heart that is full of the world, is a heart full of wants. Ah! the joy, the peace, the comfort, the confidence, the assurance, that such hearts lack! The stars which have least circuit, are nearest the pole; and men whose hearts are least entangled with the world, are always nearest to God, and to the assurance of his favour. Worldly Christians, remember this, you and the world must part, or else assurance and your souls will never meet. When a worldly Christian is saved, he is saved as by fire; and before ever he shall be assured of his salvation, he must cry out, *Omnes humanæ consolationes, sunt desolationes,* all human consolations are but desolations. God will not give the sweetmeats of heaven to those that are gorged and surfeited with the delicacies of the earth. The cock upon the dunghill prefers a barley-corn above the choicest pearl; such dunghill Christians as prefer a little barley-corn above this pearl of price, assurance; as, with Esau, prefer a morsel of meat before this blessing of blessings; as prefer Paris above Paradise, God's coin above his countenance, may at last with Esau seek, and seek with tears, this heavenly jewel assurance, and yet, as he, be rejected and repulsed, Heb. 12. 16, 17.

The cherishing of secret sins hinders assurance

(10) *The tenth impediment* that keeps Christians from assurance, is, *The secret cherishing and running out of their hearts to some bosom, darling sin.* It is dark night with the soul, when the soul will cast a propitious eye upon this or that bosom sin, and secretly say, " Is it not a little one, and my soul shall live?" Gen. 19. 20, though God and conscience hath formerly checked and whipped the soul for so doing. Ah! how many be there that dally and play with sin, even after they have put up many prayers and complaints against sin, and after they have lamented and bitterly mourned over their sins. Many there be that complain of their deadness, barrenness, frowardness, conceitedness, censoriousness, and other forms of baseness; and yet are ready at every turn to gratify, if not to justify, those very sins that they complain against. No wonder that such want assurance. After the Israelites had ate manna in the wilderness, and drunk " water out of the rock," after God had been to them a

"cloud by day, and a pillar of fire by night," after he had led them by the arms, and kept them as the apple of his eye, after he had made them spectators of his wonders, they hankered after "the flesh-pots of Egypt"; so when, after God hath given a man a new name and a white stone, after he hath made a report of his love to the soul, after he hath taken a man up into paradise, after he hath set a man upon his knee, and carried him in his bosom, after he hath spoken peace and pardon to the soul, Ps. 85. 8, for the soul to return to folly, oh! this cannot but prove a woeful hindrance to assurance, this will provoke God to change his countenance, and to act not as a friend, but as an enemy. When love is abused, justice takes up the iron rod. God will strike hard and home, when men kick against his mercy. God hath made an everlasting separation betwixt sin and peace, betwixt sin and joy, and betwixt sin and assurance. God will be out with that man, that is in with his sin. If sin and the soul be one, God and the soul must needs be two. He that is resolved to dally with any sin, he must resolve to live in many fears. Never forget this; he that savoureth any one sin, though he foregoeth many, doth but as Benhadad, recover of one disease, and die of another; yea, he takes pains to plunge himself into two hells, a hell here, and a hell hereafter. Therefore, as ever thou wouldst have assurance, offer up thy Isaac, part with thy Benjamin, pull out thy right eye, cut off thy right hand; otherwise assurance and joy will not be thy portion.

Now that I may remove this impediment, which is of such dangerous consequence to Christians' souls, and keep Christians for ever from smiling upon any bosom sin, I shall first lay down a few considerations to provoke them to dally and play no more with sin, but to put off that sin that does so easily beset them, that sticks so close unto them, Heb. 12. 1; and then in the second place, I shall propound some means that may contribute to the bringing under of bosom sins, that so it may be no longer night with the soul.

The first motive to provoke you to put out all your strength and might against bosom sins, that you are so apt to play withal, is *seriously to consider that this will be a strong and choice demonstration and evidence of the sincerity and uprightness of your hearts*: Ps. 18. 23, "I was also upright with him, and I kept myself from mine iniquity." I kept a strict and diligent watch upon that particular sin that I found myself most inclined unto. And this, says David, is a clear evidence to me of the uprightness of my heart with God. The truth is, there is no hypocrite in the world but doth dandle and dally with some bosom sin or other; and though at times, and upon carnal accounts, they seem to be very zealous against this and that sin, yet at the very same time their hearts stand strongly and affectionately engaged to some bosom sin, as might be shewed in Saul, Judas, and Herod, Job 20. 12, 13. Therefore, as ever you would have a sure argument of your uprightness, trample upon your Delilahs. This very evidence of thy uprightness may yield thee more comfort and refreshing in a day of trouble and darkness, than for the present thou dost apprehend, or hast faith to believe. Some there be that can tell thee, that neither the joy of the bridegroom nor the joy of the harvest are worthy to be compared to that joy that arises in the soul from the sense and evidence of a man's own uprightness, 2 Cor. 1. 12. Sincerity is the very queen of virtues; she holds the throne, and will be sure to keep it. Yea, the very sight of it in the soul makes a man sit cheerful and thankful, Noah-like, in the midst of all tempests and storms. Look, as the playing with a bosom sin betokens hypocrisy, so the mortifying of a bosom sin betokens sincerity.

The second motive to provoke doubting souls to trample upon their bosom sins, is *solemnly to consider that the conquest of their darling sins will render the conquests of other sins easy.*

When Goliath was slain, the rest of the Philistines fled, 1 Sam. 17. 51, 52. When a general in an army is cut off, the common soldiers are easily routed and destroyed. Ah! complaining, doubting souls, did you but take the courage and resolution to fall with all your might and spiritual strength upon those particular sins that stick so close unto you, and that do so easily captivate you, you would find, that the great

118

mountains that are before you would soon be made a plain, Zech. 4. 7. Other sins will not be long-lived, when justice is executed upon your bosom sins. Thrust but a dart through the heart of Absalom, and a complete conquest will follow, 2 Sam. 18. 14.

The third motive to provoke you to crucify your bosom sins, be they what they will, is, *seriously to consider the very great damage that your souls have already sustained by your bosom sins.*

Saul, by casting an amorous eye upon Agag, lost his crown and kingdom; Samson, by dallying with his Delilah, lost his strength, sight, light, liberty, and life. But what are these losses to thy loss of spiritual strength, to thy loss of communion with God, to thy loss of the Spirit of light, life, liberty, and glory; to thy loss of joy unspeakable, and peace that passes all understanding; and to thy loss of those fresh and sparkling hopes of glory that were once sparkling in thy breast?

Mark Antony was so far bewitched with his Cleopatra, that in the heat of the battle of Actium, when the empire of the world, his life, and all lay at stake, he fled from Augustus to pursue her, to the ruin and loss of all. So many there are bewitched to some Cleopatra, to some darling sin or other, that they pursue the enjoyment of them to the loss of God, Christ, heaven, and their souls for ever.

Ah! Christians, that the sense of what you have formerly lost, and of what you daily lose by your playing with sin, might provoke you to set upon some effectual course for the mortifying of them!

It was a blasphemous speech of Henry the Second, who said, when Le Mans, his city, was taken, " That he should never love God any more, who suffered a city so dear to him to be taken from him." But it will be a blessed and happy thing for you, in uprightness to say, Oh, we will never love, we will never favour, we will never dally with our bosom sins more; for they have injured us in our spiritual enjoyments, and in our spiritual returns from heaven. Shall the sense of outward losses by this and that instrument, work us out of love with them? And shall not the sense of our

119

spiritual losses by bosom sins, work us much more out with them. Ah, Lord! of what iron mettle is that heart that can look upon those sad losses that hath attended playing with bosom sins, and yet shall dally with those Delilahs?

The fourth motive to provoke you to be the death of your darling sins, is, *solemnly to consider, that the conquest and effectual mortifying of one bosom sin, will yield a Christian more glorious joy, comfort, and peace, than ever he hath found in the gratifying and committing of all other sins.* The pleasure and sweetness that follows victory over sin is a thousand times beyond that seeming sweetness that is in the gratifying of sin. The joy that attends the subduing of sin is a noble joy, a pure joy, a peculiar joy, an increasing joy, and a lasting joy; but that joy that attends the committing of sin is an ignoble joy, a corrupt joy, a decreasing joy, a dying joy. The truth is, were there the least real joy in sin, there could be no perfect hell, where men shall most perfectly sin, and be most perfectly tormented with their sin.

Ah! doubting Christians, as ever you would have good days, as ever you would walk in the light, as ever you would, like the angels, have always harps in your hands, and halle-lujahs in your mouths, be restless, till in the spirit and power of Jesus, you have brought under the sin that sticks so close unto you. Remember this, nothing below the conquest of bosom sins can make a jubilee in the heart. It is not a man's whining and complaining over sin, but his mortifying of sin, that will make his life a paradise of pleasure.

If, notwithstanding all that hath been said, you are still resolved to dally with sin, then you must resolve to live as a stranger to God, and as a stranger to assurance and peace; you must expect sad trials without, and sore troubles within; you must expect to find Satan playing his part both as a lion and as a serpent, both as a devil and as an angel of light. You must expect either no news from heaven, or but bad news from heaven; and you must expect that conscience will play the part both of a scolding wife and of a lion that wants his prey; and this shall be your just reward for playing with sin. If you like the reward, then take your course, and dally with sin still; if otherwise, then sacrifice your Isaac.

The fifth motive to cause you to trample upon your bosom sins is, *wisely to consider that it is your duty and glory to do that every day that you would willingly do upon a dying day.* Ah! how would you live and love upon a dying day? How would you admire God, rest upon God, delight in God, long for God, and walk with God upon a dying day? How would you hate, loathe, and abhor your bosom sins upon a dying day? How would you complain of your bosom sins, and pray against your bosom sins, and mourn over your bosom sins, and watch against your bosom sins; and fly from all occasions that should tend to draw you to close with your bosom sins upon a dying day?

Ah! doubting souls, you would not for all the world gratify your bosom sins upon a dying day, and will you gratify them on other days, which, for anything you know to the contrary, may prove your dying day? Thrice happy is that soul that labours with all his might to do that at first that he would fain do at last; that doth that on every day, that he would give a thousand worlds to do on a dying day. No way to assurance like this; no way to joy and comfort like this; no way to rest and peace like this; no way to the kingdom, to the crown, like this.

I earnestly beseech you, trembling souls, when you find your spirits running out to bosom sins, that you would lay your hands upon your hearts, and thus expostulate the case: O our souls, would you thus dally and play with sin upon a dying day? would you thus stroke and hug sin upon a dying day? would you not rather shew all the dislike and hatred that is imaginable against it? would you not tremble at sin more than at hell? and abhor the very occasions of sin more than the most venomous serpent in all the world? would you not rather suffer the worst and greatest punishments, than to smile upon a darling sin upon a dying day? Yes; oh would you fain do this upon a dying day? Why not then every day? Why not then every day, O our souls?

The sixth motive to provoke you to fall with all your might upon bosom sins is, *seriously to consider that, till this be done, fears and doubts will still haunt the soul; the soul will still be fearing that surely all is naught, and that that work that is wrought upon it is not a real but a counterfeit work; that it is not a peculiar and special work, but a common work, that a man may have and perish.* Till this be done, the soul can never be able to see grace in its own native beauty and glory. The hugging of sin in a corner, will raise such a dust in the soul, that it will not be able to see these pearls of glory sparkling and shining. Till this be done, doubting souls, you will be but babes, and scrubs, and dwarfs in Christianity. The hankering of the soul after sin is the casting of water upon the Spirit; it is the laming of grace, it is the clipping the wings of faith and prayer; so that the soul can neither be confident, nor fervent, frequent nor constant in religious services; so that it will unavoidably follow, such souls will be like Pharaoh's lean kine, poor and starveling. Look, as many men are kept low in their outward estates, by having a back door to some Herodias, Mat. 14. 3; so many doubting souls are kept low in spirituals, by their hankering after some particular sins.

Remember, Christians, sin is the soul's sickness, the soul's weakness. If the body be weak and diseased, it grows not. Sin is poison that turns all nourishment into corruption, and so hinders the growth of the soul in grace and holiness. Ah! Christians, as ever you would be rid of your fears and doubts, as ever you would see the beauty and glory of grace, as ever you would be eminent and excellent in grace and holiness, see that effectual justice be done upon that Achan, that Jonah, that darling sin, that hath occasioned storms within and tempests without.

It was a grievous vexation to King Lysimachus, that his staying to drink one draught of water lost him his kingdom. Ah! Christians, it will grievously vex you, when you come to yourselves, and when you come to taste of the admirable pleasure that attends the conquest of sin, to consider that your hankering after this or that particular sin, hath been the loss of that joy and comfort, that peace and assurance, that is worth infinitely more than all the kingdoms of the world.

Quest. But you may say to me, Oh, we would fain have our bosom sins subdued, we desire above all that they may be effectually mortified. But what course must we take to bring under our darling sins, to get off our golden fetters, to get out of these silken snares?

To this question I shall give these answers:

The first means. If ever thou wouldst have mastery over this or that bosom sin, then *engage all thy power and might against thy bosom sin, draw up thy spiritual forces, and engage them wholly against the sin that doth so easily beset thee.* As the king of Syria said to his captains, "Fight neither with small nor great, save only with the king of Israel," 2 Chron. 18. 30; so say I, your wisdom and your work, O doubting souls, lieth not in skirmishing with this or that sin, but in coming up to a close sharp fight with the king of Israel, with that darling sin that hath a kingly interest in you, and a kingly power over you.

Constantine the Great's symbol was, *Immedicabile vulnus ense rescindendum est,* when there is no hope of curing, men must fall a-cutting. Believe it, souls, you must fall a-cutting your bosom sins in pieces by the sword of the Spirit, as Samuel cut Agag in pieces in Gilgal before the Lord, or else you will never obtain a perfect cure, 1 Sam. 15. 33. Slight skirmishes will not do it; you must pursue your bosom sins to the death, or they will be the death of your souls.

The second means to bring under a bosom sin, is, *to labour to be most eminent and excellent in that particular grace that is most opposite to a man's bosom sin.* As it is a Christian's glory to be eminent in every grace, so it is a Christian's special duty to excel in that particular grace that is most contrary to his darling sins. Is it pride, is it the world, is it hypocrisy, &c., that is thy bosom sin, that is the chief favourite in thy soul? Oh then, labour above all to be clothed with humility, to abound in heavenly-mindedness, to transcend in sincerity, &c., I know no surer, no choicer, no sweeter way, effectually to crucify a bosom sin, than this. He that comes up to this counsel, will not be long held in golden fetters, it will not be long before such a soul cries out, Victory, victory!

The third means to help us to trample upon bosom sins, is, *to look upon bosom sins now, as they will appear to us at last; to look upon them in the time of health as they will appear to us in times of sickness; to look upon them in the time of our life as they will appear to us in the day of our death.* Ah! souls, of all unpardoned sins, your bosom sins will be presented by God, conscience, and Satan at last, as the most filthy and ugly, as the most terrible and dreadful. Your bosom sins at last will appear to be those monsters, those fiends of hell, that have most provoked God against you, that have shut up Christ's love and compassion from you, that have armed conscience against you, that have barred the gates of glory against you, that have prepared the hottest place in hell for you, and that have given Satan the greatest advantage eternally to triumph over you. Ah! souls, at last your bosom sins will more press and oppress you, more sadden and sink you, more terrify and amaze you, than all your other transgressions. Those sins that seem most sweet in life, will prove most bitter in death, Job 20. 11-29. Those pleasant morsels will prove thy greatest hell, when there is but a short step between thy soul and eternity. Ah! Christians, never look upon bosom sins, but with that eye with which within a few hours you must behold them; and this, you will find by experience, will be a singular means to bring under your bosom sins.

The fourth means to subdue bosom sins is, *to apply yourselves to extraordinary means, as fasting and prayer, &c.* Ordinary physic will not remove extraordinary distempers, nor will ordinary duties remove bosom sins, which, by long and familiar acquaintance with the soul, are exceedingly strengthened and advantaged. You read of some devils in the Gospel that could not be cast out but by prayer and fasting, Mat. 17. 14-22. So bosom sins are those white devils that will not, that cannot be cast out but by fervent and constant prayer, joined with fasting and humiliation. Souls that are serious and conscientious in observing of this rule will find such a divine power to attend their endeavours as will give them to "lead captivity captive," Eph. 4. 8, and to triumph over those white devils within, as Christ triumphed over principalities and powers upon the cross, Col. 2. 14, 15.

The fifth means. As you would have victory over bosom

sins, *keep off from all those occasions that tend to lead thee to the gratifying of them.* He that shuns not the occasions of sin, tempts two at once, Satan and his own heart; he tempts Satan to tempt him to taste of forbidden fruit, and he tempts his own heart to feed upon forbidden fruit. "Abstain from all appearance of evil," 1 Thes. 5. 22; "hate the garment spotted by the flesh," Jude 23. Whatever carries with it an ill show or shadow, favour or suspicion, that abstain from, that you may neither wound God nor the gospel, your own consciences nor others. If there be any fuel to feed thy bosom sin in thy house, remove it; or before thine eye, remove it; or in thy hand, remove it, put it far away. Thy soul cannot be safe, it cannot be secure, so long as the occasions of sin are thy companions. Wouldst thou have a clear evidence of the truth of thy grace, then shun the occasions of sin; wouldst thou imitate the choicest saints, then shun the occasions of sin; wouldst thou stand in shaking times, then keep off from the occasions of sin; wouldst thou keep always peace with God, and peace with conscience, then keep off from the occasions of sin; wouldst thou frustrate Satan's greatest designs, and countermine him in his deepest plots, then keep off from the occasions of sin; wouldst thou keep thy bones from breaking, and thy heart from bleeding, then keep off from the occasions of sin; wouldst thou keep down fears and doubts, and keep up faith and hope, then keep off from the occasions of sin; wouldst thou have assurance in life, and joy and peace in death, then keep off from the occasions of sin. Do this, and you do all; if you do not this, you do nothing at all.

And thus I have done with the impediments that hinder souls from assurance, as also with the means to remove those impediments.

CHAPTER IV

Motives to provoke Christians to be restless till they have obtained a well-grounded assurance of their eternal happiness and blessedness.

1. *Many have been lost who thought they were saved*

(1) *The first motive.* Now the first motive that I shall lay down to provoke you to get a well-grounded assurance, is, solemnly to consider, *That many are now dropped into hell that have formerly presumed of their going to heaven:* as those that came bouncing at heaven-gate, crying out, "Lord, Lord, open to us, for we have prophesied in thy name, and in thy name have cast out devils, and in thy name have done many wonderful works"; and yet that direful and dreadful sentence is passed upon them, "Depart from me, ye workers of iniquities," Mat. 7. 22, 26, 27.

The foolish virgins were in a golden dream that they were as happy as the best, and yet, when they were awakened, they found the bridegroom entered into his glory, and the door of mercy shut against them, Mat. 25. 10-12. Men are naturally prone to flatter themselves that their sins are not sins, when indeed they be; and that they are but small sins, when they are great and grievous, Isa. 40. 27; Deut. 29. 19; and they are apt to flatter themselves that they have grace when they have none; and that their grace is true, when it is but counterfeit; and that their condition is not so bad as that of others, when it is worse; and, with Agag, that the bitterness of death is past, when God hath his sword in his hand ready to execute the vengeance written.

I have read of a madman at Athens that laid claim to every rich ship that came into the harbour, whereas he was poor, and had no part in any. Ah! this age is full of such mad souls, that lay claim to God and Christ, and the promises and gospel privileges, and all the glory of another world, when they are poor, and blind, and miserable, and wretched, and naked, when they are Christless and graceless, &c. Ah, Christians! labour for a well-grounded assurance, so that you may not miscarry to all eternity, but may at last be found worthy to receive a crown of glory and to enter into your Master's joy, which is a joy too great and too glorious to enter into you, and therefore you must enter into it, Mat. 25. 21, 23.

2. The world is full of deceivers

(2) *The second motive* to provoke Christians to get a well-grounded assurance is this: consider, *That there be a great many soul-flatterers, soul-deceivers, and soul-cheaters in the world.* The devil hath put his angelical robes upon many of his chief agents, that they may the more easily and the more effectually deceive and delude the souls of men. This age affords many sad testimonies of this. Ah! what multitudes be there, that to some blear eyes appear as angels of light, and yet in their principles and practices are but servants to the prince of darkness, labouring with all their might to make proselytes for hell, Mat. 23. 15, and to draw men to those wild notions, opinions, and conceits that will leave them short of heaven, yea, bring them down to the hottest, darkest, and lowest place in hell, if God does not by a miracle prevent it. Therefore you had need look about you, and see that you get a well-grounded assurance, and suffer not Satan to put a cheat upon your immortal souls. Christ hath foretold us, " That in the last days there shall arise false Christs, and false prophets, that shall say, Lo, here is Christ, and lo, there is Christ," Mat. 24. 23, 24. And verily this scripture is this day fulfilled in your ears. Ah, how many blasphemous wretches there have been in these days, that have asserted themselves to be the very Christ! And it is to me no little miracle, that the very earth hath not opened her mouth and swallowed up such monsters, such firebrands of hell.

The apostle tells us of some that "lie in wait to deceive, by such sleights " as cheaters and false gamesters use at dice; he tells us of cunning crafty men that do diligently watch all advantages to work, draw, and win weak and unstable souls to those opinions, principles, and practices, that tend to drown them in everlasting perdition, Eph. 4. 14. Satan's disciples and agents are notable method-mongers, they have a method of deceiving, they are doctors in all the arts of cheating, and they will leave no means unattempted whereby they may draw men to build upon hay and stubble, upon this opinion and that notion, &c., that so men and their works may burn for ever together, 1 Cor. 3. 15.

It is reported of king Canute, that he promised to make him the highest man in England, who should kill king Edmund Ironside, his co-rival; which, when one had performed, and expected his reward, he commanded him to be hung on the highest tower in London. So Satan and his agents, they promise poor souls that such and such opinions, and notions, will thus and thus advantage them, and advance them; but in the end, poor souls shall find the promised crown turned into a halter, the promised comfort into a torment, the promised glory into ignominy, the promised exaltation into desolation, the promised heaven into a hell. This age is full of soul-flatterers, of soul-undoers, who, like evil surgeons, skin over the wound, but kill the patient. Flattery undid Ahab, and Herod, and Nero, and Alexander.

Those flatterers that told Dionysius that his spittle was as sweet as honey, undid him; and those flatterers that told Cæsar that his freckles in his face were like the stars in the firmament, ruined him. And ah! how many young and old in these days have been lost and undone by those soul-flatterers, that lie in wait to ensnare and deceive the souls of men. Oh that this very consideration might strike home by the hand of the Spirit, with that life and power upon your souls, as effectually to stir and provoke you to get a well-grounded assurance of your happiness and blessedness, that so you may stand fast, like the house built upon the rock, in the midst of all tempests and storms, that nothing may unsettle you or disquiet you, and that none may take away your crown, Mat. 7. 24, 25; Rev. 3. 11.

3. Assurance delivers from the burden of cares, fears, and doubts

(3) *The third motive* to stir you up to get a well-grounded assurance is this: consider, *That a well-grounded assurance of your happiness and blessedness will ease you, and free you of a threefold burden.* It will free you,

1. From a burden of cares.
2. From a burden of fears.
3. From a burden of doubts.

Now the burden of cares, Christian, causes thee to sit down sighing and groaning; ah! how doth the cares of getting this and that, and the cares of keeping this and that worldly content, disturb and distract, vex and rack the souls of men that live under the power of carking cares, Mat. 13. 22. Oh, but now assurance of better things makes the soul sing care away, as that martyr said, " My soul is turned to her rest; I have taken a sweet nap in Christ's lap, and therefore I will now sing care away, and will be careless according to my name." Assurance of a kingdom, of a crown, is a fire that burns up all those cares that ordinarily fill the head and distract the heart. There is no way to get off the burden of cares but by getting assurance.

Again, assurance will free you from the burden of fears, as well as from the burden of cares. Now, your hearts are filled with fears of possessing creature good, with fears of lacking creature good, with fears of losing creature good, &c. And these fears make men turn, like the chameleon, into all colours, forms, and fashions, yea, they make their lives a hell. Oh, but now assurance will scatter all these fears, as the sun doth the clouds; it will extinguish these fears, as water doth the fire. Assurance made David divinely fearless, and divinely careless: " Yea, though I walk through the valley of the shadow of death, I will fear no evil; for thou art with me, thy rod and thy staff they comfort me," Ps. 23. 3. Ah! how full of fears and perplexities was Hagar, till the Lord opened her eyes to see the well of water that was near her, Gen. 21. 16. So the soul will be full of fears and perplexities till it comes to see assurance, to enjoy assurance. Christians, when all is said that can be, this will be found at last a most certain truth, that there is no way to be effectually rid of your fears, but by obtaining a well-grounded assurance of your happiness and blessedness.

Again, assurance will rid you of your burden of doubts. Now you are still a-doubting. Sometimes you doubt whether you are a thorough Christian, and not an Agrippa, an almost Christian, an half Christian, as most professors are. Sometimes you doubt your sonship, and that leads you to doubt your heirship. Sometimes you doubt your acquaintance with God, and that leads you to doubt your access to God, and acceptance with God. Sometimes you doubt your union with God, and those doubts lead you to doubt the truth of your communion with God. The truth is. your whole life is a life of doubting, and so it will be, till you attain to a well-grounded assurance.

Though the two disciples had Christ for their companion, yet their hearts were full of fears and doubts, whilst their eyes were held that they should not know him, Luke 24. 14, 15, &c. Till a Christian's eyes be open to see his assurance, his heart will be full of doubts and perplexities. Though Mary Magdalene was very near to Christ, yet she stands sighing, mourning, and complaining that they had stolen away her Lord, because she did not see him, John 20. 13-16. Christians! though you may be very near and dear to Christ, yet till you come to see your assurance, you will spend your days in doubting, mourning, and complaining. The sum of all is this, as you would be rid of your burden of cares, your burden of fears, and your burden of doubts, get a well-grounded assurance of your happiness and blessedness; but if you are in love with your burdens, then neglect the making of your calling and election sure, and you shall certainly keep your burdens; they shall rise with you, and walk with you, and lie down with you, till they make your lives a hell.

4. Satan labours to keep Christians from assurance

(4) *The fourth motive* to provoke you to labour after a well-grounded assurance is, *To consider that Satan will*

labour with all his art and craft, with all his power and might, to keep you from attaining a well-grounded assurance of your happiness and blessedness. Such is Satan's envy and enmity against a Christian's joy and comfort, that he cannot but act to the utmost of his power to keep poor souls in doubts and darkness. Satan knows that assurance is a pearl of great price that will make the soul happy for ever; he knows that assurance turns a Christian's wilderness into a paradise; he knows that assurance begets in Christians the most noble and generous spirits; he knows that assurance is that which will make men strong to do exploits, to shake his tottering kingdom about his ears; and therefore he is as studious and industrious to keep souls from assurance, as he was to cast Adam out of paradise.

It is no wonder that Satan, who envied the first seeds of grace that divine love sowed in thy soul, should envy the increase of thy grace, yea, thy assurance, which is the top and crown of grace. When thou wast a babe, Satan cast water upon thy smoking flax, that it might not flame forth unto assurance; and now thou art grown up to some more maturity, he is raised in his enmity, so that he cannot but put out his power and policy to keep thee from assurance of felicity and glory. Satan envies thy candle-light, thy torch-light, thy star-light, how much more that the sun should shine upon thee! Satan envies thy eating of the crumbs of mercy under the table, how much more that, as a child, thou shouldst sit at Wisdom's table, and eat and drink abundantly of Wisdom's delicacies! Satan envies thy feeding on husks among the swine, how much more that thou shouldst eat of the fatted calf! Satan envies thy sitting with Mordecai at the king's gate, how much more that thou shouldst wear the king's robes! Satan envies thy tasting of the least drop of comfort, how much more thy swimming in those pleasures that be at God's right hand for evermore! He envies thy sitting upon God's knee, how much more, then, thy lying in his bosom! He envies thy being admitted into his service, how much more that thou shouldst be of his court and council!

Some say of the crystal, that it hath such a virtue in it,

that the very touching of it quickens other stones, and puts a lustre and beauty upon them. Assurance is that heavenly crystal that quickens souls, and that casts a beauty and a glory upon souls; and this makes the devil mad.

Satan knows that assurance is manna in a wilderness, it is water out of a rock, it is a cloud by day and a pillar of fire by night. He knows that assurance is a salve for all sores, a physic for all diseases, and a remedy against every malady. He knows that assurance is a Christian's anchor at sea, and his shield upon land; that it is a staff to support him, and a sword to defend him; a pavilion to hide him, and a cordial to cheer him; and therefore it is that he labours, both as a lion and as a serpent, to keep poor souls from a well-grounded assurance. This son of the morning is fallen from the top of glory to the bottom of misery, and therefore he strives to make all as miserable and unhappy as himself.

Ah! Christians, have not you need to seek assurance with all your might, who have to do with so mighty an adversary, who cares not what torments he heaps upon himself, so long as he is able to torment you, by keeping your souls and assurance asunder? Oh that this very consideration might make you restless, till you have got this "white stone" in your bosoms!

5. A well-grounded assurance is of great value to a believer

(5) *The fifth motive* to provoke you to get a well-grounded assurance is this, consider *that a well-grounded assurance is a jewel of incomparable value; it is a pearl of such great price that it will abundantly recompense the soul for all the cost and expense it shall be at to enjoy it.* Aye, the enjoyment of assurance in that hour, when the soul shall sit upon thy trembling lips, ready to take her leave of thee and of all the world, will richly recompense thee for all those prayers, tears, sighs and groans that thou hast breathed out in one place or another, in one service or another. Surely the gold in the mine will recompense the digger; the crown, in the end, will recompense the runner; the fruit in the vineyard will recompense the dresser; the corn in the barn will re-

compense the reaper; and the increase of the stock will recompense the shepherd; so assurance at last will abundantly recompense the soul for all its knocking, weeping, and waiting at mercy's door. God will never suffer "the seed of Jacob to seek his face in vain," Isa. 45. 19. There is a reward not only *in* keeping, but also *for* keeping of his commands, Ps. 19. 11. Joseph, for his thirteen years' imprisonment, had the honour to reign fourscore years like a king; David, for his seven years' banishment, had a glorious reign of forty years' continuance; Daniel, for his lying a few hours among the lions, is made chief president over a hundred and twenty princes; the three children, for taking a few turns in the fiery furnace, are advanced to great dignity and glory. Ah! doubting souls, pray hard, work hard for assurance; the pay will answer the pains. Christ will, sooner or later, say to thee, as the king of Israel said to the king of Syria, "I am thine, and all that I have," 1 Kings 20. 4. I am thine, O doubting souls, says Christ, and assurance is thine, and joy is thine; my merit is thine, my Spirit is thine, and my glory is thine; all I am is thine, and all I have is thine. Oh this is *alvearium divini mellis,* an hive full of divine honey (comfort); oh this will recompense thee for all thy wrestling and sweating to obtain assurance, Mat. 25. 34-41; Rev. 3. 11, 12.

Augustine, in his Confessions, hath this notable expression, " How sweet was it to me of a sudden to be without those sweet vanities; and those things which I was afraid to lose, I let go with joy, for thou who art the true and only sweetness, didst cast out those from me, and instead of them didst enter in thyself, who art more delightful than all pleasure, and more clear than all light." Ah! Christians, do but hold up and hold on, and assurance and joy will come, and thou shalt, after thy working and waiting, sit down and sing it out with old Simeon, " Mine eyes have seen thy salvation "; my heart hath found the sweetness of assurance, and " now, Lord, let thy servant depart in peace," Luke 2. 30.

6. *Worldlings labour hard to secure the things of this life; saints should show equal ardour for better things*

(6) *The sixth motive* to provoke you to get assurance, is this, Consider *what labour and pains worldlings take to make sure of the things of this life to them and theirs.* Ah! what riding, running, plotting, lying, swearing, stabbing, and poisoning is used by men of this world, to make sure of the poor things of this world, that are but shadows and dreams, and mere nothings! How do many with Samson lay heap upon heap, to make their crowns and kingdoms sure, to make the tottering glory of this world sure to themselves! what bloody butchers do they prove! they will have the crown, though they swim to it through blood. Men will venture life and limb to make sure of these things that hop from man to man, as the bird hops from twig to twig. Oh! how should this stir and provoke us to be up and doing, to labour as for life, to make sure of spiritual and eternal things! Is earth better than heaven? Is the glory of this world greater than the glory of the world to come? Are these riches more durable than those that corrupt not, that "are laid up in heaven, where neither moth nor rust doth corrupt, and where thieves do not break through nor steal"? Mat. 6. 19, 20. No. Oh then be ashamed, Christians, that worldlings are more studious and industrious to make sure of pebbles, than you are to make sure of pearls; to make sure of those things that at last will be their burden, their bane, their plague, their hell, than you are to make sure of those things that would be your joy and crown in life, in death, and in the day of your account.

In ecclesiastical history we read of one who wept when he saw a harlot dressed with much care and cost, partly to see one take so much pains to go to hell, and partly because he had not been so careful to please God, as she had been to please a wanton lover. Ah, Christians! what great reason you have to sit down and weep bitterly, that worldlings take more pains to make themselves miserable, than you have taken to get assurance, to get a pardon in your bosoms, to get more of Christ into your hearts!

7. Assurance renders burdens light

(7) *The seventh motive* to provoke you to get assurance, is to consider, *That assurance will enable you to bear a burden without it being a burden,* as in Heb. 10. 34, " For ye had compassion of me in my bonds, and took joyfully the spoiling of your goods, knowing in yourselves that ye have in heaven a better and an enduring substance." Here you see that assurance of heavenly things makes these worthies patiently and joyfully bear a burden without it being a burden. So the apostles, knowing that they had " a house not made with hands, eternal in the heavens, went through honour and dishonour, evil report and good report," 2 Cor. 5. 1, and 6. 8-11. They went through many weaknesses, sicknesses, wants, and deaths; they had nothing, and yet possessed all things; they had burden upon burden cast upon them by the churches, by false apostles, and by an uncharitable world, and yet they cheerfully bore all burdens without them being a burden, through the power of a well-grounded assurance. Assurance makes heavy afflictions light, long afflictions short, bitter afflictions sweet, 2 Cor. 4. 16-18. When a man lacks assurance, then the shadow of a burden frightens him, and the weight of the least burden sinks him. Such a man is still a-crying out, No man's burden equals my burden; my burden is greater than others', my burden is heavier than others'. The want of assurance oftentimes makes men's very mercies a burden, their comforts a burden, their relations a burden, yea, their very lives a burden unto them. Ah! Christians, you will never bear burdens without them being a burden, till you come to attain to an assurance of better things. This will enable you to leap under the weight of any cross, to rejoice under the weight of any mountain, Job 7. 20. Assurance fits a man's heart to his condition, and when a man's heart is fitted to his condition, nothing proves a burden to him. Assurance of better things to come takes away the sting, the poison that attends these lower things; and the sting and the poison being taken away, the very worst of these things are so far from being a burden to a man, that they become rather a pleasure and a delight

unto him. When the sting is taken out of this or that venomous creature, a man may play with it and put it in his bosom. Ah! assurance pulls out the sting that is in every cross, loss, &c., and this makes the assured soul to sit down singing, when others under far less crosses and losses, sit down sighing, mourning and complaining that their burdens are greater than they are able to bear. If there were but more assurance of better things among Christians, there would be less complaints among them of this burden, and then mole-hills would be no longer mountains. Christians, it is not new notions, new opinions, new nothings, as I may say, in your heads, but the gaining of a well-grounded assurance in your hearts, that will enable you to bear all kinds of burdens without them being a burden.

8. *God urges Christians to get assurance*

(8) *The eighth motive* to provoke you to get assurance, is drawn from *those particular commands of God, whereby he induces Christians to get assurance,* as that in 2 Peter 1. 10, "Wherefore the rather, brethren, give diligence to make your calling and election sure: for if ye do these things ye shall never fall." So 2 Cor. 13. 5, "Examine yourselves, whether ye be in the faith; prove your own selves: know ye not your own selves, how that Jesus Christ is in you, except ye be reprobates," or "unapproved," as the Greek implies. So Heb. 6. 11, "And we desire that every one of you do shew the same diligence, to the full assurance of hope unto the end." Ah! you dull, doubting, drowsy Christians, you should take all these commands of God, and press them with all the power and authority you can upon your hearts, to awaken them and provoke them to get assurance of your eternal well-being. Take one command, and charge that upon the heart; if the heart be stout and will not yield, then take another command, and press it upon your heart; if that will not do, then take another, and lay that home upon the heart; and never leave this work till your souls be effectually stirred up to labour for assurance with all your might. Christians! you should tell your souls that the commands of God bind directly and immediately, that they bind

absolutely and universally. You must obey God upon the bare sight of his will, and in one thing as well as another. Christians! if I am not much mistaken, you should make as much conscience of those commands of God that require you to get assurance of your future happiness, as you do of those commands that require you to pray, to hear, &c. It is very sad to consider that many that complain much of the want of assurance, should make no more care and conscience of those commands of God that require them to get assurance than some of the heathens have done of the commands of their gods; who, when they have called for a man, have offered a candle; or as Hercules, who offered a painted man instead of a living one. Verily, Christians! while you make light of any of God's commands, God will make as light of your comforts. If you were more conscientious in your obedience to the forementioned commands, I believe that the Sun of righteousness would certainly and speedily cause his love and glory to beam out upon you. Mind God's commands more than your own wants and complaints, and light will break in upon you. By obeying Christ's commands, you will gain more than you can give; by kissing the Son, you will even command him, and make him and assurance yours.

9. *Christians are seriously injured by the lack of assurance*

(9) *The ninth motive* to provoke you to get assurance is this, *You cannot gratify Satan more, nor injure yourselves more, than by living without assurance.* By living without assurance, you lay yourselves open to all Satan's snares and temptations; yea, you do instigate and provoke Satan to tempt you to the worst of sins, to tempt you to the greatest neglects, to tempt you to the strangest shifts, and to reduce you to the saddest straits. Ah, Christians! in what hath Satan so gratified you, that you should thus gratify him? Hath he not robbed you of your glory in innocency? Hath he not kept your souls and your Saviour long asunder? When with Joshua you have been standing before the Lord, Zech. 3. 1, 2, hath not he stood at your right hand as an

adversary to resist you? Hath he not often set the glory of the world before you, that he might bewitch you and ensnare you? Mat. 4. 8. Hath he not often cast water upon those divine motions that have been kindled in you? Have you not often found him a lion and a serpent, a tempter and a deceiver, a liar and a murderer? 1 Thes. 2. 18. Yes. Oh, then, never gratify him any longer by living without assurance. He that lives without assurance, lives without a comfortable fruition of God, and so gratifies Satan. He that lives without assurance, lives upon some creature enjoyment more than upon God, and so gratifies Satan. He that lives without assurance lives not like the beloved of God, and so gratifies Satan. He that lives without assurance is very apt to gratify Satan, sometimes by complying with him, sometimes by following after him, and sometimes by acting his part for him. Verily, Christians! there is no way effectually to prevent this sore evil, but by getting a well-grounded assurance of your everlasting happiness and blessedness. Assurance will make a man stand upon terms of defiance with Satan, it will make the soul constant in resisting, and happy in overcoming, the evil one. As assured soul will fight it out to the death with Satan; an assured soul will not fly like a coward, but will stand and triumph like a David.

And as you gratify Satan by living without assurance, so you wrong your own souls by living without assurance.

(1) In the point of comfort and joy, you wrong your own souls.

(2) In the point of peace and content, you wrong your own souls.

(3) In the point of boldness and confidence, you wrong your own souls.

A man that lives without assurance, lays his precious soul open to many blows and knocks, to many frowns and wounds, from God, from the world, from carnal friends, from hypocrites, and from Satan; therefore as you would not, Christians, gratify Satan, and wrong your own souls, and exercise over yourselves spiritual cruelty and tyranny, which is the very worst of all cruelty and tyranny, give God no rest till he hath made known to you the sweetness of his love, and the secrets of his bosom, till he hath gathered you up into himself, till he hath set you as "a seal upon his heart, as a seal upon his arm," Song of Solomon 8. 6.

10. *Ten advantages which accompany assurance*

(10) *The tenth motive,* to provoke you to get a well-grounded assurance is this, Consider *the sweet profit and glorious advantage that will redound to you by gaining assurance;* and if the gain that will certainly redound to you by assurance will not provoke you to get assurance, I know not what will.

(1) IT PRODUCES HEAVEN ON EARTH

[1] *The first advantage. It will bring down heaven into your bosoms; it will give you a possession of heaven, on this side heaven,* Heb. 11. 1. An assured soul lives in paradise, and walks in paradise, and works in paradise; and rests in paradise; he hath heaven within him, and heaven about him, and heaven over him; all his language is Heaven, heaven! Glory, glory!

(2) IT SWEETENS LIFE'S CHANGES

[2] *The second advantage. Assurance will exceedingly sweeten all the changes of this life.* This life is full of changes. Assurance will sweeten sickness and health, weakness and strength, wants and abundance, disgrace and honour, 2 Cor. 4. 16-18. While a man lives in the sense of unchangeable love, no outward changes can make any considerable change in his spirit. Let times change, let men change, let powers change, let nations change, yet a man under the power of assurance will not change his countenance, nor change his master, nor change his work, nor change his hope. Though others under changes turn, like the chameleon, into all colours to save their little all, yet the assured soul under all changes is *semper idem,* always the same.

Antistines, a philosopher, to make his life happy, desired only that he might have the spirit of Socrates, who was always in a quiet temper of spirit, whatever wrongs, injuries, crosses, losses, &c., befell him. Let the trials be what they would that did attend him, yet he continued one and the same. Ah, Christians! the want of assurance hath made many changelings in these days; but if ever you would be like Socrates, if ever you would be like the philosopher's good man, that is, *Tetragonos,* four square, that cast him where you will, like a dice, he falls always sure and square, then get assurance of everlasting happiness.

Assurance will make your souls like the laws of the Medes and Persians, that alter not; it will sweeten the darkest day, and the longest night; under variety of changes, it will make a man sit down with Habakkuk, and rejoice in the Lord, and joy in the God of his salvation, Hab. 3. 17-19.

(3) IT KEEPS THE HEART FROM DESIRING THE WORLD

[3] *The third advantage. Assurance will keep the heart from an inordinate running out after the world, and the glory thereof.* Moses having an assurance of the recompense of reward, and of the love and favour of him that is invisible, could not be drawn by all the honours, pleasures, and treasures of Egypt. He slights all, and tramples upon all the glory of the world, as men trample upon things of no worth, Heb. 11. 24-27. So after Paul had been in the third heaven, and had assurance that nothing should separate him from the love of God in Christ, he looks upon the world as a crucified thing: "The world is crucified to me," saith he, 2 Cor. 12. 1-3, and Rom. 8. 38; "and I am crucified unto the world," Gal. 6. 14. The world is dead to me, and I am dead to it: the world and I are well agreed; the world cares not a pin for me, and I care not a pin for the world.

The lodestone cannot draw the iron when the diamond is present; no more can the vanities of this world draw the soul after them, when assurance, that choice pearl of price, is present.

I have read of Lazarus, that after he was raised from the grave, he was never seen to smile. The assurance that he had of more glorious things, deadened his heart to the things of this world; he saw nothing in them worthy of a smile. Ah! were there more assurance among Christians, there would not be such tugging for the world, and such greedy hunting and pursuing after it, as is in these days, to the dishonour of God, the reproach of Christ, and the shame of the gospel. Get but more assurance, and less money will serve your turns; get but more assurance, and less places of honour and profit will serve your turns; get but assurance, and then you will neither transgress for a morsel of bread, nor yet violently pursue after the golden wedge, &c.

(4) IT ASSISTS COMMUNION WITH GOD

[4] *The fourth advantage. Assurance will exceedingly heighten you in your communion with God, and it will exceedingly sweeten your communion with God.* Assurance that a man is even now a son of God raises him high in his fellowship with God, 1 John 3. 2. There are none that have such choice and sweet communion with God as those that have the clearest assurance of their interest in God, as may be seen throughout the whole book of Solomon's Song. "My beloved is mine, and I am his," saith the spouse, chap. 2. 16. I am assured of my interest in him, says she, and therefore he shall lie all night betwixt my breasts; and upon this account it is that she holds king Jesus in the galleries, that she is sick of love, that she is raised and ravished with his kisses and embraces: "His left hand is under my head, and his right hand doth embrace me," chaps. 1. 13; 7. 5; 2. 6. None had more assurance of her interest in Christ than she, and none was higher and closer in communion with Christ than she. The wife's assurance of her interest in her husband sweetens and heightens her communion with her husband. The child's assurance of his interest in his father sweetens his dealings and fellowship with his father. So the believer's assurance of his interest in God will exceedingly heighten and sweeten his communion and fellowship with God. Assurance of a man's interest in God sweetens every thought of God, every sight of God, every taste of God, and every good word of God. God is as sweet to the assured soul when he hath a sword in his hand as when he hath a sceptre; when he hath the rod of indignation as when he hath the cup of consolation; when his garments are rolled and dyed in blood as when he appears

in his wedding robes; when he acts the part of a judge as when he acts the part of a father.

(5) IT PRESERVES FROM BACKSLIDING

[5] *The fifth advantage. Assurance will be a choice preservative to keep you from backsliding from God and his ways.* Ah! assurance will glue the soul to God and his ways, as Ruth was glued to her mother Naomi. It will make a man " stand fast in the faith, and quit himself like a good soldier of Christ," Gal. 5. 1; 2 Tim. 2. 3; 2 Peter 1. 10, 11, " Wherefore the rather, brethren, give diligence to make your calling and election sure: for if ye do these things, ye shall never fall." Stumble ye may, but assurance will keep a man from falling foully and from falling utterly. Verily, the reason why there are so many apostates in these days is, because there are so few that have a well-grounded assurance.

Pliny speaks of some fishes that swim backward. Ah! many professors in these days swim backward; they swim from God, and Christ, and conscience; yea, they swim from the very principles of morality and common honesty. Believe it, friends! it is not high notions in the brain, but sound assurance in the heart, that will keep a man close to Christ when others backslide from Christ. An assured Christian will not exchange his gold for copper; he knows that one old piece of gold is worth a thousand new counters; one old truth of Christ is worth a thousand new errors, though clothed with glistering robes; and therefore he will prize the truth, and own the truth, and keep close to the truth, when others that lack a sound assurance make merchandise of Christ, of precious truths, and of their own and others' immortal souls. Get assurance, and thou wilt stand when seeming cedars fall; lack assurance, and thou canst not but fall, to the breaking of thy bones, if not to the utter loss of thy precious soul, 2 Peter 2. 3.

(6) IT PRODUCES HOLY BOLDNESS

[6] *The sixth advantage. Assurance will very much embolden the soul with God.* It will make a man divinely

familiar with God; it will make a man knock boldly at the door of free grace; it will make a man come boldly before the mercy-seat; it will make a man enter boldly within the holy of holies. Heb. 10. 22, "Let us draw near with a true heart, in full assurance of faith, having our hearts sprinkled from an evil conscience, and our bodies washed with pure water." Assurance makes the soul converse with God as a favourite with his prince, as a bride with her bridegroom, as a Joseph with a Jacob.

Luther, under the power of assurance, lets fall this transcendent rapture of a daring faith, "*Fiat mea voluntas*, let my will be done"; and then falls off sweetly, "*Mea voluntas, Domine, quia tua*, my will, Lord, because thy will." It is the want of assurance that makes the countenance sad, the hands hang down, the knees feeble, and the heart full of fears and tremblings, Heb. 12. 13. Oh therefore get assurance, and that will scatter your fears, and raise your hopes, and cheer your spirits, and give wings to faith, and make you humbly bold with God. You will not then stand at the door of mercy with a *may I knock?* with a *may I go in?* with a *may I find audience and acceptance?* but you will, with Esther, boldly adventure yourselves upon the mercy and goodness of God. "Now verily, I think," saith one, speaking of Christ, "he cannot despise me, who is bone of my bone, and flesh of my flesh; for if he neglect me as a brother, yet he will love me as a husband: that is my comfort." Assurance will remove all strangeness from between Christ and the soul; of two, it will make Christ and the soul one.

(7) IT PREPARES A MAN FOR DEATH

[7] *The seventh advantage. Assurance will sweeten the thoughts of death, and all the aches, pains, weaknesses, sicknesses, and diseases, that are the fore-runners of it; yea, it will make a man look and long for that day.* It will make a man sick of his absence from Christ. It makes a man smile upon the king of terrors; it makes a man laugh at the shaking of the spear, at the noise of the battle, at the garments of the warriors rolled in blood. It made the martyrs to brave it out with lions, to dare and tire their persecutors,

to kiss the stake, to sing and clap their hands in the flames, to tread upon hot burning coals as upon beds of roses.

The assured soul knows that death shall be the funeral of all his sins and sorrows, of all afflictions and temptations, of all desertions and oppositions. He knows that death shall be the resurrection of his joys; he knows that death is both an outlet and an inlet; an outlet to sin, and an inlet to the soul's clear, full, and constant enjoyment of God; and this makes the assured soul to sing it out sweetly, " O death, where is thy sting? O grave, where is thy victory?" " I desire to be dissolved." "Make haste, my beloved." "Come, Lord Jesus, come quickly." 1 Cor. 15. 55-57; Philip. 1. 23; Song of Solomon 8. 14; Rev. 22. 20. Now death is more desirable than life. Now says the soul, *Ejus est timere mortem, qui ad Christum nolit ire,* let him fear death that is loath to go to Christ. So that I may be with Christ, though I go in a cloud, though I go in a fiery chariot, I care not, says the assured soul.

The Persians had a certain day in the year, in which they used to kill all serpents and venomous creatures. The assured Christian knows, that the day of death will be such a day to him, and that makes death lovely and desirable. He knows that sin was the midwife that brought death into the world, and that death shall be the grave to bury sin; and therefore death is not a terror, but a delight unto him. He fears it not as an enemy, but welcomes it as a friend; as crooked-back Richard the Third in his distress cried, " A kingdom for a horse, a kingdom for a horse!" So souls that want assurance, when they come to die, will cry out, " A kingdom for assurance, a kingdom for assurance!" and as the martyr Severus said, " If I had a thousand worlds, I would now give them all for Christ." So a soul that wants assurance, when he comes to enter upon a state of eternity, will cry out, " Oh, had I now a thousand worlds, I would give them all for assurance, whereas the assured soul would not for a thousand worlds but die. When his glass is out, and his sun is set, he cries not out, as that lady did, " A world, a world for an inch of time!" but rather, " Why is it, why is it, Lord, that thy chariots be so long a-coming?"

(8) IT MAKES MERCIES TASTE LIKE MERCIES

[8] *The eighth advantage. Assurance will very much sweeten that little oil that is in the cruse, and that handful of meal that is in the barrel,* 1 Kings 17. 8-16. Assurance will be sauce to all meats, it will make all mercies to taste like mercies. It will make Daniel's pulse to be as sweet as princes' delicacies, Daniel 1. 8, 12. It will make Lazarus's rags as pleasurable as Dives's robes, Luke 16. 20. It will make Jacob's bed upon the stones, to be as soft as those beds of down and ivory, that sinful great ones stretch themselves upon, Gen. 28. 18; Amos 6. 4.

Look, as the want of assurance embitters all a sinner's mercies, that he cannot taste the sweetness and goodness of them; so the enjoyment of assurance casts a general beauty and glory upon the believer's meanest mercy. And hence it is, that assured souls live so sweetly, and walk so cheerfully, when their little all is upon their backs and in their hands; whereas the great men of the world, that have the world at will, but lack this assurance that is more worth than the world, live as slaves and servants to these mercies, Job 20. 22. In the midst of all their abundance they are in straits and perplexities, full of fears and cares; nothing pleases them, nor is sweet unto them, because they lack that assurance that sweetens to a believer the ground he stands on, the air he breathes, the seat he sits on, the bread he eats, the clothes he wears, &c. Ah! were there more assurance among Christians, they would not count great mercies small mercies, and small mercies no mercies. No, no! then every mercy on this side hell would be a great mercy, then every mercy would be a sugared mercy, a perfumed mercy. Look, as the tree that Moses cast into the waters of Marah made those bitter waters sweet, Exod. 15. 23-25, so assurance is that tree of life that makes every bitter sweet, and every sweet more sweet.

(9) IT GIVES VIGOUR IN CHRISTIAN SERVICE

[9] *The ninth advantage. Assurance will make a man more like an angel.* It will make him full of motion, full of

action; it will make him imitate the angels, those princes of glory, that are always busy and active to advance the glory of Christ. They are still a-singing the song of the Lamb; they are still pitching their tents about them that fear the Lord, Ps. 34. 7; they are ministering spirits sent forth for the good of them that are heirs of salvation, Heb. 1. 14. Assurance will make a man fervent, constant, and abundant in the work of the Lord, as you may see in Paul. The assured Christian is more motion than notion, more work than word, more life than lip, more hand than tongue. When he hath done one work, he is a-calling out for another. What is the next, Lord, says the assured soul, what is the next? His head and his heart are set upon his work, and what he doth, he doth it with all his might, because there is no working in the grave. An assured Christian will put his hand to any work; he will put his shoulder to any burden; he will put his neck in any yoke for Christ; he never thinks that he hath done enough, he always thinks that he hath done too little; and when he hath done all he can, he sits down sighing it out, "I am but an unprofitable servant."

In a word, assurance will have a powerful influence upon thy heart. In all the duties and services of religion, nothing will make a man love like this and live like this; nothing will make a man humble and thankful, contented and cheerful, like this. Nothing will make a man more serious in prayer, more ingenuous in praises, than this; nothing will make a man more cheerful and joyful than this; nothing will make a man more fit to live and more willing to die, than this.

Ah, Christians! if ever you would act as angels in this world, get an assurance of another world; then you shall be neither dumb nor dull any more, but be active and lively, like those whose hopes and whose hearts are in heaven.

(10) IT LEADS TO THE SOUL'S ENJOYMENT OF CHRIST

[10] *The tenth advantage. Assurance will sweeten Christ, and the precious things of Christ, to thy soul.* Ah! how sweet is the person of Christ, the natures of Christ, the aims of Christ, the offices of Christ, the benefits of Christ, the blood of Christ, the word of Christ, the threatenings of

Christ, the Spirit of Christ, the ordinances of Christ, the smiles of Christ, the kisses of Christ, to an assured soul! Now thy meditations on Christ will be no more a terror, nor a horror to thee; nay, now thy heart will be always best, when you are most in pondering upon the sweetness and goodness, the kindness and loveliness, of the Lord Jesus. Now all the institutions and administrations of Christ will be precious to thee. Upon everything where Christ hath set his name, there thou wilt set thy heart. Now thou wilt call things as Christ calls them, and count things as Christ counts them; that shall not be little in thy eye that is great in the eye of Christ; neither shall that be great in thy eye that is but little in the eye of Christ.

Assurance will also exceedingly sweeten your carriage to all that bear the image of Christ. It will make you bear with those weak saints whose light is not so clear as yours, whose abilities are not so strong as yours, whose enjoyments are not so high as yours, whose judgments are not so well informed as yours, whose consciences are not so well satisfied as yours, and whose lives are not so amiable as yours.

Assurance makes men of a God-like disposition, ready to forgive, abundant in goodness, admirable in patience. It makes men to study the good of others, and joy in all opportunities wherein they may strengthen the feeble, and comfort the dejected, and enrich the impoverished, and recover the seduced, and enlarge the straitened, and build up the wasted. Verily, the reason why men are so bitter and sour and censorious, is because God hath not given into their bosoms this sweet flower of delight, assurance.

Ah! were their souls fully assured that God had loved them freely, and received them graciously, and justified them perfectly, and pardoned them absolutely, and would glorify them everlastingly, they could not but love where God loves, and own where God owns, and embrace where God embraces, and be one with every one that is one with Jesus. Were there more assurance among Christians, there would be more of David's and Jonathan's spirit among Christians than there is this day.

Were there more assurance among Christians, there would

be more life and more love, more sweetness and more tenderness. Were there more assurance, there would be less noise, less contention, less division, less distraction, less biting, and less devouring among the saints.

Assurance will make the lion and the calf, the wolf and the lamb, the leopard and the kid, the bear and the cow, lie down together, and feed together, Isa. 11. 6-8. Men that lack assurance love their brethren as flies love the pot. So long as there is any meat in the pot, the flies love it; so those men will love as long as there is an external motive to draw love, but when that ceases, their love ceases.

Dionysius loved his bottles when they were full, but hurled them away when they were empty. So many that lack assurance love the saints while their bags are full, and their houses full of the good things of this life; but when they are empty, then they throw them away, then they cast them off, as Job's friends did him.

Ah! but assurance will make a man love as God loves, and love as long as God loves. The assured Christian will not cease to love so long as the least buds and blossoms of grace appear. Lazarus in his rags is as lovely to an assured Christian as Solomon in his robes. Job is as delightful to him upon the dunghill as David is upon his throne. It is not the outward pomp and bravery, but the inward beauty and glory of saints that is attractive to the assured Christian.

(11) A WELL-GROUNDED ASSURANCE WILL KEEP A CHRISTIAN FROM BEING DECEIVED BY COUNTERFEITS

(11) *The eleventh motive* to provoke you to get a well-grounded assurance of your everlasting happiness is this, consider *that as there is a great deal of counterfeit knowledge, counterfeit faith, counterfeit love, counterfeit repentance, &c. in the world, so there is a great deal of counterfeit assurance in the world.* Many there be that talk high, and look big, and bear it out bravely that they are thus and thus, and that they have such and such glorious assurance, whereas, when their assurance comes to be weighed in the balance of the sanctuary, it is found too light; and when it comes to withstand temptations, it is found too weak; and

when it should put the soul upon divine action, it is found to be but a lazy presumption. Shall the counterfeit gold that is in the world make men active and diligent to get that which is current, and that will abide the touchstone and the fire? and shall not that counterfeit assurance that is in the world provoke your hearts to be so much the more careful and active to get the well-grounded assurance that God accounts as current, and that will abide his touchstone in the day of discovery, and that will keep a man from shame and blushing when the thrones shall be set and the books shall be opened?

I have been the longer upon these motives to provoke your soul to get a well-grounded assurance, because it is of an eternal concernment to you, and a work to which men's hearts are too backward.

Though assurance carries a reward in its own bosom, yet few seek after it; though the pains of getting it be nothing to the profit that accompanies it, yet few will sweat to gain it.

If the inducements laid down will not awaken and provoke you to be restless till you have got the " white stone " and " new name," till you have got the assurance of your pardon in your bosoms, I know not what will.

CHAPTER V

Ways and means of gaining a well-grounded assurance.

1. *Be active in exercising grace*

(1) *The first means.* If ever you will attain to assurance, then *be much in the exercise and actings of grace.* As the believing Ephesians, Eph. 1. 13, were in the very exercise and actings of grace, the Spirit of the Lord "sealed them up to the day of redemption." Assurance flows in upon the actings of grace. Assurance is bred and fed; it is raised and maintained in the soul by the actings of grace. Grace is most discernible when it is most in action, and grace is made more and more perfect by acting. Neglect of your graces is the ground of their decrease. Wells are the sweeter for drawing; you get nothing by dead and useless habits; talents hid in a napkin gather rust; the noblest faculties decline when not improved. Grace in possession is no more discernible than fire under the ashes, than gold in the ore, than a dead man in the grave; but grace, in its lively actings and operations, is as a prince upon his throne, sparkling and shining.

Ah, Christians! were your grace more active, it would be more visible; and were your grace more visible, your assurance would be more clear and full. As Paul once spake to Timothy, "Stir up the gift of God that is in thee," 2 Tim. 1. 6, so say I to you, If ever you would have assurance, stir up the grace of God that is in you; blow up that heavenly fire; raise up those noble spirits; never cease believing nor repenting, till it be clearly given into your bosoms, that you are as sure that you do believe, and that you do repent, as you are sure that you live, as you are sure that God rules in Jacob, and dwells in Zion.

Remember, Christians, all the honour that God hath from you in this life, is from the actings and exercise of your grace, and not from the possessions of grace. Remember, Christians, that all your consolations flow, not from the possession, but from the acts of grace. Remember, Christians, that the want of the exercise of grace is the reason why you do not discern your grace, and why you have no more assurance of your future happiness. He that will be rich must constantly be turning the penny; and he that will attain unto the riches of assurance must constantly be exercising his graces, Col. 2. 2. There are none but lively, active Christians, that know and feel those joys, comforts, and contents that attend the exercise of grace. If thou wouldst not be always a babe in grace, and a stranger to assurance, then see that thy lamp be always burning, see that thy golden wheels of grace be always going.

2. Assurance is obtained by obedience

(2) *The second means.* If you would, Christians, attain unto assurance, then *you must mind your work more than your wages; you must be better at obeying than disputing; at doing, at walking, than at talking and wrangling.* Assurance is heavenly wages that Christ gives, not to loiterers, but to holy labourers. Though no man merits assurance by his obedience, yet God usually crowns obedience with assurance. John 14. 21-23, "He that hath my commandments, and keepeth them, he it is that loveth me; and he that loveth me shall be loved of my Father, and I will love him, and manifest myself to him. Judas saith unto him (not Iscariot), Lord, how is it that thou wilt manifest thyself unto us, and not unto the world? Jesus answered and said unto him, If any man love me, he will keep my words: and my Father will love him, and we will come unto him, and make our abode with him." In these words you see that doing Christians, working Christians, are the only Christians that shall have most of the love of the Father and the Son, and that shall have the choicest manifestations of grace and favour, and that shall have most of their presence and company. So in Ps. 50. 23, "Unto him that ordereth his conversation aright, will I declare the salvation of God." That is, I will declare myself to be his Saviour, I will shew him salvation, and I will shew him his interest in salvation; I will save him, and I will make him see that I have saved him.

He shall see the worth of salvation, and test the sweetness of salvation. So Gal. 6. 16, "And as many as walk according to this rule" (that is, the rule of the new creature), "peace be on them, and mercy, and upon the Israel of God." The Greek word that is here rendered "*walk*," signifies not simply to walk, but to walk by rule, in order, and measure, without treading aside, but making straight steps to our feet. Now these choice souls that thus walk according to the law of the new creature, shall have peace and mercy in them, and peace and mercy with them, and peace and mercy on them. "As many as walk according to this rule, peace and mercy be on them." Assurance is a jewel of too high a price to be cast into the bosoms of any that walk contrary to the laws of the new creature. Such may talk of assurance, and make a stir and a noise about assurance, but it is the close walking Christian that shall be crowned with assurance. Assurance is a choice part of a believer's happiness, and therefore God will never give it out of a way of holiness. "The Lord hath set apart for himself the man that is godly," Ps. 4. 3. None are favourites in God's court, none are admitted to be of his counsel, but those who are all glorious within, and whose raiment is of embroidered gold. That is, those whose principles are full of spiritual glory, and whose practices are amiable and answerable in purity and sanctity. These are the persons that shall have the honour to have God's ear, and the happiness to know his heart.

3. Follow diligently the instructions of the Holy Spirit

(3) *The third means.* To gain assurance, the Christian *must be kind to the Spirit, hear his voice, follow his counsel, live up to his laws.* The Spirit is the great revealer of the Father's secrets, he lies in the bosom of the Father, he knows every name that is written in the book of life; he is best acquainted with the inward workings of the heart of God towards poor sinners; he is the great comforter, and the only sealer up of souls to the day of redemption. If you grieve by your wilful sinning he that alone can gladden you, who then will make you glad? Verily, Christians, when you turn your back upon the Spirit, he will not turn his face upon your souls. Your vexing of the Spirit will be but

the disquieting of yourselves, Isa. 63. 10. Look, as all lights cannot make up the lack of the light of the sun, so all creatures cannot make up the lack of the testimony of the Spirit. Let me speak to you, as God once spake to his people in Exod. 23. 20-23, "Behold," says God, "I send an Angel before thee, to keep thee in thy way, and to bring thee into the place which I have prepared. Beware of him, and obey his voice, provoke him not, for he will not pardon your transgressions, for my name is in him." So say I, behold the Spirit of the Lord, that is your guide and guard; he also is alone able to make a soul-satisfying report of the love and favour to you; therefore, as ever you would have assurance, beware of him and obey his voice, provoke him not; for if you do so by wilful transgressions, he will neither comfort you nor counsel you; he will neither be a sealing nor a witnessing Spirit unto you; nay, he will raise storms and tempests in your souls; he will present to you the Father frowning, and your Saviour bleeding, and himself as grieving; and these sights will certainly rack and torture your doubting souls. The Spirit of the Lord is a delicate thing, a holy thing, a blessed guest, that makes every soul happy where he lodges. "Therefore grieve not the Holy Spirit of God, whereby ye are sealed unto the day of redemption," Eph. 4. 30. You will not grieve your guests, your friends, but courteously and friendly entertain them; why then do you make so little conscience of grieving the Holy Spirit who alone can stamp the image of the Father upon you, and seal you up to life and glory?

Ah, Christians! the way to assurance is not to sit down sighing and complaining of the want of assurance, but it lies in your looking to the Spirit, in your complying with the Spirit, in your cleaving to the Spirit, in your following of the Spirit, in your welcoming of the Spirit, and in your honouring and obeying of the Spirit. As David said of the sword of Goliath, "None like to that," 1 Sam. 21. 9; so say I, no means like to this, to gain a well-grounded assurance of a man's happiness and blessedness. And as one said, "If there be any way to heaven on horseback, it is by prayer"; so say I, if there be any way in the world to assurance, it is by being fearful to offend, and careful to please the Spirit of the Lord, whose office it is to witness to poor souls the remission of their sins, and the salvation of their souls.

4. *Be diligent in attendance upon ordinances*

(4) *The fourth means.* If you would obtain assurance, then *be sincere, be diligent and constant in assuring ordinances.* He that will meet the king, must wait on him in his walks, Isa. 64. 5. Christ's ordinances are Christ's walks; and he that would see the beauty of Christ and taste of the sweetness of Christ, and be ravished with the love of Christ, must wait at wisdom's door; he must attend Christ in his own appointments and institutions, Rev. 2. 1; Prov. 8. 34, 35. That comfort and assurance that flows not in through the golden pipes of the sanctuary, will not better the soul, nor long abide with the soul; it will be as the morning dew, and as the flowers of the field that soon fade away, Hosea 6. 4; 1 Pet. 1. 24.

I have in the former discourse shewed at large how the Lord is graciously pleased to cause his love and glory to beam forth upon souls in ordinances; and therefore I shall say no more on this particular at this time.

5. *Pay particular attention to the scope of God's promises of mercy*

(5) *The fifth means* to obtain assurance is, *wisely and seriously to observe what gift of God there is in thee, that brings thee within the compass of the promises of eternal mercy.* Now, let the gift be this or that, if it be a gift that brings thee within the compass of the promise of eternal mercy, that gift is an infallible evidence of thy salvation.

For the better and further opening of this truth, take note of these three things:

[1] *First,* No man can have any sure evidence to himself of his happiness and blessedness from absolute promises. Absolute promises do not describe to whom salvation and all eternal blessings do belong. The promises of giving Christ, of giving the Spirit, of giving a new heart, and of pardoning and blotting out sin, are all absolute promises. Now God is free to make good these to whom he pleases; therefore he

often passes over the rich and chooses the poor; the learned, and chooses the ignorant; the strong, and chooses the weak; the noble, and chooses the ignoble; the sweet nature, and chooses the rugged nature, &c., that no flesh may glory, and that all may shout out, Grace, grace! 1 Cor. 1. 25-29.

[2] *Secondly*, Though no man can have any sure evidence of his happiness and blessedness from absolute promises, because absolute promises do not describe the persons to whom salvation and all eternal blessings do belong, yet absolute promises are of most choice and singular use.

(1) In that they reveal to us that our salvation is only from free grace, and not from anything in us or done by us.

(2) They are a most sure and glorious foundation for the very worst of sinners to stay their filthy, guilty, wearied, burdened, perplexed souls upon. Seeing that God looks not for any penny or pennyworth, for any portion or proportion in the creature to draw his love, but he will justify, pardon, and save for his name's sake, Isa. 55. 1, 2; seeing all the motives that move God to shew mercy are in his own bosom; seeing they are all within doors, there is no reason why the vilest of sinners should sit down and say, There is no hope, there is no help, Deut. 7. 7, 8; Ps. 68. 18.

[3] *Thirdly*, Absolute promises may, and doubtless often are, choice cordials to many precious souls, who unhappily have lost the sense and feeling of divine favour. Absolute promises are waters of life to many precious sons of Sion. They are a heavenly fire at which they can sit down and warm themselves when they cannot blow their own spark into a flame, and when all candle-light, torch-light and star-light fails them. When all other comforts can yield a perplexed, distressed soul no comfort, then absolute promises will prove full breasts of consolation to the distressed soul, as John 10. 29; Isa. 31. 3 and 57. 15; Heb. 10. 37.

These things being premised, see now what gift of God there is in thee that brings thee within the compass of the promise of everlasting happiness and blessedness; and to help you a little in this, I shall put you in mind of these following particulars.

1. *The first gift.* **Faith** is a gift of God that brings the

155

soul within the promise of everlasting blessedness, as the Scripture doth everywhere evidence: "He that believes shall be saved"; "he that believes shall not come into condemnation"; "he shall not perish"; "he shall have eternal life," Mark 16. 16; John 3. 15, 16, &c.; John 1. 12. Now believing is nothing else but the accepting of Christ for thy Lord and Saviour as he is offered to thee in the gospel; and this accepting is principally, if not only, the act of thy will; so that if thou art sincerely and cordially willing to have Christ upon his own terms, upon gospel terms, that is, to save thee and rule thee, to redeem thee and to reign over thee, then thou art a believer. Thy sincere willingness to believe is thy faith; and this gift brings thee within the compass of the promise of eternal happiness and blessedness.

Christian reader, in the discourse that follows this, thou wilt find the nature, the properties, and the excellencies of a sound saving faith clearly and largely laid open before thee; and therefore I shall say no more to it in this place, but refer thee to what follows.

2. *The second gift. Waiting patiently on God* is a gift that brings thee within the promise of everlasting happiness and blessedness. And he that hath but a waiting frame of heart, hath that which God will eternally own and crown: Isa. 30. 18, "And therefore will the Lord wait that he may be gracious unto you; and therefore will he be exalted that he may have mercy upon you; for the Lord is a God of judgment: blessed are all they that wait for him." Verily, it is no iniquity to pronounce them blessed that God pronounces blessed. It is no piety, but cruelty and inhumanity, for any not to be as merciful to themselves as God is merciful to them; not to have as sweet and precious thoughts of their present condition as God hath. If God says the waiting soul is blessed, who dares judge, who dares say it is not blessed? "Let God be true, and every man a liar," Rom. 3. 4; Isa. 64. 4, "For since the beginning of the world, men have not heard nor perceived by the ear, neither hath the eye seen, O God, besides thee, what he hath prepared for him that waiteth for him"; Prov. 8. 34, "Blessed is the man that heareth me, watching daily at my gates, and waiting at the

posts of my doors"; Isa. 49. 23, "They shall not be ashamed that wait for me"; that is, I will never fail the waiting soul; I will never put him to blushing by frustrating his patient waiting on me. The waiting soul shall bear the belt, and carry away the crown at last. Verily, glorious love and power is as much seen in keeping up a poor soul in a patient waiting on God, as it was in raising Christ from the grave, and as it is in bringing souls to glory. Nothing can make the waiting soul miserable. Hold out faith and patience but a little, "and he that shall come will come, and bring his reward with him," Rev. 22. 11, 12.

3. *The third gift. Hungering and thirsting after righteousness* is a gift that brings the soul within the compass of the promise of everlasting happiness and blessedness: Mat. 5. 6, " Blessed are they which do hunger and thirst after righteousness: for they shall be filled"; or as it runs in the Greek, " Blessed are they that are hungering and thirsting," intimating that wherever this is the present disposition of men's souls, they are blessed, and may expect spiritual repletion.

In relation to this we read in Isa. 44. 2-5: "Thus saith the Lord that made thee, and formed thee from the womb, which will help thee: Fear not, O Jacob my servant; and thou, Jeshurun, whom I have chosen. For I will pour water upon him that is thirsty, and floods upon the dry ground; I will pour my Spirit upon thy seed, and my blessing upon thy offspring. And they shall spring up as among the grass, as willows by the water-courses. One shall say, I am the Lord's, and another shall call himself by the name of Jacob; and another shall subscribe with his hand unto the Lord, and surname himself by the name of Israel."

Of the like consideration is that of Isa. 35. 6, 7, "Then shall the lame man leap as an hart, and the tongue of the dumb sing; for in the wilderness shall waters break forth, and streams in the desert. And the parched ground shall become a pool, and the thirsty land springs of water: in the habitation of dragons, where each lay, shall be grass, with reeds and rushes."

To the like purpose is that in Ps. 107. 9, " For he satisfieth the longing soul, and filleth the hungry soul with goodness."

But that none may mistake or miscarry in this business, that is of eternal concern to them, I shall desire them to note these following things, for a better and fuller clearing of this particular truth that we are at present considering.

First, All real hungerings and thirstings after righteousness are earnest and vehement thirstings and longings. They are like Rachel's longing for children, and like Samson's longing for water: Ps. 42. 2, "As the hart panteth after the water-brook, so panteth my soul after thee, O God. My soul thirsteth for God, for the living God: when shall I come and appear before God?" Philosophers observe, that of all the beasts the hart is most thirsty by nature, but most of all thirsty when she is hunted and pursued by dogs. Says David: "As the hunted hart, as the wounded hart, yea, as the she-hart, in whom the passions of thirst are strongest, panteth after the water-brooks, so doth my soul pant after thee, O God." A gracious soul panteth and fainteth, it breatheth and breaketh, for the longing it hath at all times after the righteousness of Christ imputed and infused, Ps. 119. 20. The Greeks derive their word for *desire* from a root that signifies to *burn.* Ah, Christians! real desires are burning desires; they set the soul all in a holy flame after God and Christ. If they are not vehement; if they do not put an edge upon thy affections, if they do not make thee like the burning seraphim, Christ will take no pleasure in them; they shall return into thy own bosom without working any wonders in heaven, as those desires do that flow from the soul's being touched with a coal from the altar.

Secondly, All real hungerings in the soul after righteousness arise from spiritual and heavenly considerations, Ps. 63. 1-4; 27. 4; Philip. 3. 7-10. They spring in the soul from some convictions, some apprehensions, some persuasions that the soul hath, of a real worth, of a real beauty, glory, and excellency that is in Christ, and in his righteousness, imputed and imparted. Such desires after righteousness that flow from external considerations, are of no worth, weight, or continuance, but those desires after righteousness that flow from spiritual considerations, are full of spirit, life, and glory;

158

they are such that God will not only observe but accept, not only record but reward, Ps. 145. 19.

Thirdly, Real hungerings and thirstings after Christ and his righteousness will put the soul upon lively endeavours. If they are true-born desires, they will not make the soul idle but active, not negligent but diligent, in the use of all holy means, whereby the soul may enjoy Christ and his righteousness: Isa. 26. 9, "With my soul have I desired thee in the night, yea, with my spirit within me will I seek thee early." Real desires will make us earnest and early in seeking to obtain the thing desired, as the Hebrew word imports. A thirsty man will not only long for drink, but labour for it; the condemned man will not only desire his pardon, but he will write, and entreat, and weep, and set this friend and that to solicit for him; the covetous man doth not only wish for wealth, but will rise early and go to bed late, he will turn every stone, and make attempts upon all hopeful opportunities, whereby he may fill his bags and his barns. Even so, all holy desires will put souls upon the use of the means, whereby the mercy desired may be gained. And thus to run, is to attain; thus to will, is to work; thus to desire, is to do the will of our Father, who accepts of pence for pounds, of mites for millions.

The Persian monarch was not so famous for accepting a little water from the hand of a loving subject, as our God is for accepting a handful of meal for a sacrifice, and a gripe of goat's hair for an oblation; for accepting of that little we have, and for accounting our little much, Lev. 2. 2; Exod. 35. 6; 2 Cor. 8. 12.

Noah's sacrifice could not be great, and yet it was greatly accepted and highly accounted of by God. Such is God's condescending love to weak worms, that he looks more at their will than at their work; he minds more what they would do, than what they actually do; he always prefers the willing mind before the worthiest work, and where desires and endeavours are sincere, there God judges such to be as good as they desire and endeavour to be.

Fourthly, Spiritual hungerings and thirstings are only satisfied with spiritual things. John 14. 8, "Shew us the
159

Father, and it sufficeth us." All things in the world cannot suffice us, but a sight of the Father, that will satisfy us: Ps. 63. 5, 6, " My soul shall be satisfied as with marrow and fatness; and my mouth shall praise thee with joyful lips; when I remember thee upon my bed, and meditate on thee in the night-watches." Ps. 65. 4, " We shall be satisfied with the goodness of thy house, even of thy holy temple." It is only God, and the precious things of his house, that can satisfy a thirsty soul.

It was a sweet saying of one, " As what I have, if offered to thee, pleaseth thee not, O Lord, without myself; so the good things we have from thee, though they may refresh us, yet they cannot satisfy us, without thyself." The rattle without the breast will not satisfy the child, the house without the husband will not satisfy the wife, the cabinet without the jewel will not satisfy the virgin, and the world without Christ will not satisfy the soul.

Luther, in a time of want, receiving unexpectedly a good sum of money from one of the electors of Germany, being somewhat amazed, turned himself to God and protested, that God should not put him off with such poor low things. The hungry soul will not be put off with any bread but with the bread of life; the thirsty soul will not be put off with any water but with the well-springs of life. As the king of Sodom said once, " Take you the goods, give me the persons," Gen. 14. 21; so says the hungry soul, Take you the goods, take your honours, and riches, and the favour of creatures, take you the corn, the oil, and the wine; give me Christ, give me the light of his countenance, give me the joy of his Spirit. Oh, the answering of spiritual breathings is very sweet to the soul: Prov. 13. 19, " The desire accomplished is sweet to the soul." Returns from heaven make a paradise in the soul.

I have read of Darius, that when he fled from his enemy, being in great thirst, and meeting with a dirty puddle of water with carrion lying in it, he sucked in and drank very heartily of it, and professed, " That it was the sweetest draught that ever he drank in his life." Ah, how sweet then are those waters of life that be at God's right hand! How sweet are the droppings of God's honeycomb upon the hungry soul! Water out of the rock, and manna in the wilderness, was not so sweet to the hungry, thirsty Israelites, as spiritual answers and spiritual returns are to those that hunger and thirst after spiritual things.

6. Six matters in which Christ's true followers are distinguished from all others

(6) *The sixth means* to obtain a well-grounded assurance of your everlasting happiness is *to be much, yea, to excel, in those choice particular things that may clearly and fully difference and distinguish you, not only from the profane, but also from the highest and most glistering hypocrites in all the world.* It is nothing to be much in those duties and performances wherein the worst of sinners may equalize, yea, go beyond the best of saints. Oh! but to excel in those things that the most refined hypocrites cannot reach to, this cannot but much help you on to assurance. He that hath those jewels in his bosom that God gives only to his choicest favourites, needs not question whether he be a favourite. If he doth so, it is his sin, and will hereafter be his shame.

But you may say to me, What are those choice and particular things that may difference and distinguish Christ's true Nathanaels from all other persons in the world?

Now, to this question I shall give these following answers:

[1] *The first distinction.* A true Nathanael, in his constant course, *labours in all duties and services to be approved and accepted of God.* He is most studious and industrious to approve his heart to God in all that he puts his hand to. So David, " Search me, O God, and know my heart; try me, and know my thoughts; and see if there be any wicked way in me, and lead me in the way everlasting," Ps. 139. 23, 24. So Peter approves his heart to Christ three several times together: " Lord, thou knowest that I love thee; Lord thou knowest that I love thee; Lord, thou knowest all things, thou knowest that I love thee," John 21. 15-17. Thou knowest the sincerity and reality of my love, and therefore to thee I do appeal. To the same purpose the apostle speaks: 2 Cor. 5. 9, " Wherefore we labour, that, whether

present or absent, we may be accepted of him." The Greek word that is here rendered *labour*, is a very emphatical word; it signifies to labour and endeavour with all earnestness and might, to endeavour with a high and holy ambition to be accepted of God, judging it the greatest honour in the world to be owned and accepted of the Lord. Ambitious men are not more diligent, earnest, studious, and laborious to get honour among men, than we are, saith the apostle, to get acceptance with God. Ah! but your most refined hypocrites labour only to approve themselves to men in their praying, fasting, talking, hearing, giving, &c. Let them have but man's eye to see them, and man's ear to hear them, and man's tongue to commend them, and man's hand to reward them, and they will sit down and bless themselves, saying it is enough; "aha! so would we have it."

They say of the nightingale, that when she is solitary in the woods, she is careless of her note; but when she conceives that she hath any auditors, or is near houses, then she composes herself more quaintly and elegantly. Verily, this is the frame and temper of the best of hypocrites. Oh! but a sincere Nathanael labours in all places, and in all cases and services, to approve himself to God; he labours as much to approve himself to God in a wood, where no eye sees him, as he doth when the eyes of thousands are fixed upon him. The sun would shine bright though all men were asleep at high noon, and no eyes open to see the glory of his beams: so a sincere heart will shine, he will labour to do good; though all the world should shut their eyes, yet he will eye his work, and eye his God. He knows that God is *totus oculus*, all eye, and therefore he cares not though others have never an eye to observe him, to applaud him. Let God but secretly whisper to him in the ear, and say, "Well done, good and faithful servant!" and it is enough to his soul, enough to satisfy him, enough to cheer him, and enough to encourage him in the ways and the work of his God.

[2] *The second distinction.* He *labours to get up to the very top of holiness; he labours to live up to his own principles.* He cannot be satisfied with so much grace as will bring him to glory, but he labours to be high in grace, that

he may be high in glory: Philip. 3. 11, "I desire if by any means I might attain unto the resurrection of the dead," that is, to that perfection that the dead shall attain to in the morning of the resurrection. Verily, that man is ripe for heaven who counts it his greatest happiness to be high in holiness; that man shall never be low in heaven, a doorkeeper in heaven, that cannot be satisfied till he be got up to the very top of Jacob's ladder, till he hath attained to the highest perfection in grace and holiness. Ps. 45. 13, "The king's daughter is all glorious within; her clothing is of wrought gold." Her inward principles are all glorious, and her outward practice echoes to her inward principles: "her clothing is of wrought gold."

It was the honour and glory of Joshua and Caleb, that they followed the Lord fully, Num. 14. 24, that is, they lived up to their own principles. So those virgins in Rev. 14. 4, 5, that were without spot before the throne of God, they followed the Lamb wheresoever he went, that is, they lived up to their profession; there was a sweet harmony betwixt their principles and practices. And thus the apostles lived: 2 Cor. 1. 12, "For our rejoicing is this, the testimony of our conscience, that in simplicity and godly sincerity, not with fleshly wisdom, but by the grace of God, we have had our conversation in the world, and more abundantly to you-ward." 1 Thes. 2. 10, "Ye are witnesses, and God also, how holily, and justly, and unblameably, we behaved ourselves among you that believe." Thus we see these worthies living up to their own principles. Blessed Bradford and Bucer lived so up to their principles, that their friends could not sufficiently praise them, nor their foes find anything justly to fasten on them.

Believers know,

(1) That their living up to their own principles, doth best evidence Christ living in them, and their union with him, Gal. 2. 20.

(2) They know that it is not their profession, but living up to their principles, that will effectually stop the mouths, and convince the consciences of vain men: 1 Pet. 2. 15, "For so is the will of God, that by well-doing," that is, by living up

to your own principles, " you may put to silence the ignorance of foolish men." There is no better way in the world to still and silence wicked men, to make them dumb and speechless, to muzzle and tie up their mouths, as the Greek word notes, as by living up to your own principles. The lives of men convince more strongly than their words; the tongue persuades, but the life commands.

(3) They know that by living up to their principles, they cast a general glory upon Christ and his ways. This makes Christ and his ways to be well thought of and well spoken of, Mat. 5. 16; 1 Pet. 2. 11, 12; 2 Pet. 1. 5-13.

(4) They know that the ready way, the only way to get and keep assurance, joy, peace, &c., is to live up to their principles.

(5) They know that by living below their own principles, or contrary to their own principles, they do but gratify Satan, and provoke wicked men to blaspheme that worthy name by which they are called; they know that by their not living up to their own principles they do but multiply their own fears and doubts, and put a sword into the hand of conscience, and make sad work for future repentance.

Now these and such like considerations do exceedingly stir and provoke believers to labour with all their might to live up to their own principles, to get to the very top of holiness, to be more and more a-pressing towards the mark, and to think that nothing is done till they have attained the highest perfections that are attainable in this life. It is true, many hypocrites may go up some rounds of Jacob's ladder, such as make for their profit, pleasure, applause, and yet tumble down at last to the bottom of hell, as Judas and others have done. Hypocrites do not look, nor like, nor love to come up to the top of Jacob's ladder, Gen. 28. 12, to the top of holiness, as you may see in the Scribes and Pharisees, and all other hypocrites that the Scripture speaks of.

[3] *The third distinction. It is their greatest desire and endeavour that sin may be cured, rather than covered.* Sin most afflicts a gracious soul. David cries out, not *Perii*, but *Peccavi*, not " I am undone," but " I have done foolishly," Ps. 51. 3. Daniel complains not, " we are reproached and

oppressed," but "we have rebelled," Dan. 9. 5. Paul cries not out of his persecutors, but of the law in his members rebelling against the law of his mind, Rom. 7. 23. A gracious soul grieves more that God by his sin is grieved and dishonoured, than that for it he is afflicted and chastened.

The hart feeling within her the operation of the serpent's poison, runs from the thorns and thickets, and runs over the green and pleasant pastures, that she may drink of the foun tain and be cured. So gracious souls, being sensible of the poison and venom of sin, run from the creatures, that are but as thorns and thickets, and run over their own duties and righteousness, which are but as pleasant pastures, to come to Christ the fountain of life, that they may drink of those waters of consolation, of those wells of salvation that be in him, and cast up and cast out their spiritual poison, and be cured for ever. Believers know that their sins do most pierce and grieve the Lord, they lie hardest and heaviest upon his heart, and are most obvious to his eye, Amos 2. 13. The sin of Judah is written with a pen of iron, and with the point of a diamond, Jer. 17. 1; their sins are against beams of strongest light, they are against God's tenderest mercy, they are against the manifestations of greatest love, they are against the nearest and dearest relations, they are against the choicest and highest expectations; and this makes believing souls cry out, "Oh, a cure, Lord! a cure, Lord! Oh give me purging grace, give me purging grace; though I should never taste of pardoning mercy, yet give me purging grace."

It was a notable speech of Cosmus, duke of Florence, "I have read," saith he, "that I must forgive my enemies, but never that I must forgive my friends." The sins of God's friends, of God's people, provoke him most, and sadden him most, and this makes them sigh and groan out, "Who shall deliver us from this body of death?" Rom. 7. 24. Oh! but now wicked men labour, not that sin may be cured, but only that sin might be covered, Hosea 7. 10-16; and that the consequents of sin, viz., affliction and the stinging of conscience, may be removed, as you may see in Cain, Saul, Judas, and divers others: Hosea 5, 14, 15, "In their affliction they will seek me early," saith God; they will then seek to be rid of their affliction, but not to be rid of their sins that hath brought down the affliction upon them: like the patient that would fain be rid of his pain and torment, under which he groans, but cares not to be rid of those evil habits that have brought the pain and torment upon him. Ps. 78, 34-37, "When he slew them, then they sought him; but they returned and inquired early after God: and they remembered that God was their rock, and the high God their Redeemer. Nevertheless they did flatter him with their mouth, and they lied unto him with their tongues. For their heart was not upright with him, neither were they stedfast in his covenant." In these words you see plainly, that these people are very early and earnest in seeking God, to take off his hand, to remove the judgments that were upon them, but not that God would cure them of those sins that provoked him to draw his sword, and to make it drunk with their blood; for, notwithstanding the sad slaughters that divine justice had made among them, they did but flatter and lie, and play the hypocrites with God; they would fain be rid of their sufferings, but did not care to be rid of their sins. Ah! but a gracious soul cries out, "Lord, do but take away my sins, and it will satisfy me and cheer me, though thou shouldst never take off thy heavy hand." A true Nathanael sighs it out under his greatest affliction, as that good man did, *A me, me salva domine,* deliver me, O Lord, from that evil man myself. No burden is equal to the burden of sin. "Lord!" says the believing soul; "deliver me from my inward burden, and lay upon me what outward burden thou pleasest."

(4) *The fourth distinction. Are not your souls taken with Christ as chief? is he not in your eye the chiefest of ten thousand? is he not altogether lovely?* Song of Solomon 10. 16. Yes, have you any in heaven but he, and is there any on earth that you desire in comparison with him? Prov. 3. 16; Ps. 73. 25, 26; Philip. 3. 7, 8. No! Do not you lift up Jesus Christ as high as God the Father lifts him? God the Father lifts up Christ above all principalities and powers, Eph. 1. 21, Philip. 2. 9; he lifts up Christ above all your duties, above all your privileges, above all your mercies, above all

your graces, above all your contentments, above all your enjoyments; do not you thus lift up Jesus Christ? Yes! As he is the Father's chiefest jewel, so he is your choicest jewel, is he not? Yes! Verily none can lift up Christ as chief, unless Christ have their hearts, and they dearly love him, and believe in him, for Christ is only precious to them that believe, 1 Pet. 2. 7. Luther had rather be in hell with Christ, than in heaven without him; is not that the frame of thy heart? Yes! Why then dost thou say thou hast no grace, thou hast no Christ. Surely none but those that have union with Christ, and that shall eternally reign with Christ, can set such a high value upon the person of Christ. The true believer, *amat Christum propter Christum*, loves Christ for Christ; he loves Christ for his personal excellencies, Song of Solomon 5. 10-16.

What Alexander said of his two friends, is applicable to many in our day; says he, " Hæphestion loves me as I am Alexander, but Craterus loves me as I am King Alexander." One loved him for his person, the other for the benefits he received by him. So some Nathanaels there be that love Christ for his person, for his personal excellency, for his personal beauty, for his personal glory; they see those perfections of grace and holiness in Christ that would render him very lovely and desirable in their eyes, though they should never get a kingdom or a crown by it. But most of those that bear any love and good-will to Christ, do it only in respect of the benefits they receive by him.

It was Augustine's complaint of old that scarce any love Christ for his rewards. Few follow him for love, but for loaves, John 6. 26; few follow him for his inward excellencies, many follow him for their outward advantages; few follow him that they may be made good by him, but many follow him that they may be great by him. Certainly, you are the bosom friends of Christ, you are in the very heart of Christ, who prize Christ above all, who lift up Jesus Christ as high as God the Father lifts him, and that because of his rich anointings, and because all his garments smell of myrrh, aloes, and cassia, Ps. 45. 6-8. This is a work too high and too hard, too great and too noble, for all that are not new-born, that are not twice born, that are not of the blood-royal, that are not partakers of the divine nature.

[5] *The fifth distinction. Are not your greatest and your hottest conflicts against inward pollutions, against those secret sins that are only obvious to the eye of God and your own souls?* The light of nature's education, and some common convictions of the Spirit, may put men upon combating those sins that are obvious to every eye, but it must be a supernatural power and principle that puts men upon conflicting with the inward motions and secret operations of sin, Rom. 7. 23. The apostle complains of a law in his members warring against the law of his mind. The war was within doors, the fight was inward. The apostle was deeply engaged against a law within him, which made him sigh it out, "O wretched man that I am, who shall deliver me from this body of death?" So David cries out, "Who can understand his errors? cleanse thou me from secret faults," Ps. 19. 12. So Hezekiah humbled himself for the pride of his heart, or for the uplifting of his heart, as the Hebrew hath it, 2 Chron. 32. 26. His recovery from sickness, his victories over his enemies, and his rich treasures, lifted up his heart. Oh! for those outward risings and vauntings of heart Hezekiah humbles himself, he abases and lays himself low before the Lord. A sincere heart weeps and laments bitterly over those secret and inward corruptions that others will scarce acknowledge to be sins. Many a man there is that bleeds inwardly, and dies for ever; many a soul is eternally slain by the inward workings of sin, and he sees it not, he knows it not, till it be too late.

Oh! but a true Nathanael mourns over the inward motions and first risings of sin in his soul, and so prevents an eternal danger. Upon every stirring of sin in the soul the believer cries out, "O Lord, help; O Lord, undertake for me; oh dash these brats of Babylon in pieces." Oh! stifle the first motions of sin, that they may never conceive and bring forth, to the wounding of two at once, thy honour and my own conscience!

[6] *The sixth distinction. Are you not subject to Christ as a Head?* Yes! Devils and wicked men are subject to

168

Christ as a Lord, but those that are by faith united to him, and that have a spiritual interest in him, are subject to him as a Head.

I shall open this particular thus unto you.

First, The members are willingly and sweetly subject to the head; their subjection is voluntary, not compulsory. It is so with a believing soul: Ps. 27. 8, "When thou saidst, Seek ye my face, my heart said unto thee, Thy face, Lord, will I seek." So Ps. 110. 3, "Thy people shall be willing in the day of thy power, in the beauties of holiness." Paul cries out, "What wilt thou have me to do?" Acts 9. 6, and professes that he is willing not to be bound only, but also to die at Jerusalem for the name of Christ, Acts 21. 13. A gracious soul is in some measure naturalised to the work of Christ, and Christ's work is in some measure naturalised to the soul.

Secondly, The members are subject to the head universally, they do all the head enjoineth; so the real members of Christ do in sincerity endeavour universally to be subject to all that Christ their Head requires, without any exception or reservation: Luke 1. 5, 6, "Zacharias and Elizabeth walked in all the commandments and ordinances of the Lord blameless." They walked without halting or halving of it with God; they fell in with every part and point of God's revealed will, without prejudice or partiality, without tilting the balance to one side or the other: Acts 13. 22, "I have found David the son of Jesse a man after my own heart, which shall fulfil all my will," or rather "all my wills," as the Greek hath it, to note the universality and sincerity of his obedience.

Thirdly, The members are subject to the head constantly, unweariedly. The members are never weary of obeying the head; they obey in all places, cases, and times; so are the real members of Christ: Acts 24. 16, "And herein do I exercise myself, to have always a conscience void of offence toward God and toward men." I use all diligence, skill, cunning, and conscience, to be sincere and inoffensive in all my motions and actions towards God and towards men. So David, Ps. 119. 112, "I have inclined my heart" (or rather, as the

Hebrew word signifies, "I have stretched out my heart," as a man would do a piece of parchment) "to do thy statutes" (the Hebrew word signifies to do accurately, exactly, perfectly) "alway, even unto the end." A gracious soul is not like a deceitful bow, nor like the morning dew, but he is like the sun, that rejoiceth to run his race; he is like the stone in Thracia, that neither burneth in the fire nor sinketh in the water. Now tell me, pray tell me, O you doubting souls, whether you do not,

(1) Labour in all duties and services to approve your hearts to God?

(2) Whether you do not endeavour to get up to the very top of holiness, and to live up to your own principles?

(3) Whether it be not your greatest desire and endeavour that sin may be cured rather than covered?

(4) Whether you are not taken with Christ as chief? whether you do not, in your judgments and affections, lift up Christ above all, as God the Father doth?

(5) Whether your greatest and hottest conflicts and combats be not against inward pollutions, against those secret stirrings and operations of sin, which are only obvious to the eye of God and your own souls?

(6) Whether you do not, in respect of the general bent and frame of your hearts, submit to Christ as your Head?

[1] Freely and sweetly.

[2] Universally, in one thing as well as another, without any exception or reservation.

[3] Constantly and unwearily.

Yes! we do these things; we should belie the grace of God if we should say otherwise. These things the Lord hath wrought in us and for us, Isa. 26. 12. Well, then, know,

First, That your estate is good; you have certainly a blessed interest in the Lord Jesus. None can do these things but souls that have union with Christ, that are interested in Christ, that are moved by the peculiar and special influences of Christ, and that are highly beloved of Christ. Verily, these are flowers of paradise that cannot be gathered in nature's garden; they are pearls of that price that God bestows upon none but those that are the price of Christ's blood. All the men in the world cannot prove by the Scripture that these jewels can be found in any men's breasts but in those that have union and communion with Christ, and that shall reign for ever with Christ.

Secondly, Know that it is no iniquity, but rather your duty, for you to suck sweetness out of these honeycombs, and to look upon these things as infallible pledges and evidences of divine favour, and of your everlasting happiness and blessedness. Some there be that make the witness of the Spirit, of which I shall, towards the close of this discourse, speak at large, the only evidence of our interest in Christ, and deny all other evidences from the fruit of the Spirit; but this is to deny the fruit, growing upon the tree, to be an evidence that the tree is alive, whereas all know, that the fruit growing upon the tree is an infallible and undeniable evidence that there is life in the tree. Certainly it is one thing to judge by our graces, and another thing to rest upon our graces, or to put trust in our graces. When one argues from the beams of the sun, that there is a sun, one would think that the most cavilling spirit in the world should lie quiet and still.

7. *Seek to grow in grace*

(1) *The seventh means* to get a well-grounded assurance of your everlasting happiness and blessedness is, *to grow and increase more and more in grace.* 2 Pet. 1. 5-11, " Add to your faith, virtue; and to virtue, knowledge. . . . For so an entrance shall be ministered unto you abundantly into the everlasting kingdom of our Lord and Saviour Jesus Christ." By entrance into the everlasting kingdom of Christ, is not meant a local entrance into heaven; for heaven is nowhere called the kingdom of Christ, but the Father's kingdom. The opposition, ver. 9, sheweth clearly that it is meant of assurance. Now the way to full assurance is by adding grace to grace. The Greek word that is here rendered " *add*," hath a greater emphasis; it signifies to link our graces together, as virgins in a dance do link their hands together. Oh! we must be still a-joining grace to grace, we must still be adding one grace to another, we must still be a-leading

up the dance of graces. Great measures of grace carry with them great evidence of truth, little measures carry with them but little evidence; great measures of grace carry with them the greatest evidence of the soul's union and communion with Christ; and the more evident your union and communion with Christ is, the more clear and full will your assurance be.

Great measures of grace carry with them the greatest and clearest evidences of the glorious indwellings of the Spirit in you, and the more you are persuaded of the real indwellings of the Spirit in you, the higher will your assurance rise. Great measures of grace will be a fire that will consume and burn up the dross, the stubble, the fears and doubts that perplex the soul, and that cause darkness to surround the soul. Now, the more you are rid of your fears, doubts, and darkness, the more easily, and the more effectually will your hearts be persuaded that the thoughts of God towards you are thoughts of love; that you are precious in his eyes, and that he will rejoice over you, to do you good for ever, Jer. 32. 41.

8. *Seek assurance when the soul is in its best frames*

(8) *The eighth means* to gain a well-grounded assurance of your everlasting happiness and blessedness is, *to take your hearts when they are in the best and most spiritual frame and temper God-wards, heaven-wards, and holiness-wards.* Times of temptation and desertion are praying times, hearing times, mourning times, and believing times; but they are not seasonable times for doubting souls to set themselves about so great and so solemn a work as that of searching and examining how things stand, and are likely to stand, between God and them for ever, 2 Cor. 13. 5.

Be diligent and constant, be studious and conscientious in observing the frame and temper of your own hearts, and when you find them most plain, most melting, most yielding, most tender and humble, most sweetly raised, and most divinely composed, then, oh then, is the time to single out the most convenient place where thou mayest with greatest freedom open thy heart to God, and plead with him as for thy life, that he would shew thee how things stand between him and thee, and how it must fare with thy soul for ever. And when thou hast thus set thyself before God, and opened thy heart to God, then wisely observe what report God and thy own renewed conscience do make concerning thy eternal condition: "I will hear what God the Lord will speak," saith David; "for he will speak peace unto his people, and they shall not return to folly," so the Hebrew may be read, Ps. 85. 8, 9. Oh! so must thou stand still, when thou hast sincerely unbosomed thyself before the Lord. and listen and hearken what God will say unto thee. Surely he will speak peace unto thee; he will say, "Son, be of good cheer, thy sins be forgiven thee," thy heart is upright with me; my soul is set upon thee; I have already blessed thee, and I will hereafter glorify thee.

I have read of one who was kept from destroying himself, —being much tempted by Satan thereunto,—by remembering that there was a time when he solemnly set himself in prayer and self-examination before the Lord, and made a diligent inquiry into his spiritual condition; and in the close of that work, it was evidenced to him that his heart was upright with God, and this kept him from laying violent hands upon himself. Oh! a wise and serious observing of the testimony that God, conscience, and the Word gives upon solemn prayer and self-examination may beget strong consolation, and support the soul under the greatest affliction, and strengthen the soul against the most violent temptations, and make the soul look and long for the day of dissolution, as princes do for their day of coronation.

9. *Ascertain whether you have the things that accompany salvation; notably knowledge, faith, repentance, obedience, love, prayer, perseverance, and hope*

(9) *The ninth means* to gain a well-grounded assurance is, *to make a diligent inquiry whether thou hast those things that do accompany eternal salvation:* Heb. 6. 9, "But, beloved, we are persuaded better things of you, and things that accompany salvation"; that comprehend salvation and that touch upon salvation.

173

Oh! beloved, if you have those choice things that accompany salvation, that comprehend salvation, you may be abundantly assured of your salvation.

But you may say to me,

What are those things that accompany salvation?

To this question I shall give this answer, viz., that there are eight special things that accompany salvation, and they are these:

1, *Knowledge;* 2. *Faith;* 3. *Repentance;* 4. *Obedience;* 5, *Love;* 6, *Prayer;* 7, *Perseverance;* 8, *Hope.*

(1) *Knowledge* is one of those special things that accompanies salvation: John 17. 3, "And this is life eternal, that they may know thee, the only true God, and Jesus Christ, whom thou hast sent." Divine knowledge is the beginning of eternal life; it is a spark of glory, it works life in the soul, it is a taste and pledge of eternal life: 1 John 5. 20, "And we know that the Son of God is come, and hath given us an understanding, that we may know him that is true: and we are in him that is true, even in his Son Jesus Christ; this is the true God, and eternal life." 2 Pet. 1. 3, "According as his divine power hath given unto us all things that pertain unto life and godliness, through the knowledge of him that hath called us to glory and virtue." What this knowledge is that accompanies salvation, I shall shew you anon.

(2) Secondly, *Faith* is another of those special things that accompanies salvation: 2 Thes. 2. 13, "But we are bound to give thanks alway to God for you, brethren beloved of the Lord, because God hath from the beginning chosen you to salvation, through sanctification of the Spirit, and belief of the truth." 1 Pet. 1. 5, "You who are kept by the power of God through faith unto salvation." Heb. 10. 39, "But we are not of them who draw back to perdition, but of them that believe to the saving of the soul." John 3. 14-16, "And as Moses lifted up the serpent in the wilderness, even so must the Son of man be lifted up, that whosoever believeth in him should not perish, but have everlasting life." Ver. 36, "He that believeth on the Son hath everlasting life." Chap. 5. 24, "Verily, verily, I say unto you, he that heareth my word, and believeth on him that sent me, hath everlasting

life, and shall not come into condemnation, but is passed from death unto life." Chap 6. 40, " And this is the will of him that sent me, that every one that seeth the Son, and believeth on him, may have everlasting life, and I will raise him up at the last day." Ver. 47, " Verily, verily, I say unto you, he that believeth on me hath everlasting life."

(3) Thirdly, *Repentance* is another of those choice things that accompanies salvation: 2 Cor. 7. 10, " For godly sorrow worketh repentance to salvation, not to be repented of; but the sorrow of the world worketh death." Jer. 4. 14, " O Jerusalem, wash thy heart from wickedness, that thou mayest be saved." Acts 11. 18, " When they heard these things, they held their peace, and glorified God, saying, Then hath God also to the Gentiles granted repentance unto life." Mat. 18. 3, " And Jesus said, Verily I say unto you, except ye be converted, and become as little children, ye shall not enter into the kingdom of heaven." Acts 3. 19, " Repent ye, therefore, and be converted, that your sins may be blotted out, when the times of refreshing shall come from the presence of the Lord."

(4) Fourthly, *Obedience* is another of those precious things that accompanies salvation. Heb. 5. 9, " And being made perfect," speaking of Christ, " he became the author of eternal salvation unto all them that obey him." Ps. 50. 23, " Whoso offereth praise, glorifieth me; and to him that ordereth his conversation aright, will I declare the salvation of God."

(5) Fifthly, *Love* is another of those singular things that accompanies salvation. 2 Tim. 4. 8, " Henceforth there is laid up for me a crown of righteousness, which the Lord, the righteous Judge, shall give me at that day; and not to me only, but unto all them also that love his appearing." James 2. 5, " Hearken, my beloved brethren, hath not God chosen the poor of this world to be rich in faith, and heirs of the kingdom, which he hath promised to them that love him?" 1 Cor. 2. 9, " It is written, eye hath not seen, nor ear heard, neither hath it entered into the heart of man, the things which God hath prepared for them that love him." James 1. 12, " Blessed is the man that endureth temptation,

175

for when he is tried he shall receive a crown of life, which the Lord hath promised to them that love him." Mat. 19. 28, "And Jesus said unto them, Verily I say unto you, that ye which have followed me, in the regeneration, when the Son of man shall sit in the throne of his glory, ye shall sit upon twelve thrones, judging the twelve tribes of Israel. And every one that hath forsaken houses, or brethren, or sisters, or father, or mother, or wife, or children, or lands for my name's sake, shall receive an hundred-fold, and shall inherit everlasting life." The whole is as if Christ had said, Whosoever shall shew love to me, this way or that, in one thing or another, out of respect to my name, to my honour, mercy shall be his portion here, and glory shall be his portion hereafter.

(6) Sixthly, *Prayer* is another of those sweet things that accompanies salvation. Rom. 10. 10, 13, "For with the heart man believeth unto righteousness, and with the mouth confession is made unto salvation. For whosoever shall call on the name of the Lord shall be saved." Acts 2. 21, "And it shall come to pass, that whosoever shall call on the name of the Lord shall be saved." That is, saith one, he shall be certainly sealed up to salvation. Or as another saith, He that hath this grace of prayer, it is an evident sign and assurance to him, that he shall be saved. Therefore to have grace to pray, is a better and a greater mercy than to have gifts to prophesy, Mat. 7, 22. Praying souls shall find the gates of heaven open to them, when prophesying souls shall find them shut against them.

(7) Seventhly and lastly, *perseverance* is another of those prime things that accompanies salvation. Mat. 10. 22, "And ye shall be hated of all men for my name's sake, but he that endureth to the end, the same shall be saved." Chap. 24. 12, 13, "And because iniquity shall abound, the love of many shall wax cold; but he that endurth unto the end, the same shall be saved." Rev. 2. 10, "Fear none of those things which thou shalt suffer; behold the devil shall cast some of you into prison, that ye may be tried, and ye shall have tribulation ten days. Be thou faithful unto death, and I will give thee a crown of life." Chap. 3. 5, "He that overcometh,

the same shall be clothed in white raiment, and I will not blot out his name out of the book of life, but I will confess his name before my Father, and before his angels. To him that overcometh, will I grant to sit with me in my throne, as I also overcame, and am set down with my Father in his throne."

Thus you see these seven choice things that accompany salvation. But for your further and fuller edification, satisfaction, confirmation, and consolation, it will be very necessary that I shew you,

(1) What knowledge that is that accompanies salvation, that borders, that touches upon salvation.

(2) What faith that is that accompanies salvation.

(3) What repentance that is that accompanies salvation.

(4) What obedience that is that accompanies salvation.

(5) What love that is that accompanies salvation.

(6) What prayer that is that accompanies salvation.

(7) What perseverance that is that accompanies salvation.

I hope when I have fully opened these precious things to you, that you will be able to sit down much satisfied and cheered in a holy confidence and blessed assurance of your everlasting well-being.

I shall begin with the first, and shew you what that knowledge is that accompanies salvation, that comprehends salvation, that touches upon salvation; and that I shall open in these following particulars:

The things that accompany salvation: KNOWLEDGE.

KNOWLEDGE IS OPERATIVE

(1) That knowledge that accompanies salvation is *a working knowledge, an operative knowledge*: 2 Cor. 4. 6, " God, who commanded the light to shine out of darkness, hath shined in our hearts, to give us the light of the knowledge of the glory of God in the face of Jesus Christ." Divine light reaches the heart as well as the head. The beams of divine light shining in upon the soul through the glorious face of Christ are very working; they warm the heart, they affect the heart, they new-mould the heart. Divine knowledge masters the heart, it guides the heart, it governs the heart, it sustains

the heart, it relieves the heart: Rom. 6. 6, "We know that our old man is crucified with him, that the body of sin might be destroyed, that henceforth we should not serve sin." Divine knowledge puts a man upon crucifying of sin; it keeps a man from being a servant, a slave to sin, which no other knowledge can do. Under all other knowledge, men remain servants to their lusts, and are taken prisoners by Satan at his will. No knowledge lifts a man up above his lusts but that which accompanies salvation. The wisest philosophers and the greatest doctors, as Socrates and others, under all their sublime notions and rare speculations, have been kept in bondage by their lusts. That knowledge that accompanies salvation is operative knowledge: 1 John 2. 3, 4, "And hereby we do know that we know him, if we keep his commandments. He that saith, I know him, and keepeth not his commandments, is a liar, and the truth is not in him." By keeping his commandments they did know that they did know him; that is, they were assured that they did know him. To know that we know, is to be assured that we know: So James 3. 17, "But the wisdom that is from above is first pure, then peaceable, gentle, and easy to be entreated, full of mercy and good fruits, without partiality, and without hypocrisy." Ver. 13, "Who is a wise man, and endued with knowledge amongst you? Let him shew out of a good conversation his works, with meekness of wisdom." Divine knowledge fills a man full of spiritual activity; it will make a man work as if he would be saved by his works, and yet it will make a man believe that he is saved only upon the account of free grace, Eph. 2. 8. That knowledge that is not operative and working, will only serve to light souls to hell, and to double damn all that have it, Mat. 23. 14.

KNOWLEDGE IS TRANSFORMING

(2) That knowledge that accompanies salvation is *transforming knowledge, it is metamorphosing knowledge.* It is knowledge that transforms, that metamorphoses the soul: 2 Cor. 3. 18, "But we with open face, beholding the glory of the Lord as in a glass, are changed into the same image, from glory to glory." Divine light beating on the heart,

178

warms it, and betters it; it transforms and changes it, it moulds and fashions it into the very likeness of Christ.

The naturalists observe that the pearl, by the often beating of the sunbeams upon it, becomes radiant; so the often beating and shining of the Sun of righteousness, with his divine beams, upon the saints, causes them to glister and shine in holiness, righteousness, heavenly-mindedness, and humbleness. Divine light casts a general beauty and glory upon the soul; it transforms a man more and more into the glorious image of Christ. Look, as the child receiveth from his parents member for member, limb for limb, or as the paper from the press receiveth letter for letter, the wax from the seal print for print, or as the face in the glass answers to the face of the man, or as indenture answers to indenture, so the beams of divine light and knowledge shining into the soul, stamp the lively image of Christ upon the soul, and make it put on the Lord Jesus, and resemble him to the life. Notional knowledge may make a man excellent at praising the glorious and worthy acts and virtues of Christ; but that transforming knowledge that accompanies salvation, will cause a man divinely to imitate the glorious acts and virtues of Christ: 1 Pet. 2. 9, "But ye are a chosen generation, a royal priesthood, an holy nation, a peculiar people, that ye should shew forth the praises (virtues) of him who hath called you out of darkness into his marvellous light." When God causes his divine light, his marvellous light, to shine in upon the soul, then a Christian will preach forth the virtues of Christ in an imitable practice, and till then a man, under all other knowledge, will remain an incarnate devil. When a beam of divine light shone from heaven upon Paul, ah, how it changed and metamorphosed him. How it altered and transformed him! It made his rebellious soul obedient: Acts 9. 6, "Lord, what wilt thou have me to do?" God bids him arise and go into the city, and it should be told him what he should do; and he obeys the heavenly vision, chap. 26. 19. Divine light makes this lion a lamb, this persecutor a preacher, this destroyer of the saints a builder up of the saints, this tormentor a comforter, this monster an angel, this notorious blasphemer a very great admirer of God, and the actings of his free grace, as you may see by comparing Acts 9 and 26 together.

So when a spark of this heavenly fire fell upon the heart of Mary Magdalene, Luke 7. 36, 37, oh what a change, what a turn doth it make in her! Now she loves much, and believes much, and repents much, and weeps much. Oh what a change did divine light make in Zacchæus, and in the jailor! Verily, if thy light, thy knowledge doth not better thee, if it doth not change and transform thee, if, under all thy light and knowledge thou remainest as vile and base as ever, thy light, thy knowledge, thy notions, thy speculations, will be like unto fire, not on the hearth, but in the room, that will burn the house and the inhabitant too; it will be like mettle in a blind horse, that serves for nothing but to break the neck of the rider. That knowledge that is not a transforming knowledge, will torment a man at last more than all the devils in hell; it will be a sword to cut him, a rod to lash him, a serpent to bite him, a scorpion to sting him, and a vulture, a worm eternally gnawing him.

When Tamberlaine was in his wars, one having found and dug up a great pot of gold, brought it to him; Tamberlaine asked whether it had his father's stamp upon it; but when he saw it had the Roman stamp, and not his father's, he would not own it. So God at last will own no knowledge, but that which leaves the stamp of Christ, the print of Christ, the image of Christ upon the heart; that which changes and transforms the soul; that which makes a man a new man, another man than what he was before divine light shined upon him.

KNOWLEDGE IS EXPERIMENTAL

(3) That knowledge that accompanies salvation is *experimental knowledge*. It is knowledge that springs from a spiritual sense and taste of holy and heavenly things. Song of Solomon 1. 2, "Let him kiss me with the kisses of his mouth, for thy love is better than wine." The spouse had experienced the sweetness of Christ's love; " his loves," says she, " being better than wine," though wine is an excellent creature, a useful creature, a comfortable and delightful

180

creature, a reviving and restorative creature. And this draws out her heart, and makes her insatiable in longing, and very earnest in coveting, not a kiss, but kisses, not a little, but much of Christ. Her knowledge being experimental, she is impatient and restless, till she is drawn into the nearest and highest communion and fellowship with Christ. So in ver. 13, "A bundle of myrrh is my well-beloved unto me; he shall lie all night betwixt my breasts." Myrrh is marvellous sweet and savoury, "so is my well-beloved unto me," says the spouse; I have found Jesus Christ to be marvellous sweet and savoury to my soul. Myrrh is bitter to the taste, though it be sweet to the smell; "so is my well-beloved unto me," says the spouse, Ps. 45. 8; Prov. 7. 17. I have found him to be bitter to the old man, to the ignoble and worse part of man; and I have found him to be sweet and lovely to the new man, to the regenerate man, to the noble part of man. I have found him to be a bitter enemy to my sins, and at the same time to be a sweet and precious friend unto my soul. Myrrh is of a preserving nature; it is hot and dry in the second degree, as the naturalists observe; "so is my well-beloved unto me," says the spouse. Oh! I have found the Lord Jesus preserving my soul from closing with such and such temptations, and from falling under the power of such and such afflictions.

In relation to this we read in Philip. 1. 9, "And this I pray, that your love may abound yet more and more in knowledge, and in all judgment." The Greek word that is here rendered "*judgment*," properly signifies sense, not a corporeal, but a spiritual sense and taste, an inward experimental knowledge of holy and heavenly things. The apostle well knew that all notional and speculative knowledge would leave men on this side heaven, and therefore he earnestly prays that their knowledge might be experimental, it being the knowledge that accompanies salvation, and will give a man at last a possession of salvation. Verily, that knowledge that is only notional, speculative, and general, that is gathered out of books, discourses, and other outward advantages, is such a knowledge that will make men sit down on this side salvation, as it did Judas, Demas, and the scribes and pharisees. Christ will at last shut the door of hope, of help, of consolation and salvation, upon all those that know much of him notionally, but nothing feelingly, as you may see in his shutting the door of happiness against the foolish virgins, Mat. 25. 11, 12, and against those froward professors, preachers, and workers of miracles, Mat. 7. 22, who had much speculative knowledge, but no experimental knowledge; who had much outward general knowledge of Christ, but no spiritual inward acquaintance with Christ.

A man that hath that experimental knowledge that accompanies salvation, will from his experience tell you that sin is the greatest evil in the world, for he hath found it so, Rom. 7; that Christ is the one thing necessary, for he hath found him so, Ps. 27. 4; that the favour of God is better than life, for he hath found it so, Ps. 63. 3; that pardoning mercy alone makes a man happy, for he hath found it so, Ps. 32. 1, 2; that a wounded spirit is such a burden that none can bear, for he hath found it so, Prov. 18. 14; that an humble and a broken heart is an acceptable sacrifice to God, for he hath found it so, Ps. 51. 17; that the promises are precious pearls, for he hath found them so, 2 Pet. 1. 4; that the smiles of God will make up for the absence of any outward mercy, for he hath found it so, Ps. 5. 6, 7; that communion with God can alone make a heaven in a believer's heart, for he hath found it so, Ps. 48. 10; that if the Spirit be pleased and obeyed, he will be a comforter to the soul, for he hath found it so, John 16. 7; but if his motions and laws be slighted and neglected, he will stand far off from the soul, he will vex and gall the soul, Lam. 1. 16, Isa. 63, 10, 11. Well! souls, remember this, that knowledge that is not experimental will never turn to your account, it will only increase your guilt and torment, as it did the scribes' and Pharisees'. What advantage had the men of the old world by their knowing that there was an ark, or by their clambering about the ark, when they were shut out and drowned in the flood! What doth it profit a man to see heaps of jewels and pearls, and mountains of gold and silver, when he is moneyless and penniless? It is rather a torment than a comfort to know that there is a pardon for other malefactors, but none for

me; that there is water and wine to cheer, comfort, and refresh others, but not a sip, a drop, for me; my bottle is
empty, and I may die of thirst, whilst others are drinking
at the fountain-head; that there are houses and clothes to
shelter others from colds, storms, and tempests, whilst I lie
naked with Lazarus at Dives's door, exposed to the misery
of all weathers. This kind of knowledge doth rather torment men than comfort them, it does but add fuel to the
fire, and make their hell the hotter. The knowledge that
devils and apostates have of God, Christ, and the Scriptures, being only notional, is so far from being a comfort to
them, that it is their greatest torment; it is a worm that is
eternally gnawing them, it makes them ten thousand times
more miserable than otherwise they would be. They are
still a-crying out, Oh that our light, our light were put out!
Oh that our knowledge, our knowledge were extinguished!
Oh that we might but change rooms, change places with the
heathens, with the barbarians, that never knew what we have
known! Oh how happy would damned devils and apostates
judge themselves in hell, if they should escape with those
dreadful stripes that shall be eternally laid upon the backs
of fools! Remember, reader, that a little heart-knowledge,
a little experimental knowledge, is of greater efficacy and
worth than the highest notions of the most acute wits. He
doth well that discourses of Christ, but he doth infinitely
better that, by experimental knowledge, feeds and lives on
Christ. It was not Adam's seeing, but his tasting, of forbidden fruit that made him miserable; and it is not your
seeing of Christ, but your experimental tasting of Christ,
that will make you truly happy. As no knowledge will save
but what is experimental, so let no knowledge satisfy you
but what is experimental, Ps. 34. 8.

KNOWLEDGE IS HEART-AFFECTING

(4) That knowledge that accompanies salvation is *a
heart-affecting knowledge*. It affects the heart with Christ
and all spiritual things. Oh, it doth wonderfully endear
Christ and the things of Christ to the soul: Song of Solomon 2. 5, " Stay me with flagons, and comfort me with

apples, for I am sick of love." Oh, saith the spouse, my heart is taken with Christ, it is raised and ravished with his love; my soul is burning, my soul is beating towards Christ. Oh, none but Christ, none but Christ! I cannot live in myself, I cannot live in my duties, I cannot live in external privileges, I cannot live in outward mercies, I cannot live in common providences; I can live only in Christ, who is my life, my love, my joy, my crown, my all in all. Oh, the hearing of Christ affects me, the seeing of Christ affects me, the taste of Christ affects me, the glimmerings of Christ affect me; the more I come to know him in his natures, in his names, in his offices, in his discoveries, in his appearances, in his beauties, the more I find my heart and affections to prize Christ, to run after Christ, to be affected with Christ, and to be wonderfully endeared to Christ, Song of Solomon 5. 10. "He is white and ruddy, the chiefest of ten thousand," Ps. 73. 25, 26. The knowledge that she had of Christ did so affect and endear her heart to Christ, that she cannot but make use of all her rhetoric to set forth Christ in the most lovely and lively colours. Gal. 6. 14, "God forbid that I should glory in anything, save in Christ Jesus." Oh, God forbid that my heart should be affected or taken with anything in comparison of Christ. The more I know him, the more I like him; the more I know him, the more I love him; the more I know him, the more I desire him; the more I know him, the more my heart is knit unto him. His beauty is taking, his love is ravishing, his goodness is drawing, his manifestations are enticing, and his person is enamouring. His lovely looks please me, his pleasant voice delights me, his precious Spirit comforts me, his holy Word rules me; and these things make Christ to be a heaven unto me. Oh, but now all that notional knowledge, that speculative knowledge, that leaves a man on this side salvation, never affects the heart; it never draws it, it never endears the heart to Christ, or to the precious things of Christ. Hence it is that such men, under all their notions, under all their light and knowledge, have no affection to Christ, no delight in Christ, no workings of heart after Christ.

Well, reader! remember this, if thy knowledge doth not

now affect thy heart, it will at last with a witness afflict thy heart; if it doth not now endear Christ to thee, it will at last the more provoke Christ against thee; if it doth not make all the things of Christ to be very precious in thy eyes, it will at last make thee the more vile in Christ's eyes. A little knowledge that divinely affects the heart, is infinitely better than a world of that swimming knowledge that swims in the head, but never sinks down into the heart, to the bettering, to the warming, and to the affecting of it. Therefore strive not so much to know, as to have thy heart affected with what thou knowest; for heart-affecting knowledge is the only knowledge that accompanies salvation, that will possess thee of salvation.

KNOWLEDGE IS WORLD-DESPISING

(5) That knowledge that accompanies salvation, is *a world-despising, a world-crucifying, and a world-contemning knowledge*. It makes a man have low, poor, mean thoughts of the world; it makes a man slight it, and trample upon it as a thing of no value. That divine light that accompanies salvation, makes a man to look upon the world as mixed, as mutable, as but for moment; it makes a man look upon the world as a liar, as a deceiver, as a flatterer, as a murderer, and as a witch that hath bewitched the souls of thousands to their eternal overthrow, by her golden offers and proffers. Divine knowledge put Paul upon trampling upon all the bravery and glory of the world, Philip. 3. 4-9. I shall only transcribe the seventh and eighth verses, and leave you to turn to the rest. "But what things were gain to me, those I counted loss for Christ. Yea, doubtless, and I count all things but loss for the excellency of the knowledge of Christ Jesus my Lord, for whom I have suffered the loss of all things, and do count them but dung" (the Greek signifies dog's dung or dog's meat, coarse and contemptible), "that I may win Christ." Divine knowledge raises his heart so high above the world, that he looks upon it with an eye of scorn and disdain, and makes him count it as an excrement, yea, as the very worst of excrements, as dogs' dung, as dogs' meat. Of the like import is that of Heb. 10. 34.

"For ye had compassion of me in my bonds, and took joyfully the spoiling of your goods, knowing in yourselves that ye have in heaven a better and an enduring substance." Divine knowledge will make a man rejoice, when his enemies make a bonfire of his goods. This man hath bills of exchange under God's own hand, to receive a pound for every penny, a million for every mite, that he loses for him. And this makes him to rejoice, and to trample upon all the glory of this world, as one did upon the philosopher's crown, Mat. 19. 27-30.

It was heavenly knowledge that made Moses disdain and scorn the pomp and pleasures, the bravery and glory, the riches and advantages of Egypt, and of Ethiopia too, as some writers observe, Heb. 11. 24-26. So when a beam of divine light had shined upon Zacchæus, Oh, how doth it cause him to part with the world, to cast off the world, to slight it and trample upon it, as a thing of nought! "And Zacchæus stood and said unto the Lord, Behold, Lord! the half of my goods I give to the poor; and if I have taken anything from any man by false accusation, I restore him fourfold. And Jesus said unto him, This day is salvation come to this house forsomuch as he also is the son of Abraham," Luke 19. 2-10. Before the candle of the Lord was set up in Zacchæus's soul, he dearly loved the world, he highly prized the world, he eagerly pursued after the world; he would have it right or wrong, his heart was set upon it, he was resolved to gather riches, though it was out of others' ruin. Ay, but when once he was divinely enlightened, he throws off the world, he easily parts with it, he sets very light by it, he looks with an eye of disdain upon it. His knowledge lifts him up above the smiles of the world, and above the frowns of the world; the world is no longer a snare, a bait, a temptation to him. He knows that it is better to be a son of Abraham, that is, to be taken into covenant with Abraham, to tread in the steps of Abraham's faith, as children tread in the steps of their fathers, and to lie and rest in the bosom of Abraham, as sons do in their fathers' bosoms, than to be rich, great, and honourable in the world, Rom. 4. 12, 16, and 9. 1. And this made him part with the world, and say to it, as he to his idols, "Get you hence, for what have I more to do with you?" Isa. 30. 22; Hos. 14. 8. Verily, that light, that knowledge, will never lead thee to heaven, it will never possess thee of salvation, that leaves thee under the power of the world, that leaves thee in league and friendship with the world, 1 John 2. 15; James 4. 4. If thy knowledge doth not put the world under thy feet, it will never put a crown of glory upon thy head. The church that is clothed with the sun, and that hath a crown upon her head, hath the moon under her feet, Rev. 12. 1.

Ah, knowing souls, knowing souls! do not deceive yourselves! Verily, if you are clothed with the comeliness and righteousness of the sun, which is Jesus Christ, and have a crown of victory and glory upon your heads, you will have the moon under your feet, you will tread and trample upon the trash of this world; all the riches, glories, and braveries of the world will be under your feet, by reason of your non-subjection to it and your holy contempt of it. If thy knowledge doth not enable thee to set thy feet upon those things that most set their hearts on, thou art undone for ever; thy knowledge will be so far from lifting thee up to heaven, that it will cast thee the lower into hell. Therefore let no knowledge satisfy thee, but that which lifts thee above the world, that which weans thee from the world, that which makes the world a footstool. This knowledge, this light will at last lead thee into everlasting light.

KNOWLEDGE IS SOUL-HUMBLING

(6) That knowledge that accompanies salvation is *soul-abasing, soul-humbling knowledge*. It makes a man very, very little and low in his own eyes, as you may see in the most knowing apostle: Eph. 3. 8, "Unto me, who am less than the least of all saints, is this grace given, that I should preach among the Gentiles the unsearchable riches of Christ." Paul's great light makes him very little. Though he was the greatest apostle, yet he looks upon himself as less than the least of all saints.

Likewise is it with the Lord's forerunner, John the Baptist. Oh how little, how low is John in his own eyes!

John 1. 26, 27, " John answered them saying, I baptize with water; but there standeth one among you whom ye know not. He it is, who, coming after me, is preferred before me, whose shoe's latchet I am not worthy to unloose." In this phrase John alludes to the custom of the Hebrews. Those among them which were more noble than others, had boys who carried their shoes, and untied them when they laid them by. Oh! says John, I am a poor, weak, worthless creature; I am not worthy to be admitted to the meanest, to the lowest service under Christ; I am not worthy to carry his shoes, to unloose his shoes. Peter too cries out, " Depart from me, O Lord, for I am a sinful man," a man, a sinner, a very mixture and compound of dirt and sin, of vileness and baseness. Abraham, with all his light and knowledge, acknowledges himself to be but dust and ashes, Gen. 18. 27. Jacob, with all his knowledge, acknowledges himself to be unworthy of the least of all mercies, Gen. 32. 10. David, with all his knowledge, acknowledges himself to be a worm, and no man. Ps. 22. 6. Asaph acknowledges himself to be foolish and ignorant, and as a beast before the Lord, Ps. 73. 22. Job, with all his knowledge, acknowledges that he hath much reason to abhor himself in dust and ashes, Job 42. 1-5. Agur was very good and his knowledge very great; and yet with all his knowledge, oh, how did he vilify, yea, nullify himself! " Surely," saith he, " I am more brutish than any man, and have not the understanding of a man. I neither learned wisdom, nor have the knowledge of the holy," Prov. 30. 1, 4. The evangelical prophet Isaiah, with all his knowledge and visions, which were very great and glorious, acknowledges himself to be a man of unclean lips, and to dwell in the midst of a people of unclean lips," Isa. 6. 1-8. Divine and heavenly knowledge brings a man near to God; it gives a man the clearest and fullest sight of God; and the nearer any man comes to God, and the clearer visions he hath of God, the more low and humble will that man lie before God. None so humble as they that have nearest communion with God. The angels that are near unto him cover their faces with their wings, in token of humility. Divine knowledge makes a man look inwards;

and analyse himself; it is a glass that shews a man the spots of his own soul, and this makes him little and low in his own eyes.

In the beams of this heavenly light, a Christian comes to see his own pride, ignorance, impatience, unworthiness, conceitedness, worthlessness, frowardness and nothingness. That knowledge that swells thee will undo thee; that knowledge that puffs thee will sink thee; that knowledge that makes thee delightful in thy own eyes will make thee despicable in God's and good men's eyes: 1 Cor. 8. 1, 2, "Knowledge puffeth up"; that is, notional knowledge, speculative knowledge, knowledge that ripens a man for destruction, that will leave him short of salvation. This knowledge puffs and swells a man, and makes him think himself something when he is nothing: "And if any man thinketh that he knoweth anything, he knoweth nothing yet as he ought to know," saith the apostle.

Will not that philosopher rise in judgment against many of our high-flown professing *Christians,* who swell, who look big, and talk big under their notional knowledge, who said of himself: *Hoc tantum scio, quod nihil scio,* "This only do I know, that I know nothing." Well! if that knowledge thou hast be that knowledge that accompanies salvation, it is a soul-humbling and a soul-abasing knowledge. If it be otherwise, then will thy knowledge make thee both a prisoner and a slave to the devil at once.

KNOWLEDGE IS APPROPRIATING

(7) That knowledge that accompanies salvation is *an appropriating knowledge,* a knowledge that appropriates and applies spiritual and heavenly benefits to a man's own particular soul. As you may see in Job, "my Redeemer lives," and "my witness is in heaven," and "my record is on high," Job. 19. 25, and 16. 19; so David, "the Lord is my portion," Ps. 16. 5. In Ps. 18. 2, he useth this word of personal possession eight times together, "The Lord is *my rock,* and *my* fortress, and *my* deliverer; *my* God, *my* strength, in whom I will trust; *my* buckler, and the horn of *my* salvation, and *my* high tower." So the spouse, "My beloved is

mine, and I am his," Song of Solomon 2. 16; so Thomas, "My Lord and my God," John 20. 28; so Paul, "I am crucified with Christ: nevertheless I live; yet not I, but Christ liveth in me: and the life which I now live in the flesh I live by the faith of the Son of God, who loved me. and gave himself for me," Gal. 2. 20. Applicatory knowledge (*i.e.*, applied knowledge) is the sweetest knowledge; it revives the heart, it cheers the spirits, it rejoices the soul, it makes a man go singing to duties, and go singing to his grave, and singing to heaven; whereas others, though gracious, that lack this kind of knowledge, have their hearts full of fears, and their lives full of sorrows, and so go sighing and mourning to heaven.

But lest any precious soul should turn this truth into a sword to cut and wound himself, let me desire him to remember, that every believer that hath such knowledge that accompanies salvation, hath not this applicatory knowledge, that makes so much for the soul's consolation, and that doth accompany some men's salvation, I say not all men's salvation. If thou findest thy knowledge to be such a knowledge as is before described in the six former particulars, though thou hast not attained to this applicatory knowledge, yet hast thou attained to that knowledge that accompanies salvation, and that will, my soul for thine. give thee a possession of salvation. This applicatory knowledge that accompanies salvation is only to be found in certain eminent saints that are high in their communion with God, and that have attained some considerable assurance of their interest in God. Many men's salvation is accompanied with an applicatory knowledge, but all men's salvation is not accompanied with an applicatory knowledge of man's particular interest in Christ, and those blessed favours and benefits that come by him. Thy soul may be safe, and thy salvation may be sure, though thou hast not attained unto this appropriating knowledge, but thy life cannot be comfortable without this appropriating knowledge; therefore, if thou hast it not, labour for it as for life. It is a pearl of price, and if thou findest it, it will make thy soul amends for all thy digging, seeking, working, sweating and weeping.

(8) That knowledge that accompanies salvation is accompanied and attended with these things:

[1] *The first attendant.* That knowledge that accompanies salvation is attended *with holy endeavours, and with heavenly desires, thirstings, and pantings after a further knowledge of God, after clearer visions of God.* Prov. 15. 14, " The heart of him that hath understanding seeketh knowledge: but the mouth of fools feedeth on foolishness." The Hebrew word that is here rendered " *seeketh*" signifies an earnest and *diligent seeking*; to seek as an hungry man seeks for meat, or as a covetous man for gold; the more he hath, the more he desires; or as a condemned man seeks for his pardon, or as the diseased man seeks for his cure. The word in the text signifies *to seek studiously,* laboriously, industriously; to seek by suing, praying, inquiring, and walking up and down, that we may find what we seek: so it is in Prov. 18. 15, " The heart of the prudent getteth knowledge, and the ear of the wise seeketh knowledge." A man that divinely knows, will set his heart and his ear, his inward and outward man, to know more and more. Divine knowledge is marvellously sweet, pleasing, comforting, satisfying, refreshing, strengthening, and supporting; and souls that have found the sweetness and usefulness of it, cannot but look and long, breathe and pant after more and more of it. The new-born babe doth not more naturally and more earnestly long for the breasts, than a soul that hath tasted that the Lord is gracious doth long for further and further tastes of God; 1 Pet. 2. 2, 3. David, with all his knowledge, cries out, " I am a stranger in the land, hide not thy commandments from me. Open thou mine eyes, that I may behold wondrous things out of thy law," Ps. 119. 18, 19. Job, with all his knowledge, which was very great, cries out, " That which I see not, teach thou me: if I have done iniquity, I will do no more," Job 34. 32.

[2] *The second attendant.* A second thing that attends and accompanies that knowledge that accompanies salvation, is *holy endeavours to edify others, to instruct others,*

to enlighten and inform others in the knowledge of spiritual and heavenly things. Heavenly light cannot be hid under a bushel. You may as easily hinder the sun from shining, as you may hinder a gracious soul from diffusing and spreading abroad that knowledge and light that God hath given him. Divine light in the soul is like a light in a bright lantern, that shines forth every way, or like a light in a room, or on a beacon, that gives light to others. A Christian that divinely knows, is like the lamp in the story, that was always burning and shining and never went out. So in Gen. 18. 17, 19, " And the Lord said, Shall I hide from Abraham that which I do; for I know him, that he will command his children and his household after him, and they shall keep the way of the Lord, to do justice and judgment; that the Lord may bring upon Abraham that which he hath spoken of him." He that communicates his knowledge to others, shall be both of God's court and counsel; he shall lie in the bosom of God, he shall know the secrets of God. Prov. 15. 7. " The lips of the wise disperse knowledge, but the heart of the foolish doeth not so." The Hebrew word that is here rendered " *disperse*," is a metaphor taken from seedsmen scattering abroad their seed in the furrows of the field. Heavenly knowledge is very spreading and diffusive; it is like the sun: the sun casteth his beams upward and downward, upon good and upon bad; so divine light in a gracious soul will break forth for the advantage and profit of friends and enemies, of those that be in a state of nature, and of those that be in a state of grace. Acts 4. 18-20, " And they called them, and commanded them not to speak at all, nor teach, in the name of Jesus. But Peter and John answered and said unto them, Whether it be right in the sight of God to hearken unto you more than unto God, judge ye. For we cannot but speak the things that we have seen and heard." The bee doth store her hive out of all sorts of flowers for the common benefit; so a heavenly Christian sucks sweetness out of every mercy and every duty, out of every providence and out of, every ordinance, out of every promise and out of every privilege, that he may give out the more sweetness to others. " We learn, that we may teach," is a proverb among the

Rabbins. "And I do therefore lay in, and lay up," saith the heathen, "that I may draw forth again, and lay out for the good of many." The heathen [Socrates and others] will rise in judgment against those that monopolise knowledge to themselves, that imprison their light within their own breasts, lest others should outshine and darken them.

Synesius speaks of some, who, having a treasure of rare abilities in themselves, would as soon part with their hearts as with their thoughts. Verily, such men are far off from that knowledge that accompanies salvation; for that knowledge will make a man willing to spend and be spent for the edification, consolation, and salvation of others, 2 Cor. 6. 10; Gal. 4. 19; Prov. 10. 21, "The lips of the righteous feed many."

[3] *The third attendant.* A third thing that attends and accompanies that knowledge that accompanies salvation, is *holy zeal, courage, and resolution for God.* Divine knowledge makes a man as bold as a lion, Prov. 28. 1. Dan. 11. 32, "The people that do know their God shall be strong, and do exploits." So Prov. 24. 5, "A wise man is strong; yea, a man of knowledge increaseth strength," or, "He strengtheneth might," as it is in the Hebrew. Divine light makes a man full of mettle for God; it makes the soul divinely fearless and careless. Josh. 24. 15, "Choose ye whom you will serve, I and my household will serve the Lord." Come what will of it, we will never change our Master, nor quit his service.

Those beams of light that shined in upon Chrysostom, did so heat and warm his heart, that he stoutly tells Eudoxia the empress, that for her covetousness she would be called a second Jezebel; whereupon she sent him a threatening message, to which he returned this answer, "Go tell her," *nil nisi peccatum timeo,* "I fear nothing but sin."

A prophetical man, mentioned in ecclesiastical history, went to the pillars a little before an earthquake, and bade them stand fast, for they should shortly be shaken. Ah, Christians! there is an earthquake a-coming, and therefore as you would stand fast, as you would not have any earthquakes to make your hearts quake, get this zeal and courage

193

that attends divine knowledge, and then you shall in the midst of all earthquakes be as mount Zion that cannot be removed, Ps. 125. 1, 2.

They that write the story of the travels of the apostles, report that Simon Zelotes preached here in England. Ah, England, England! if ever thou needest some zealots, it is now. Oh how secure, how dull, how drowsy, how sleepy in the midst of dangers art thou! For this and other of thy abominations, I desire my soul may weep in secret.

[4] *The fourth attendant.* The fourth and last thing that attends or accompanies that knowledge that accompanies salvation is, *faith and confidence in God.* Ps. 9. 10, "They that know thy name will put their trust in thee; for thou, Lord, hast not forsaken them that seek thee." 2 Tim. 1. 12, "For the which cause I also suffer these things, nevertheless I am not ashamed; for I know whom I have believed, and I am persuaded that he is able to keep that which I have committed unto him against that day." I shall not enlarge upon this branch, because I shall speak at large concerning faith in the next particular.

And thus I have shewed you from the Scriptures what that knowledge is that accompanies salvation.

The things that accompany salvation: FAITH

Now, the second thing that I am to shew you is, what that faith is that accompanies salvation. I have formerly shewed you that faith doth accompany salvation, but now I will shew you what faith that is that doth accompany salvation; and that I shall do, by divine assistance, thus:

First, That faith that accompanies salvation, that comprehends salvation, that will possess a man of salvation, is known,

(1) By the objects about which it is exercised. And,
(2) By the properties of it.

The objects of faith

First, By the objects about which it is exercised. Now the objects of faith are these.

1. THE PERSON OF CHRIST

(1) *The first object of faith.* First, *The person of Christ* is the object of faith. It is Christ in the promises that faith deals with. The promise is but the shell, Christ is the kernel; the promise is but the casket, Christ is the jewel in it; the promise is but the field, Christ is the treasure that is hid in that field; the promise is a ring of gold, and Christ is the pearl in that ring; and upon this sparkling, shining pearl, faith delights most to look. Song of Solomon 3. 4, " It was but a little that I passed from them, but I found him whom my soul loveth. I held him, and I would not let him go, until I had brought him into my mother's house, and into the chamber of her that conceived me." So Song of Solomon 7. 5, " The king is held in the galleries." Faith hath two hands, and with both she lays earnest and fast hold on King Jesus. Christ's beauty and glory is very taking and drawing; as soon as faith sees it, it lays hold on it. Christ is the principal object about which faith is exercised, for the obtaining of righteousness and everlasting happiness. Acts 16. 30, 31, " And the jailor said, Sirs, what must I do to be saved? And they said, Believe on the Lord Jesus Christ, and thou shalt be saved." Christ is in all the scriptures held forth to be the object about which faith is most conversant; and the more faith is exercised upon the person of Christ, the more it buds and blossoms, like Aaron's rod. Faith looks upon him as the express image and character of his Father; faith beholds him as the chiefest of ten thousand; faith sees him to be the most glorious object in all the world.

2. THE RIGHTEOUSNESS OF CHRIST

(2) *The second object of faith.* Secondly, The second object that faith is exercised about is *the righteousness of Jesus Christ:* Philip. 3. 9, " I desire to be found in Christ, not having my own righteousness, which is of the law, but that which is through the faith of Christ, the righteousness which is of God by faith." Paul would not be found in a legal righteousness, for he knew all his legal righteousness

was but as " filthy rags," Isa. 64. 6. All his legal righteousness, sewed together, would but make up a coat of patches, a beggar's coat, that is good for nothing but to be cast away; therefore he desired to be found in the righteousness of Christ by faith. He knew that Christ's righteousness was a pure righteousness, a spotless righteousness, a matchless righteousness, a complete righteousness, a perfect righteousness, an absolute righteousness, a glorious righteousness. Faith loves to fix her eye upon that rich and royal robe, that blameless and spotless righteousness of Christ, wherewith the soul stands gloriously clothed before God, as being all fair, as being without spot or wrinkle in divine account. Oh, it is the actings of faith upon this blessed object, this glorious righteousness of Christ, that makes a man familiar and bold with God, that makes a man active and resolute for God, that strengthens a man against temptations, that supports a man under afflictions, that makes a man long for the day of his dissolution, that makes him prefer his coffin above a prince's crown, the day of his death above the day of his birth; that makes him triumph over sin and Satan, hell and wrath. Adam's righteousness was but the righteousness of a creature, but the righteousness about which faith is exercised is the righteousness of a God, Rom. 3. 21, and 10. 3. Adam's righteousness was a mutable righteousness, a righteousness that might be sinned away; but the righteousness that a believer's faith is exercised about is an everlasting righteousness, a righteousness that cannot be sinned away, 2 Cor. 5. 21; Prov. 8. 18. Dan. 9. 24: " Seventy weeks are determined upon thy people and upon thy holy city, to finish the transgression, and to make an end of sins, and to make reconciliation for iniquity, and to bring in everlasting righteousness, and to seal up the vision and prophecy, and to anoint the most holy "; Ps. 119. 142, " Thy righteousness is an everlasting righteousness, and thy law is the truth." The righteousness of Adam was a righteousness subject to shaking, and we know that Satan did shake all his righteousness about his ears, as I may say. But that glorious righteousness about which faith is conversant is an unshaken righteousness, a righteousness that cannot be shaken: Ps.

36. 6, "Thy righteousness is like the great mountains," or rather, as it is in the Hebrew, "Thy righteousness is like the mountains of God." What more stable than a mountain! and what mountain so stable as the mountain of God! The mountains cannot be shaken, no more can that glorious righteousness of Christ, about which a believer's faith is exercised. Adam's righteousness was a low righteousness, a righteousness within his own reach, and a righteousness within Satan's reach; it was not so high, but Adam could lay his hand upon it, as I may say; it was not so high, but Satan could reach to the top of it, yea, to the over-topping of it, as we have all found by woeful experience. But that righteousness that faith is conversant about, is a righteousness of such a height, as that neither Satan nor the world can reach to it: Ps. 76. 15, 16, 19, "My mouth shall shew forth thy righteousness and thy salvation all the day; for I know not the numbers thereof. I will go in the strength of the Lord God: I will make mention of thy righteousness, even of thine only. Thy righteousness also, O God, is very high, who hath done great things: O God, who is like unto thee?" This glorious righteousness of Christ, about which faith is busied, is called the righteousness of faith, because faith apprehends it, and applies it, and feeds upon it, and delights in it, Rom. 3. 28. Rom. 4. 13, "For the promise, that he should be the heir of the world, was not to Abraham, or to his seed, through the law, but through the righteousness of faith." Chap. 9. 30, "What shall we say then? That the Gentiles which followed not after righteousness, have attained to righteousness, even the righteousness which is of faith." The righteousness of Christ about which faith is employed, is called the righteousness of faith, because faith puts this righteousness upon the soul. Faith wraps the soul up in this righteousness of Christ, and so justifieth it before God instrumentally. The actings of faith on this glorious righteousness greatly strengthen the soul: Isa. 45. 24, "Surely shall one say, In the Lord have I righteousness and strength." The actings of faith on this blessed righteousness, greatly gladden and rejoice the soul: Isa. 61. 10, "I will greatly rejoice in the Lord, my soul shall be joyful in my God; for he

hath clothed me with the garment of salvation, he hath covered me with the robe of righteousness." The actings of faith upon this complete righteousness of Christ, render souls just and righteous, pure and holy, in the account of God: Rom. 10. 4, "For Christ is the end of the law for righteousness to every one that believeth." Christ fulfils the law for believers, and they by believing do fulfil the law in him; and so Christ by doing, and they by believing in him that doth it, do fulfil the law, and so are reputed fair and spotless, complete and perfect, before the throne of God. Faith's putting this righteousness on the soul, brings down blessings upon the soul. When Jacob had put on his elder brother's garment, he carried the blessing away. The actings of faith upon this peerless righteousness of Christ, bring down the blessing of peace, and the blessing of joy, and the blessing of remission of sins; and, in a word, all other blessings that contribute to the making us blessed here and happy hereafter.

3. THE PROMISES OF GOD

(3) *The third object of faith.* Thirdly, The third object that faith is exercised about is, *the precious promises,* which are a Christian's *magna charta.* As every precious stone hath a peculiar virtue in it, so hath every promise. The promises are a special book; every leaf drops myrrh and mercy; and upon these precious promises, precious faith looks and lives. From these breasts faith sucks comfort and sweetness. Ps. 119. 49, 50, "Remember thy word (that is, thy promise) unto thy servant, upon which thou hast caused me to hope. This is my comfort in my affliction, for thy word hath quickened me." So in Ps. 27. 13, "I had fainted, unless I had believed to see the goodness of the Lord in the land of the living"; Heb. 11. 13, "These all died in faith (or according to faith), not having received the promises, but having seen them afar off, and were persuaded of them, and embraced them" (or, as the Greek hath it, *saluted* them by faith; they kissed the promises, and kissed Christ in the promises), "and confessed that they were strangers and pilgrims on the earth." It would be an endless thing to shew

you how the faith of the patriarchs, prophets, apostles, and other saints have been acted and exercised upon promises of sanctification, upon promises of justification, upon promises of salvation, upon promises of glorification, upon promises of protection, upon promises of direction, upon promises of support. Look, as the lamp lives upon the oil, and the child upon the breasts, so doth faith upon the promises.

For the further advantage and comfort of your souls in eyeing the promises, let me give you these two sweet hints:

First, In your looking upon the promises, mind most, eye most, spiritual promises, absolute promises, such as Jer. 32. 40, 41; Ezek. 11. 19, 20; 36. 25-27; Isa. 42. 1; Ezek. 20. 41-43; Ps. 91. 15; Isa. 65. 24; Jer. 33. 3; Isa. 32. 15; Ezek. 34. 30, 31, with many others of the like import. These spiritual and absolute promises are of nearest and greatest concernment to you; these carry in them most of the heart of Christ, the love of Christ, the good-will of Christ; these are of greatest use to satisfy you, and to settle you when you are wavering; to support you when you are falling; to recall you when you are wandering; to comfort you when you are fainting; and to counsel you when you are staggering. Therefore make these your choicest and your chiefest companions, especially when it is night within your souls, when you are sensible of much sin and but a little grace, of much corruption but of little consolation, of much deadness but of little quickness, of much hardness but of little tenderness, of many fears but a little faith. The Jews under the law had more temporal promises than spiritual, but we under the gospel have far more spiritual promises than temporal; therefore sit down at this fire, and be warmed; drink of these springs, and be satisfied; taste of these delicacies, and be cheered. Let the eye of faith be cast upon all the promises, but fixed upon spiritual promises, upon absolute promises; they will have the greatest influence upon the heart to holiness, and to prepare it for everlasting happiness.

Look not only upon some of the riches, the jewels, the pearls, that be wrapped up in the promises, but enlarge and expatiate your understandings to an effectual contemplation of all those riches and treasures that God hath laid up in the promises. Cast not the eye of your faith only upon one beam of the sun, but endeavour to see all the beams of the sun; look not upon one branch only of the tree of life, but upon every branch of that tree; look not upon one bunch only of the grapes of Canaan, but look upon the whole land. As understanding heirs, when they come to read over their evidences and writings, they will see what they have in houses, what in goods, what in lands, what in money, what in jewels, what at home, what abroad; they will not sit down and say, Well! we find in our evidences, that such and such land is ours, and look no further; no, no, they will look all over, and take exact notice of everything; they will say, We have so much land, and so much money, &c. O beloved, there is much marrow and fatness, there is much honey and sweetness, much grace and glory wrapped up in the promises. Oh press them and distil them till you have got forth all the riches and sweetness that is in them.

Ah, Christians! if you did this, God would be more honoured, the promises more prized, your graces more strengthened, your fears more abated, your hearts more warmed and engaged, and your lives more regulated, and Satan more easily and frequently vanquished. And so much for this third object, about which faith is exercised.

4. THE FUTURE GLORY

(4) Fourthly, *The fourth object of faith.* The fourth object and last that I shall mention that faith is set and fixed upon is, *that glory, blessedness, and life, which God hath laid up for them that love him,* 2 Tim. 4. 8. The things of eternity are the greatest things, they are the most excellent things. They are most excellent in their natures, in their causes, in their operations, in their effects, in their ends; and upon these faith looks and lives. Faith realiseth things; it makes absent things present. "Faith is the substance of things hoped for, the evidence of things not seen," Heb. 11. 1. Faith makes absent glory present, absent riches present, absent pleasures present, absent favours present. Faith

brings an invisible God, and sets him before the soul. Moses by faith saw him that was invisible. Faith brings down the recompense of reward, and sets it really though spiritually before the soul. Faith sets divine favour before the soul. It sets peace, it sets pardon of sin, it sets the righteousness of Christ, it sets the joy of heaven, it sets salvation, before the soul; it makes all these things very near and obvious to the soul: "Faith is the evidence of things not seen." Faith makes invisible things visible, absent things present, things that are afar off to be very near unto the soul, by convincing demonstrations, by arguments and reasons drawn from the Word, as the Greek word signifies: 2 Cor. 4. 17, 18, "For our light affliction, which is but for a moment, worketh for us a far more exceeding and eternal weight of glory. While we look not at the things which are seen, but at the things which are not seen: for the things which are seen are temporal, but the things which are not seen are eternal." Faith trades in invisible things, in eternal things. Its eye is always upwards, like a certain fish, that hath but one eye, which looks continually up to heaven. Faith enters within the veil, and fixes her eye upon those glorious things of eternity, that are so many that they exceed number, so great that they exceed measure, so precious that they are above all estimation. Says faith, The spangled firmament is but the footstool of my Father's house; and if the footstool, the outside, be so glorious, oh how glorious is his throne! Verily, in heaven there is that life that cannot be expressed, that light that cannot be comprehended, that joy that cannot be fathomed, that sweetness that cannot be dissipated, that feast that cannot be consumed; and upon these pearls of glory I look and live, says faith.

And thus I have shewed you the choice and precious objects about which that faith is exercised that accompanies salvation.

The properties of faith

I shall now in the next place shew you the properties of that faith that accompanies salvation, and they are these that follow.

[1] *The first property* of that faith that accompanies salvation is this: *it puts forth itself in vital operation.* It makes a man full of life and activity for God; it will make a man diligent and venturous in the work and ways of God. Faith is a most active quality in itself, and so it makes a Christian most active. It is a doing thing, and it sets the person doing. Faith will not suffer the soul to be idle. Faith is like the virtuous woman in the last of the Proverbs, who puts her hand to every work, who would suffer none of her handmaids to be idle. Faith puts the soul upon grieving for sin, upon combating with sin, upon weeping over sin, upon trembling at the occasions of sin, upon resisting temptations that lead to sin, upon fighting it out to the death with sin, Zech. 12. 10. Faith puts a man upon walking with God, upon waiting on God, upon working for God, upon wrestling with God, upon bearing for God, and upon parting with anything for God. Faith makes religious duties to be easy to the soul, to be delightful to the soul, to be profitable to the soul. Faith makes the soul to be serious and conscientious in doing, to be careful and faithful in doing, to be delightful and cheerful in doing, to be diligent and faithful in doing. The faith that is not a working faith is no faith; the faith that is not a working faith is a dead faith; the faith that is not a working faith is a deluding faith; the faith that is not a working faith is a worthless faith; the faith that is not a working faith will leave a man short of heaven and happiness in the latter day. Faith that accompanies salvation is better at doing than at thinking, at obeying than at disputing, at walking than at talking: Titus 3. 8, "This is a faithful saying; and these things I will that thou affirm constantly, that they which have believed in God might be careful to maintain good works." Faith will make a man endeavour to be good, yea, to be best, at everything he undertakes. It is not leaves but fruit, not words but works, that God expects; and if we cross his expectation, we frustrate our own salvation, we further our own condemnation. Faith makes the soul much in doing, abundant in

working, and that partly by persuading the soul that all its works, all its duties and services, shall be owned and accepted of God, as in Isa. 56. 7, "Even them will I bring to my holy mountain, and make them joyful in my house of prayer: their burnt-offerings and their sacrifices shall be accepted upon mine altar; for mine house shall be called an house of prayer for all people." Faith assures the soul that every prayer, every sigh, every groan, every tear is accepted. And this makes the soul pray much, and sigh much, and mourn much.

Again, faith spreads the promises of divine assistance before the soul. Oh! says faith, here, O soul, is assistance suitable to the work required. And this makes a man work, as for life; it makes a man work and sweat, and sweat and work.

Again, faith sets the recompense, the reward, before the soul, Heb. 11. 25, 26. Oh, says faith, look here, soul, here is a great reward for a little work; here is great wages for weak and imperfect services; here is an infinite reward for a finite work. Work, yea, work hard, says faith, O believing soul, for thy actions in passing pass not away; every good work is as a grain of seed for eternal life. There is a resurrection of works as well as of persons, and in that day wicked men shall see that it is not a vain thing to serve God; they shall see the most doing souls to be the most shining souls, to be the most advanced and rewarded. Oh, the sight of this crown, of this recompense, makes souls to abound in the work of the Lord, they knowing that their labour is not in vain in the Lord, 1 Cor. 15. 58.

Again, faith draws from Christ's fulness; it sucks virtue and strength from Christ's breasts. Faith looks upon Christ as a head, and so draws from him; it looks upon Christ as a husband, and so draws from him; it looks upon him as a fountain, and so draws from him; it looks upon him as a sea, as an ocean of goodness, and so draws from him; it looks upon him as a father, Col. 1. 19, and so draws from him; it looks upon him as a friend, and so draws from him, John 1. 16. And this divine power and strength sets the soul a-working hard for God; it makes the soul full of motion, full of action. In a word, faith is such a working grace as sets all other graces a-working. Faith hath an influence upon every grace; it is like a silver thread that runs through a chain of pearls; it puts strength and vivacity into all other virtues. Love touched by a hand of faith flames forth; hope fed at faith's table grows strong, and casts anchor within the veil, Rom. 15. 13. Joy, courage, and zeal being smiled upon by faith, are made invincible and unconquerable Look, what oil is to the wheels, what weights are to the clock, what wings are to the bird, what sails are to the ship, that faith is to all religious duties and services, except it be winter with the soul.

And thus you see, that that faith that accompanies salvation is a working faith, a lively faith, and not such a dead faith as most please and deceive themselves with for ever.

2. IT GROWS

[2] *The second property* of that faith that accompanies salvation is this: *it is of a growing and increasing nature.* It is like the waters of the sanctuary, that rise higher and higher, as Ezekiel speaks. It is like a tender plant, that naturally grows higher and higher; it is like a grain of mustard-seed, which though it be the least of all seeds, yet by a divine power it grows up beyond all human expectations, Mat. 13. 32. Faith is imperfect, as all other graces are, but yet it grows and increases gradually: Rom. 1. 17, "For therein is the righteousness of God revealed from faith to faith: as it is written, The just shall live by faith." As a gracious soul is always adding knowledge to knowledge, love to love, fear to fear, zeal to zeal, so he is always adding faith to faith. A gracious soul knows, that if he be rich in faith, he cannot be poor in other graces; he knows the growth of faith will be as " the former and the latter rain " to all other graces; he knows that there is no way to outgrow his fears but by growing in faith; he knows that all the pleasant fruits of paradise, viz., joy, comfort, and peace, flourish as faith flourishes; he knows that he hath much work upon his hands, that he hath many things to do, many temptations to withstand, many mercies to improve, many burdens to bear,

many corruptions to conquer, many duties to perform. And this makes the believing soul thus to reason with God: Ah, Lord! whatever I am weak in, let me be strong in faith; whatever dies, let faith live; whatever decays, let faith flourish. Lord, let me be low in repute, low in abilities, low in estate, if only thou wilt make me high in faith. Lord! let me be poor in anything, poor in everything, if only thou wilt make me rich in faith. Lord, let the eye of faith be more opened, let the eye of faith be more quick-sighted, let the eye of faith be the more raised, and it shall be enough to me, though Joseph be not, though Benjamin be not.

It was the glory of the Thessalonians, that " their faith grew exceedingly," 2 Thes. 1. 3. A growth in faith will render a man glorious in life, lovely in death, and twice blessed in the morning of the resurrection. So will not a growth in honours, a growth in riches, a growth in notions, a growth in opinions. The faith that accompanies salvation unites the soul to Christ, and keeps the soul in communion with Christ. And from that union and communion that the soul hath with Christ, flows the divine power and virtue that causes faith to grow.

Yet that no weak believers may be stumbled, or made sad, let them remember,

(1) That though that faith that accompanies salvation be a growing faith, yet there are some certain seasons and cases wherein a man may decay in his faith, and wherein he may not have the exercise and the actings of his faith. This blessed babe of grace may be cast into a deep slumber; this heavenly pearl may be so buried under the thick clay of this world, and under the ashes of corruption and temptation, as that for a time it may neither stir, nor grow, as might be shewn in Abraham, David, Solomon, Peter, and others.

(2) Secondly, Remember this, that the strongest faith at times is subject to shakings, as the strongest men are to faintings, as the stoutest ships are to tossings, as the wisest men are to doubtings, as the brightest stars are to twinklings. Therefore, if at certain times thou shouldest not be sensible of the growth of thy faith, yet do not conclude that thou

hast no faith. Faith may be truly present when it is not active. There may be life in the root of the tree, when there is neither leaves, blossoms, nor fruit upon the tree; the life that is in the root will shew itself at the spring, and so will true faith break forth into acts, when the Sun of righteousness shall shine forth, and make it a pleasant spring to thy soul. And thus much for this second particular.

3. IT BELITTLES THE GLORIES OF THE WORLD

[3] *The third property* of that faith that accompanies salvation is this: *it makes those things that are great and glorious in the world's account to be very little and low in the eyes of the believer.* Faith makes a believer to live in the land of promise as in a strange country, Heb. 11. 9. It is nothing to live as a stranger in a strange land, but to live as a stranger in the land of promise, this is the excellency and glory of faith.

Faith will make a man set his feet where other men set their hearts. Faith looks with an eye of scorn and disdain upon the things of this world. What, says faith, are earthly treasures to the treasures of heaven? What are stones to silver, dross to gold, darkness to light, hell to heaven? Mat. 6. 19, 20. No more, says faith, are all the treasures, pleasures, and delights of this world, to the light of thy countenance, to the joy of thy Spirit, to the influences of thy grace, Ps. 4. 6, 7. I see nothing, says David, in this wide world, only "thy commandments are exceeding broad." Faith makes David account his crown nothing, his treasures nothing, his victories nothing, his attendants nothing. Faith will make a man write *nothing* upon the best of worldly things; it will make a man trample upon the pearls of this world, as upon dross and dung, Heb. 11. 24-26. Faith deadens a man's heart to the things of this world: "I am crucified to the world, and the world is crucified to me," says Paul, Philip. 3. 8; Gal. 6. 14. This world, says faith, is not my house, my habitation, my home; I look for a better country, for a better city, for a better home, 2 Cor. 5. 1, 2. He that is adopted heir to a crown, a kingdom, looks with an eye of scorn and disdain upon everything below a kingdom, below a crown. Faith tells the soul that it hath a crown, a kingdom in reversion; and this makes the soul to set light by the things of this world, 2 Tim. 4. 8. Faith raises and sets the soul high. "And hath raised us up together, and hath made us sit together in heavenly places in Christ Jesus," saith the apostle, Eph. 2. 6. Faith makes a man live high: "Our conversation is in heaven," Philip. 3. 20; and the higher any man lives, the less, the lower will the things of this world be in his eye. The fancy of Lucian is very pleasant, who places Charon on the top of an high hill, viewing all the affairs of men, and looking on their greatest, richest, and most glorious cities, as little birds' nests. Faith sets the soul upon the hill of God, the mountain of God, that is, a high mountain; and from thence, faith gives the soul a sight, a prospect of all things here below. And, ah! how like birds' nests do all the riches, braveries, and glories of this world look and appear to them that faith hath set upon God's high hill. Faith having set Luther upon this high hill, he protests that God should not put him off with these poor low things. Faith set Moses high, it set him among invisibles; and that made him look upon all the treasures, pleasures, riches, and glories of Egypt, as little birds' nests, as mole-hills, as dross and dung, as things that were too little and too low for him to set his heart upon. Verily, when once faith hath given a man a sight, a prospect of heaven, all things on earth will be looked upon as little and low. And so much for this third property of faith.

4. IT PURIFIES THE HEART

[4] *The fourth property* of that faith that accompanies salvation is this: *it purifies the heart, it is a heart-purifying faith.* "Purifying their hearts by faith," Acts 15. 9. Faith hath two hands, one to lay hold on Christ, and another to sweep the heart, which is Christ's house. Faith knows that Christ is of a dove-like nature; he loves to lie clean and sweet. Faith hath a neat housewife's hand, as well as an eagle's eye. Faith is as good at purging out of sin, as it is at discovering of sin. There is a cleansing quality in faith, as well as a healing quality in faith. Sound faith will purge the soul

from the love of sin, from a delight in sin, and from the reign and dominion of sin, Ezek. 16. "Sin shall not have dominion over you; for ye are not under the law, but under grace," Rom. 6. 14, 21. Now faith purgeth and cleanseth the heart from sin, sometimes by pressing and putting God to make good the promises of sanctification. Faith takes that promise in Jer. 33. 8, "And I will cleanse them from all their iniquity, whereby they have sinned against me"; and that promise in Micah 7. 19. "He will turn again, he will have compassion upon us; he will subdue our iniquities, and thou wilt cast all their sins into the depths of the sea"; and that promise in Ps. 65. 3, "Iniquities prevail against me; as for our transgressions, thou shalt purge them away"; and that promise in Isa. 1. 25, "And I will turn my hand upon thee, and purely purge away thy dross, and take away all thy tin"; and spreads them before the Lord, and will never leave urging and pressing, seeking and suing, till God makes them good. Faith makes the soul divinely impudent, divinely shameless. Lord! says faith, are not these thine own words? Hast thou said it, and shall it not come to pass? Art thou not a faithful God? Is not thine honour engaged to make good the promises that thou hast made? Arise, O God, and let my sins be scattered; turn thy hand upon me, and let my sins be purged. And thus faith purifies the heart.

Again, sometimes faith purifies the heart from sin, by engaging against sin in Christ's strength, as David engaged against Goliath, 1 Sam. 17. 47, not in his own strength, but in the strength and name of the Lord of hosts. Faith leads the soul directly to God, and engages God against sin, so that the combat, by the wisdom of faith, is changed, and made now rather between God and sin than between sin and the soul; and so sin comes to fall before the power and glorious presence of God. That is a choice word, Ps. 61. 2, "From the ends of the earth will I cry to thee, when my heart is overwhelmed: lead me to the rock that is higher than I." Look, as a child that is set upon by one that is stronger than he, cries out to his father to help him, to stand by him, and to engage for him against his enemy; so faith, being sensible of its own weakness and inability to get the victory over sin, cries out to Christ, and engages Christ, who is stronger than the strong man, and so Christ binds the strong man, and casts him out. Faith tells the soul that all purposes, resolutions, and endeavours, unless Christ be engaged, will never set the soul above its sins, they will never purify the heart from sin; therefore faith engages Christ, and casts the main of the work upon Christ, and so it purges the soul from sin. Luther reports of Staupicius, a German divine, that he acknowledged, before he came to understand the free and powerful grace of Christ, that he vowed and resolved an hundred times against some particular sin, and could never get power over it; he could never get his heart purified from it, till he came to see that he trusted too much to his own resolutions, and too little to Jesus Christ; but when his faith had engaged Christ against his sin, he had the victory.

Again, faith purifies the heart from sin, by the application of Christ's blood. Faith makes a plaster of Christ's blessed blood, and lays it upon the soul's sores, and so cures it. Faith tells the soul, that it is not all the tears in the world, nor all the water in the sea, that can wash away the uncleanness of the soul; it is only the blood of Christ that can make a blackamoor white; it is only the blood of Christ that can cure a leprous Naaman, that can cure a leprous soul. This fountain of blood, says faith, is the *only* fountain for Judah and Jerusalem to wash themselves, to wash their hearts from all uncleanness and filthiness of flesh and spirit, Zech. 13. 1. Those spots a Christian finds in his own heart, can only be washed out in the blood of the Lamb, by the hand of faith.

Again, faith purifieth the soul from sin, by putting the soul upon heart-purifying ordinances, and by mixing and mingling itself with ordinances: "The word profited them not," saith the apostle, "because it was not mixed with faith in them that heard it," Heb. 4. 2. Faith is such an excellent ingredient, that it makes all potions work for the good of the soul, for the purifying of the soul, and for the bettering of the soul; and no potion, no means, will profit the soul, if this heavenly ingredient be not mixed with it. Faith puts a man upon praying, upon hearing, upon the fellowship of the saints, upon public duties, upon family duties, and upon private duties; and faith in these comes and joins with the soul, and mixes herself with these soul-purifying ordinances, and so makes them effectual for the purifying of the soul more and more from all filthiness and uncleanness. Faith puts out all her virtue and efficacy in ordinances, to the purging of souls from their dross and tin; not that faith in this life shall wholly purify the soul from the being of sin, or from the motions or operations of sin; no, for then we should have our heaven in this world, and then we might bid ordinances adieu; but that faith that accompanies salvation doth naturally purify and cleanse the heart by degrees from the remainders of sin. Sound faith is always a-making the heart more and more neat and clean, that the king of glory may delight in his habitation, that he may not remove his court, but may abide with the soul for ever. And thus you see that that faith that accompanies salvation is a heart-purifying faith.

5. IT MELTS THE SOUL

(5) *The fifth property* of that faith that accompanies salvation is this: *it is soul-softening, it is soul-mollifying.* Oh, nothing breaks the heart of a sinner like faith. Peter believes soundly, and weeps bitterly, Mat. 26. 75; Mary Magdalene believes much, and weeps much, Luke 7. 44. Faith sets a wounded Christ, a bruised Christ, a despised Christ, a pierced Christ, a bleeding Christ before the soul, and this makes the soul sit down and weep bitterly: "I will pour upon the house of David the Spirit of grace and of supplications; and they shall look upon him whom they have pierced, and they shall mourn for him" (all gospel-mourning flows from believing), "as one mourneth for his only son, and shall be in bitterness for him, as one that is in bitterness for his first-born," Zech. 12. 10. Oh! the sight of those wounds that their sins have made will wound their hearts through and through; it will make them lament over Christ with a bitter lamentation. Men say that nothing will dissolve the

210

adamant but the blood of a goat. Ah! nothing will kindly, sweetly, and effectually break the hardened heart of a sinner, but faith's beholding the blood of Christ trickling down his sides. Pliny reports of a serpent, that when it stings, it fetches all the blood out of the body; but it was never heard that any ever sweat blood but Christ, and the very thought of this makes the believing soul to sit down sweating and weeping. That Christ should love man when he was most unlovely, that man's extreme misery should but inflame Christ's love and mercy, this melts the believing soul. That Christ should leave the eternal bosom of his Father; that he that was equal with God should come in the form of a servant; that he that was clothed with glory, and born a king, should be wrapped in rags; that he that the heaven of heavens could not contain should be cradled in a manger; that from his cradle to his cross, his whole life should be a life of sorrows and sufferings; that the Judge of all flesh should be condemned; that the Lord of life should be put to death; that he that was his Father's joy should in anguish of spirit cry out, " My God, my God, why hast thou forsaken me?"; that that head that was crowned with honour should be crowned with thorns; that those eyes that were as a flame of fire, that were clearer than the sun, should be closed up by the darkness of death; that those ears which were wont to hear nothing but hallelujahs should hear nothing but blasphemies; that that face that was white and ruddy should be spit upon by the Jews; that that tongue that spake as never man spake, yea, as never angel spake, should be accused of blasphemy; that those hands which swayed both a golden sceptre and a iron rod, and those feet that were as fine brass should be nailed to the cross; and all this for man's transgression, for man's rebellion: Oh! the sight of these things, the believing of these things, the acting of faith on these things, makes a gracious soul to break and bleed, to sigh and groan, to mourn and lament. The faith that accompanies salvation is more or less a heart-breaking, a heart-melting faith.

6. IT OVERCOMES THE WORLD

(6) *The sixth property* of that faith that accompanies salvation is this: *it is a world-conquering faith, it is a world-overcoming faith.* 1 John 5. 4, "For whatsoever is born of God overcometh the world; and this is the victory that overcometh the world, even our faith." Faith overcomes the frowning world, the fawning world, the tempting world, and the persecuting world; and this it doth thus:

(1) Faith, by uniting the soul to Christ, gives the soul an interest in all the victories and conquests of Christ, and so makes the soul a conqueror with Christ: John 16. 33, "These things have I spoken unto you, that in me ye might have peace; in the world ye shall have tribulation, but be of good cheer, I have overcome the world." We have to deal but with a conquered enemy; our Jesus hath given the world a mortal wound; we have nothing to do but to set our feet upon a subdued enemy, and to sing it out with the apostle, "Over all these we are more than conquerors," Rom. 8. 37.

(2) Faith overcomes the world by out-bidding sights; faith out-bids the world, and so makes the soul victorious. The world sets honours, pleasures, &c., before Moses, but his faith out-bid the world. It presents the recompense of reward, it brings down all the glory, pleasures, and treasures of heaven, of that other world, and sets them before the soul; and so it overtops and overcomes the world by out-bidding it. So Christ, "for the joy that was set before him, endured the cross, despising the shame," Heb. 12. 2.

(3) Faith overcomes the world by telling the soul that all things are its own. Says faith, This God is thy God, this Christ is thy Christ, this righteousness is thy righteousness, this promise is thy promise, this crown is thy crown, this glory is thy glory, these treasures are thy treasures, these pleasures are thy pleasures. "All things are yours," saith the apostle, "things present are yours, and things to come are yours," 1 Cor. 3. 22. Thus the faith of the martyrs acted, and so made them victorious over a tempting and a persecuting world, Heb. 11. 35.

(4) Faith overcomes the world by valuing the things of

this world as they are. Most men overvalue them, they put too great a price upon them, they make the world a god, and then they cry, "Great is Diana of the Ephesians." Oh, but faith now turns the inside of all creatures outward, faith presents all worldly things as impotent, as mixed, as mutable, as things of a moment to the soul, and so makes the soul victorious. Faith makes a man to see the prickles that be in every rose, the thorns that be in every crown, the scabs that be under every gown, the poison that is in the golden cup, the snare that is in the delicate dish, the spot that is in the shining pearl, and so makes a Christian count and call all these things, as indeed they are, "vanity of vanities," and so the believing soul slights the world, and tramples upon it as dung and dross. And lastly,

(5) Faith overcomes the world, by presenting Jesus Christ to the soul as a most excellent, glorious, and comprehensive good, a good that comprehends all good. Christ is that one good that comprehends all good, that one thing that comprehends all things. All the beauties, all the rarities, all the excellencies, all the riches, all the glories of all created creatures are comprehended in Christ. As the worth and value of many pieces of silver is collected in one piece of gold, or in one precious jewel, so the whole volume of perfections which is spread through heaven and earth is epitomised in Christ; and the sight and sense of this makes the soul to triumph over the world. Faith presents more excellencies and better excellencies in Christ than can be lost for Christ, and so it makes the soul a conqueror.

I have been long upon these things, because they are of much weight and worth: I shall be the briefer in what follows. But before I leave this point, I shall give you these hints:

Strong faith and weak faith

In the first place, I shall give you some hints concerning strong faith.

In the second place, I shall give you some hints concerning weak faith.

My design in both is, to keep precious souls from mistaking and fainting. Concerning strong faith, I shall give you these short hints:

(1) *The first hint.* Strong faith will make a soul resolute in resisting, and happy in conquering the strongest temptations, Heb. 11. 3; Dan. 6. 10.

(2) *The second hint.* It will make a man own God, and cleave to God, and hang upon God, in the face of the greatest difficulties and dangers, Rom. 4. 18; Ps. 44. 16-18. So Job will trust in God though he slay him, Job 13. 15, 16.

(3) *The third hint.* It will enable men to prefer Christ's cross before the world's crown, to prefer tortures before deliverance, Heb. 11. 3.

(4) *The fourth hint.* Strong faith will make a soul divinely fearless, and divinely careless; it will make a man live as the child lives in the family, without fear or care, Ps. 23. 4. Dan. 3. 16, "We are not careful to answer thee, O king; our God whom we serve is able to deliver us, and he will deliver us." Micah 7. 7-9.

(5) *The fifth hint.* Strong faith will make a man cleave to the promise when providence runs cross to the promise, Num. 10. 29; 2 Chron. 20. 9-11. Ps. 60. 6, 7, "God hath spoken in his holiness," saith David; "I will rejoice: I will divide Shechem, and mete out the valley of Succoth. Gilead is mine, and Manasseh is mine," &c. Though David was in his banishment, yet his faith accounts all his as if he had all in possession, and that because God had spoken in his holiness. His faith hangs upon the promise, though present providences did run cross to the promise.

(6) *The sixth hint.* Strong faith will make men comply with those commands that do most cross them in their most desirable comforts, Heb. 11. 8, 9, and 10. 34; Gen. 22.

Now, O precious souls! you are not to argue against your own souls, that surely you have no faith, because your faith doth not lead you forth to such and such noble things. Thou mayest have true faith, though thou hast not so great faith as others of the Lord's worthies have had.

The philosophers say that there are eight degrees of heat: we discern three. Now, if a man should define heat only by the highest degree, then all other degrees will be cast out from being heat. So if a man should define faith only by the highest degrees and operations of it, then that will be denied to be faith that indeed is faith, as I shall presently shew.

In the second place, I shall give you some hints concerning weak faith.

(1) *The first hint.* A weak faith doth as much justify and as much unite a man to Christ as a strong faith. It gives a man as much title to and interest in Christ as the strongest faith in the world. The babe hath as much interest in the father as he that is of grown years. A weak faith gives a man as good a title to Christ, and all the precious things of eternity, as the strongest faith in the world. A weak hand may receive a pearl as well as the strong hand of a giant. Faith is a receiving of Christ, John 1. 12.

(2) *The second hint.* The promises of eternal happiness and blessedness are not made over to the strength of faith, but to the truth of faith; not to the degrees of faith, but to the reality of faith. He that believes shall be saved, though he hath not such a strength of faith as to stop the mouth of lions, as to work miracles, as to remove mountains, as to subdue kingdoms, as to quench the violence of fire, as to resist strong temptations, as to rejoice under great persecutions, Heb. 11. 33-35. No man that is saved is saved upon the account of the strength of his faith, but upon the account of the truth of his faith. In the great day Christ will not bring balances to weigh men's graces, but a touch-stone to try their graces; he will not look so much at the strength as at the truth of their graces.

(3) *The third hint.* The weakest faith shall grow stronger and stronger. A weak believer shall go on from faith to faith. Christ is the finisher as well as the author of our faith, Rom. 1. 17; Heb. 12. 2. Christ will nurse up this blessed babe, and will not suffer it to be strangled in its infancy. He that hath begun a good work will perfect it, Philip. 1. 6; 1 Pet. 1. 5. Christ is as well bound to look after our graces as he is to look after our souls. Grace is Christ's work, therefore it must prosper in his hand; he is the great builder and re-pairer of our graces; he will turn thy spark into a flame, thy

drop into an ocean, thy penny into a pound, thy mite into a million, Mat. 12. 20, and 13. 32. Therefore do not sit down discouraged because thy faith is weak. That which is sown in weakness, shall rise in power. Thy weak faith shall have a glorious resurrection. Christ will not suffer such a pearl of price to be buried under a clod of earth.

(4) *The fourth hint.* A little faith is faith, as a spark of fire is fire, a drop of water is water, a little star is a star, a little pearl is a pearl. Verily, thy little faith is a jewel that God doth highly prize and value; and thy little faith will make thee put a higher price upon Christ and grace than upon all the world, Mat. 18. 10; 1 Pet. 2. 7. Well! remember this, that the least measure of true faith will bring thee to salvation, and possess thee of salvation, as well as the greatest measure. A little faith accompanies salvation as well as a great faith, a weak faith as well as a strong. Therefore do not say, O precious soul, that thou hast not that faith that accompanies salvation, because thou hast not such a strong faith, or such and such degrees of faith. A great faith will yield a man a heaven here, a little faith will yield him a heaven hereafter.

The things that accompany salvation: REPENTANCE

The third thing that I am to shew you is, what repentance that is that accompanies salvation. That repentance doth accompany salvation I have formerly shewed. Now, I shall manifest in the following particulars what repentance that is that accompanies salvation, that comprehends salvation, that borders upon salvation.

The properties of repentance

1. IT EFFECTS A CHANGE IN EVERY PART OF A MAN

(1) *First,* That repentance that accompanies salvation, *is a general, a universal change of the whole man; a change in every part, though it be but in part.* That repentance that accompanies salvation changes both heart and life, word and work; it makes an Ethiopian an Israelite, a leper an angel. " Wash you, make you clean "; there is the change of your

hearts. "Put away the evil of your doings from before mine eyes, cease to do evil, learn to do well," Isa. 1. 16-18; there is the change of their practices.

So the prophet Ezekiel, "Cast away all your transgressions," saith he, "whereby you have transgressed"; there is the change of life: "And make you a new heart, and a new spirit," Ezek. 18. 30-32; there is the change of the heart. That repentance that accompanies salvation works a change in the whole man; in all the qualities of the inward man, and in all the actions of the outward man. The understanding is turned from darkness to light; the will from a sinful servility to a holy liberty; the affections from disorder into order; the heart from hardness into softness. So in the outward man, the wanton eye is turned into an eye of chastity; the uncircumcised ear is turned into an obedient ear; the hands of bribery are turned into hands of liberality; and the wandering feet of vanity are turned into ways of purity. And verily, that repentance that changes a man in some part, but not in every part, that only makes a man a Herod, or an Agrippa, a half Christian, an almost Christian, that repentance will never bring down heaven into a man's bosom here, and never bring a man up to heaven hereafter. That repentance that accompanies salvation makes a man all glorious within, and his raiment to be of embroidered gold, Ps. 45. 13; it stamps the image of God both upon the inward and the outward man; it makes the heart like the ark, all gold within; and it makes the life like the sun, all glorious without.

2. IT IS A TURNING FROM ALL SIN

(2) *Secondly*, That repentance that accompanies salvation is *a total turning as well as a universal turning*; a turning from all sin, without any reservation or exception. "I hate and abhor every false way, but thy law do I love," Ps. 119. 163. So in Ezek. 18. 30, "Therefore I will judge you, O house of Israel, every one according to his ways, saith the Lord God. Repent, and turn yourselves from all your transgressions; so iniquity shall not be your ruin." So in Ezek. 33. 11. As Noah's flood drowned his nearest and his dearest friends, so the flood of penitent tears drowns men's nearest

and dearest lusts. Be they Isaacs or Benjamins, be they right eyes or right hands, repentance that accompanies salvation puts all to the sword; it spares neither father nor mother, neither Agag nor Achan; it casts off all the rags of old Adam; it leaves not a horn nor a hoof behind; it throws down every stone of the old building; it scrapes off all leviathan's scales; it washeth away all leprous spots. Ezek. 14. 6, "Therefore say unto the house of Israel, Thus saith the Lord God, Repent, and turn yourselves from your idols; and turn away your faces from all your abominations." Sin is a turning the back upon God, and the face towards hell; but repentance is a turning the back upon sin, and a setting the face towards God. He that looks upon Jerusalem and upon Babylon with a leering eye at the same time; he that looks upon God, and at the same time looks upon any sin with a leering eye, hath not yet reached unto this repentance that accompanies salvation; his repentance and profession cannot secure him from double damnation. He that serves God in some things, and his lusts in other things, says to God as David said to Mephibosheth concerning his lands, "Thou and Ziba divide the lands," 1 Sam. 19. 29; so thou and Satan divide my soul, my heart between you. Ah! doth not such a soul deserve a double hell? Christ takes every sin at a penitent man's hands, as Cæsar did his wounds from him of whom he merited better usage, with, "And thou, my son!" What, thou wound me! what, thou stab me! that shouldst venture thy own blood to save mine?

There are no wounds that are so grievous and terrible to Christ, as those that he receives in the house of his friends, and this sets the penitent man's heart and hand against everything that makes against Christ. A true penitent looks upon every sin as poison, as the vomit of a dog, as the mire of the street. And his looking thus upon every sin, turns his heart against every sin, and makes him not only to refrain from sin, but to forsake it, and to loathe it more than hell.

3. IT IS A TURNING TO GOD

(3) *Thirdly*, That repentance that accompanies salvation is not only a turning from all sin, but *it is also a turning*

unto God. It is not only a ceasing from doing evil, but it is also a learning to do well; it is not only a turning from darkness, but it is also a turning to light; as the apostle speaks, Acts 26. 18, "To open their eyes, and to turn them from darkness to light, and from the power of Satan unto God." So in Isa. 55. 7, "Let the wicked forsake his ways, and the unrighteous man his thoughts, and let him return unto the Lord," &c. It is not enough for the man of iniquity to forsake his evil way, but he must also return unto the Lord; he must subject his heart to the power of divine grace, and his life to the will and word of God. As negative goodness can never satisfy a gracious soul, so negative goodness can never save a sinful soul. It is not enough that thou art thus and thus bad, but thou must be thus and thus good, or thou art undone for ever: Ezek. 18. 21, "But if the wicked will turn from all his sins that he hath committed, and keep all my statutes, and do that which is lawful and right, he shall surely live, he shall not die." Negative righteousness and holiness is no righteousness, no holiness, in the account of God. It was not the pharisee's negative righteousness, nor his comparative goodness, that could prevent his being rejected of God, his being shut out of heaven, his burning in hell, Luke 18. 5; Mat. 20. 13, 14. It is not enough that the tree bears no ill fruit, but it must bring forth good fruit, else it must be cut down and cast into the fire. That tree that is not for fruit is for the fire. "Every tree that brings not forth good fruit," says Christ, "is hewn down, and cast into the fire," Mat. 7. 19. Men that content themselves with negative righteousness, shall find at last heaven-gates bolted upon them with a double bolt. All that negative righteousness and holiness can do, is to help a man to one of the best chambers and easiest beds in hell. That repentance that accompanies salvation brings the heart and life not only off from sin, but on to God; it makes a man not only cease from walking in the ways of death, but it makes him walk in the ways of life: "They do no iniquity, they walk in his ways," Ps. 119. 3.

(4) *Fourthly*, That repentance that accompanies salvation, *strikes most effectually and particularly against that sin or sins that the sinner was most apt and prone to before his conversion.* The hand of repentance is most against that sin, it is most upon that sin that the soul hath looked most with a leering eye upon. The chief and principal sins that Israel was guilty of, were idolatry and sinful compliance. Now, when God works kindly upon them, they put the hand of repentance upon those particular sins, as you may see: Isa. 27. 9, " By this, therefore, shall the iniquity of Jacob be purged, and this is all the fruit to take away his sin: when he maketh all the stones of the altar as chalk stones, that are beaten in sunder, the groves and images shall not stand up." Here you see, when God appears and acts graciously for and towards his people, they put the hand of repentance upon their groves and images; these must come down, these must no longer stand. The groves and the images shall not stand up, they shall be utterly abandoned and destroyed, demolished, and abolished. So in Isa. 30. 22, " Ye shall defile also the covering of thy graven images of silver, and the ornament of thy molten images of gold . . . thou shalt say unto it, Get thee hence." Here you see the hand of repentance is against their idols of silver and gold; and not only against their idols, but also against whatsoever had any relation to them. Now they shew nothing but a detestation of their idols, and a holy indignation against them: " Get you hence." The hand of repentance makes a divorce between them and their idols, between their souls and their especial sins. Now they are as much in hating, abhorring, abominating, and contemning their idols and images, as they were formerly in adoring, worshipping, and honouring of them. So Mary Magdalene, Luke 7, walks quite cross and contrary to her former self, her sinful self; she crosses the flesh in those very things wherein formerly she did gratify the flesh. So the penitent jailor, Acts 16, washes those very wounds that his own hands had made. He acts in ways of mercy, quite contrary to his

former cruelty. At first there was none so fierce, so furious, so cruel, so inhuman in his carriage to the apostles; at last, none so gentle, so soft, so sweet, so courteous, so affectionate to them. The same you may see in Zacchæus, Luke 19. 8, in Paul, Acts 9, and in Manasseh, in 2 Chron. 33. 6.

5. IT IS COMPREHENSIVE IN ITS SCOPE

(5) *Fifthly,* That repentance that accompanies salvation, *is very large and comprehensive.* It comprehends and takes in these following particulars, besides those already named.

[1] *It takes in a sight and sense of sin.* Men must first see their sins, they must be sensible of their sins, before they can repent of their sins. Ephraim had first a sight of his sin, and then he repents and turns from his sin. "After I was instructed, I smote upon my thigh," Jer. 31. 18, 19. A man first sees himself out of the way, before he returns into the way. Till he sees that he is out of the way, he walks still on, but when he perceives that he is out of the way, then he begins to make inquiry after the right way. So when the sinner comes to see his way to be a way of death, then he cries out, "Oh lead me in the way of life, lead me in the way everlasting," Ps. 139. 24.

[2] The repentance that accompanies salvation, doth include not only a sight and sense of sin, but also *confession and acknowledgment of sin.* Ps. 51, and Ps. 32. 3-5, "While I kept close my sin, my bones consumed; but I said, I will confess my sin, and thou forgavest the iniquity of my sin"; see also Job 33. 21-27. The promise of remission is made to confession. 1 John 1. 9, "If we confess our sins, God is faithful and just to forgive us our sins." So Prov. 28. 13, "He that hideth his sin, shall not prosper, but he that confesseth and forsaketh it, shall find mercy." If we confess our sins sincerely, seriously, humbly, cordially, pardon attends us. *Homo agnoscit, deus ignoscit* (Man confesses, God pardons). Confession of sin must be joined with the slaying of sin, or all is lost, God is lost, Christ is lost, heaven lost, and the soul lost for ever.

The true penitent can say, with Vivaldus, "I hide not my sins, but I shew them; I wipe them not away, but I sprinkle them; I do not excuse them, but I accuse them." *Peccata enim non nocent, si non placent* (My sins hurt me not, if I like them not); the beginning of my salvation is the knowledge of my transgression.

[3] That repentance that accompanies salvation doth include, not only confession of sin, but also *contrition for sin*; Ps. 51. 4; Sam. 7. 2; Zech. 12. 10, 11; Ezra 10. 1, 2; 2 Cor. 7. 11, &c. It breaks the heart with sighs, sobs, and groans, for that a loving Father is offended, a blessed Saviour crucified, and the sweet Comforter grieved. Penitent Mary Magdalene weeps much, as well as loves much. Tears, instead of gems, were the ornaments of penitent David's bed; and surely that sweet singer never sang more melodiously than when his heart was broken most penitentially. How shall God wipe away my tears in heaven, if I shed none on earth? And how shall I reap in joy, if I sow not in tears? I was born with tears, and shall die with tears; why should I then live without them in this valley of tears? saith the true penitent. The sweetest joys are from the sourest tears; penitent tears are the breeders of spiritual joy. When Hannah had wept, she went away and was no more sad, 1 Sam. 1. 18. The bee gathers the best honey off the bitterest herbs. Christ made the best wine of water; the strongest, the purest, the truest, the most permanent, and the most excellent joy is made of the waters of repentance. If God be God, "they that sow in tears shall reap in joy," Ps. 126. 5.

But that no mourner may drown himself in his own tears, let me give this caution, viz., that there is nothing beyond remedy but the tears of the damned. A man who may persist in the way to paradise, should not place himself in the condition of a little hell; and he that may or can hope for paradise ought not to be dejected nor overwhelmed for anything.

[4] That repentance that accompanies salvation doth include not only contrition for sin, but also *a holy shame and blushing for sin*: Ezra 9. 6; Jer. 3. 24, 25; 31. 19; Ezek. 16. 61, 63, "And thou shalt be confounded, and never open thy mouth any more, because of thy shame, when I am pacified towards thee for all that thou hast done, saith the Lord God." When the penitent soul sees his sins pardoned, the

anger of God pacified, and divine justice satisfied, then he sits down ashamed: so Rom. 6. 21, "What fruit had ye then in those things whereof ye are now ashamed?" Sin and shame are inseparable companions. A man cannot have the seeming sweet of sin without the real shame that accompanies sin. These two God hath joined together, and all the world cannot put them asunder.

It was an impenitent Caligula that said of himself "that he loved nothing better in himself than that he could not be ashamed." That should grieve most which is shameful in itself, and done against conscience. And doubtless those things are only shameful that are sinful. A soul that hath sinned away all shame is a soul ripe for hell, and given up to Satan. A greater plague cannot befall a man in this life than to sin and not to blush.

[5] That repentance that accompanies salvation, comprehends *loathing and abhorring of sin, and of ourselves for sin, as well as shame and blushing for sin*, Job 42. 6; Ezek. 16. 61, 62, 63; Amos 5. 15; Ezek. 20. 41, 42, 43, "And ye shall remember your ways, and all your doings, wherein ye have been defiled; and ye shall loathe yourselves in your own sight, for all the evils that you have committed." The sincere penitent loathes his sins, and he loathes himself also because of his sins. He cries out, Oh these wanton eyes! oh these wicked hands; oh this deceitful tongue! oh this crooked will! oh this corrupt heart! oh how do I loathe my sins, how do I loathe myself, how do I loathe sinful self, and how do I loathe my natural self, because of sinful self! My sins are a burden to me, and they make me a burden to myself; my sins are an abhorrence to me, and they make me abhor myself in dust and ashes. A true penitent hath not only low thoughts of himself, but loathsome thoughts of himself. None can think or speak so vilely of him, as he doth and will think and speak of himself. Ezek. 6. 9, "And they that escape of you shall remember me among the nations whither they shall be carried captives, because I am broken with their whorish heart" (as the heart of a husband is at the adulterous behaviour of his wife), "which hath departed from me, and with their eyes, which go a-whoring after their

idols: and they shall loathe themselves for the evils which they have committed in all their abominations." If thy repentance do not work thee out with thy sins, and thy sins work thee out of love with thyself, thy repentance is not that repentance that accompanies salvation. And thus you see the particular things that the repentance that accompanies salvation comprehends and includes.

6. IT HAS APPROPRIATE ATTENDANTS

(6) *Sixthly,* That repentance that accompanies salvation hath these choice companions attending it.

[1] *Faith.* Zech. 12. 10, 11, "They shall look upon him whom they have pierced, and mourn," &c. Mourning and believing go together. So in Mat. 4. 17; Mark 1. 14, 15, "Now, after that John was put in prison, Jesus came into Galilee, preaching the gospel of the kingdom of God, and saying, The time is fulfilled, and the kingdom of God is at hand; repent ye, and believe the gospel."

[2] *Love to Christ* doth always accompany that repentance that accompanies salvation, as you may see in Mary Magdalene, Luke 7.

[3] *A filial fear of offending God, and a holy care to honour God,* doth always accompany that repentance that accompanies salvation: 2 Cor. 7. 10, "For godly sorrow worketh repentance to salvation not to be repented of: for, behold, this self-same thing, that ye sorrowed after a godly sort, what carefulness it wrought in you, yea, what clearing of yourselves, yea, what indignation, yea, what fear, yea, what vehement desire, yea, what zeal, yea, what revenge! In all things ye have approved yourselves to be clear in this matter." Verily, repentance to life hath all these lively companions attending it; they are born together and will live together, till the penitent soul changes earth for heaven, grace for glory.

7. IT IS A CONTINUED ACT

(7) *Seventhly and lastly,* That repentance that accompanies salvation is *a continued act, a repentance never to be repented of,* 2 Cor. 7. 10. Repentance is a continual spring,

where the waters of godly sorrow are always flowing. A sound penitent is always a-turning nearer and nearer to God; he is always a-turning further and further from sin. This makes the penitent soul to sigh and mourn that he can get no nearer to God, that he can get no further from sin, Rom. 7. The work of repentance is not the work of an hour, a day, a year, but the work of a life-time. A sincere penitent makes as much conscience of repenting daily as he doth of believing daily; and he can as easily content himself with one act of faith, or love, or joy, as he can content himself with one act of repentance: "My sins are ever before me," says David, Ps. 51. 3. Next to my being kept from sin, I count it the greatest mercy in the world to be still a-mourning over sin, says the penitent soul. The penitent soul never ceases repenting till he ceases living. He goes to heaven with the joyful tears of repentance in his eyes. He knows that his whole life is but a day of sowing tears that he may at last reap everlasting joys. That repentance that accompanies salvation is a final forsaking of sin. It is a bidding sin an everlasting adieu; it is a taking an eternal farewell of sin; a never turning to folly more: "What have I to do any more with idols?" says Ephraim, Hosea 14. 8. I have tasted of the bitterness that is in sin; I have tasted of the sweetness of divine mercy in pardoning of sin; therefore, away, sin; I will never have to do with you more! You have robbed Christ of his service, and me of my comfort and crown. Away, away, sin! you shall never be courted nor countenanced by me more. That man that only puts off his sins in the day of adversity, as he doth his garments at night when he goes to bed, with an intent to put them on again in the morning of prosperity, never yet truly repented: he is a dog that returneth to the vomit again; he is like the swine that return to their wallowing in the mire. So it was with Judas; so it was with Demas.

It is an extraordinary vanity in some men to lay aside their sins before solemn duties, but with a purpose to return to them again, as the serpent layeth aside his poison when he goeth to drink, and when he hath drunk, he returns to it again, as they fable it. It is sad when men say to their lusts, as Abraham said to his servants, "Abide you here, and I will go and worship, and return again to you," Gen. 22. 5. Verily such souls are far off from that repentance that accompanies salvation, for that makes a final and everlasting separation between sin and the soul. It makes such a divorce between sin and the soul, and puts them so far asunder, that all the world can never bring them to meet as two lovers together. The penitent soul looks upon sin and deals with sin, not as a friend, but as an enemy. It deals with sin as Amnon dealt with Tamar: 2 Sam. 13. 15, "And Amnon hated her exceedingly, so that the hatred wherewith he hated her was greater than the love wherewith he had loved her. And Amnon said unto her, Arise, begone." Just thus doth the penitent soul carry itself towards sin.

And thus you see what repentance that is that accompanies salvation.

The things that accompany salvation: OBEDIENCE

The fourth thing I am to shew is, what obedience that is that doth accompany salvation. That obedience doth accompany salvation, I have formerly proved. Now what this obedience is that doth accompany or comprehend salvation, I shall shew you in these following particulars:

1. IT IS HEARTY

[1] *First*, That obedience that accompanies salvation is *cordial and hearty*. The heart, the inward man, doth answer and echo to the word and will of God. The believer knows that no obedience but heart obedience is acceptable to Christ. He knows that nothing takes Christ's heart but what comes from the heart. Christ was hearty in his obedience for me, says the believer; and shall not I be hearty in my obedience to him? Christ will lay his hand of love, his hand of acceptance, upon no obedience but what flows from the heart: Rom. 6. 17, "Ye have obeyed from the heart that form of doctrine which was delivered you." So in Rom. 7. 25, "So then with the mind, I myself serve the law of God." My heart, says Paul, is in my obedience. So in Rom. 1. 9, "God is my witness, whom I serve with my spirit in the

gospel of his Son." Many serve God with their bodies, but I serve him with my spirit; many serve him with the outward man, but I serve him with my inward man, Ezek. 36. 26, 27. God hath written his law in believers' hearts, and therefore they cannot but obey it from the heart: "I delight to do thy will, O my God." How so? Why, "thy law is within my heart." Ps. 40. 8. The heart within echoes and answers to the commandments without, as a book written answers to his mind that writes it; as face answers to face; as the impression on the wax answers to the character engraven on the seal. The scribes and Pharisees were much in the outward obedience of the law, but their hearts were not in their obedience; and therefore all they did signified nothing in the account of Christ, who is only taken with outward actions as they flow from the heart and affections. Their souls were not in their services, and therefore all their services were lost services. They were very glorious in their outward profession, but their hearts were as filthy sepulchres. Their outsides shone as the sun, but their insides were as black as hell, Mat. 23. They were like the Egyptians' temples, beautiful without, but filthy within. Well! remember this: No action, no service, goes for current in heaven, but that which is sealed up with integrity of heart. God will not be put off with the shell, when we give the devil the kernel.

2. IT SEEKS TO PERFORM ALL GOD'S WILL

(2) *Secondly*, That obedience that accompanies salvation is *universal as well as cordial*. The soul falls in with every part and point of God's will, so far as he knows it, without prejudice or partiality, without tilting the balance on one side or another. A soul sincerely obedient will not pick and choose what commands to obey and what to reject, as hypocrites do; he hath an eye to see, an ear to hear, and a heart to obey the first table as well as the second, and the second table as well as the first; he doth not adhere to the first and neglect the second, as hypocrites do; neither doth he adhere to the second and contemn the first, as profane men do; he obeys out of a sense of duty; he obeys out of conscience: Ps. 119. 6, "Then shall I not be ashamed, when I have re-

spect unto *all* thy commandments." Look, faith never singles out its object, but lays hold on every object God holds forth for it to close with. Faith doth not choose this truth and reject that, it doth not close with one and reject another. Faith doth not say, I will trust God in this case but not in that, I will trust him for this mercy but not for that mercy, I will trust him in this way but not in that way. Faith doth not choose its object. Faith knows that he is powerful and faithful that hath promised, and therefore faith closes with one object as well as another. So a true obedient soul singles not out the commands of God, as to obey one and rebel against another; it dares not, it cannot, say I will serve God in this command but not in that. No! in an evangelical sense it obeys all: Luke 1. 5, 6, "Zacharias and Elizabeth were both righteous before God, walking in all the commandments and ordinances of the Lord blameless." They walked not only in commandments, but also in ordinances; not only in ordinances, but also in commandments. They were good souls, and good at both. A man sincerely obedient lays such a charge upon his whole man, as Mary, the mother of Christ, did upon all the servants at the feast: John 2. 5, "Whatever the Lord saith unto you do it." Eyes, ears, hands, heart, lips, legs, body, and soul, do you all seriously and affectionately observe whatever Jesus Christ says unto you, and do it. So David doth: Ps. 119. 34, 69, "Give me understanding, and I shall keep thy law; yea, I shall observe it with my whole heart." "The proud have forged a lie against me; but I will keep thy precepts with my whole heart." The whole heart includes all the faculties of the soul and all the members of the body. Says David, I will put hand and heart, body and soul, all within me and all without me, to the keeping and observing of thy precepts. Here is a soul thorough-paced in his obedience; he stands not halting nor halving of it; he knows the Lord loves to be served truly and totally, and therefore he obeys with an entire heart and a sincere spirit.

I have read of a very strange speech that dropped out of the mouth of Epictetus, a heathen: "If it be thy will," says he, "O Lord, command me what thou wilt, send me whither thou wilt; I will not withdraw myself from anything that seems good to thee." Ah! how will this heathen at last rise in judgment against all Sauls, Jehus, Judases, Demases, scribes, pharisees, time-servers, who are partial in their obedience, who while they yield obedience to some commands, live in the habitual breach of other commands! Verily, he that lives in the habitual breach of one command, shall at last be reputed by God guilty of the breach of every command, James 2. 10, and God accordingly will in a way of justice proceed against him, Ezek. 18. 10-13. It was the glory of Caleb and Joshua, that they followed the Lord fully in one thing, as well as another, Num. 14. 24. So Cornelius: "We are present before God, to hear whatsoever shall be commanded us of God," Acts 10. 33. He doth not pick and choose. So in Acts 13. 22, "I have found David, the son of Jesse, a man after mine own heart, which shall fulfil all my will"; or rather as it is in the Greek, "he shall fulfil all my wills," to denote the universality and sincerity of his obedience. A sincere heart loves all commands of God, and prizes all commands of God, and sees a divine image stamped upon all the commands of God; and therefore the main bent and disposition of his soul, is to obey all, to submit to all. God commands universal obedience, Josh. 1. 8; Deut. 5. 29; Ezek. 18. The promise of reward is made over to universal obedience, Ps. 19. 11; Josh. 1. 8. Universal obedience is a jewel that all will wish for or rejoice in, at the day of death and the day of account; and the remembrance of these things, with others of the like nature, provokes all upright souls to be impartial, to be universal in their obedience.

3. IT FLOWS FROM FAITH

[3] *Thirdly*, That obedience that accompanies salvation *springs from inward spiritual causes, and from holy and heavenly motives.* It flows from faith. Hence it is called "the obedience of faith," Rom. 16. 26. So in 1 Tim. 1. 5, "Now the end of the commandment is love out of a pure heart, and of a good conscience, and of faith unfeigned." Faith draws down that divine virtue and power into the soul

that makes it lively and active, abundant and constant, in the work and way of the Lord. And as faith, so love, puts the soul forward in ways of obedience. John 14. 21, 23, "If any man love me, he will keep my commandments." So Ps. 119. 48, "My hands also will I lift up to thy commandments, which I have loved." Divine love is said to be the keeping the commandments, because it puts the soul upon keeping them. Divine love makes every weight light, every yoke easy, every command joyous. It knows no difficulties, it facilitates obedience, it divinely constrains the soul to obey, to walk, to run the ways of God's commands. And as sound obedience springs from faith and love, so it flows from a filial fear of God: Ps. 119. 161, "Mine heart stands in awe of thy word." So Heb. 11. 7, "Noah, being warned of God concerning things not seen as yet, moved with fear, prepared an ark."

Ah! but hypocrites and time-servers are not carried forth in their obedience from such precious and glorious principles, and therefore it is that God casts all their services back in their faces, Isa. 1. 11, 12. And as that obedience which accompanies salvation flows from inward spiritual principles, so it flows from holy and heavenly motives, as from the tastes of divine love, and the sweetness and excellency of communion with God, and the choice and precious discoveries that the soul in ways of obedience hath had of the beauty and glory of God, Isa. 64. 5. The sweet looks, the heavenly words, the glorious kisses, the holy embraces that the obedient soul hath had, make it freely and fully obedient to the word and will of God. Ah! but all the motives that move hypocrites and carnal professors to obedience are only external and carnal, as the eye of the creature, the ear of the creature, the applause of the creature, the rewards of the creature; either the love of the loaves, or the gain of custom, or the desire of ambition, Hosea 7. 14. Sometimes they are moved to obedience by the fear of the creature, and sometimes by the absence of the creature, and sometimes by the example of the creature, and sometimes by vows made to the creature. Sometimes the frowns of God, the displeasure of God, the rod of God, move them to obedience, Hosea 5. 15; Ps. 78. 34. Sometimes the quieting and stilling of conscience, the stopping of the mouth of conscience, and the disarming of conscience of all her whipping, racking, wounding, condemning, terrifying, and torturing power, puts them upon some ways of obedience. Their obedience always flows from some low, base, carnal, corrupt consideration or other. Oh! but that obedience that accompanies salvation doth always flow, as you see, from inward and spiritual causes, and from holy and heavenly motives.

4. IT IS READY, FREE, WILLING, AND CHEERFUL

[4] *Fourthly,* That obedience that accompanies salvation is *a ready, free, willing, and cheerful obedience.*

(1) *It is ready obedience.* Ps. 27. 8, "When thou saidst, Seek ye my face, my heart said unto thee, Thy face, Lord, will I seek"; Ps. 119. 60, "I made haste, and delayed not to keep thy commandments"; Ps. 18. 44, "As soon as they hear of me, they shall obey me; the strangers shall submit themselves unto me."

I have read of one who readily fetched water nearly two miles every day for a whole year together to pour upon a dry stick, upon the bare command of a superior, when no reason could be given for the thing. Oh how ready, then, doth grace make the soul to obey those divine commands that are backed with the highest, strongest, and choicest arguments.

(2) As that obedience that accompanies salvation is ready obedience, so it is *free and willing obedience.* Acts 21. 13, "Then Paul answered, What mean ye to weep, and to break mine heart? for I am willing not to be bound only, but also to die at Jerusalem for the name of the Lord Jesus." The beamings out of divine love and glory make gracious souls "willing in the day of his power," Ps. 110. 3. Those divine principles that be in them make them willingly obey. So 2 Cor. 8. 3. The Macedonians were willingly obedient, or, as the Greek signifies, they were volunteers not only to their power, but beyond their power. All the motions and actings of Christ towards his people, for his people, and in his people, are free; he loves them freely, he pardons them freely,

he intercedes for them freely, he acts towards them freely, and he saves them freely, and so they move and act towards Christ freely; they hear, they pray, they wait, they weep, they work, they watch freely and willingly. That Spirit of grace and holiness that is in them makes them volunteers in all religious duties and services. 1 Chron. 29. 6-18; 1 Tim. 6. 18; 1 Thes. 2. 8.

It is reported of Socrates, that when a tyrant ruler threatened death unto him, he answered, " I am willing." " Nay then," says the tyrant, "you shall live against your will." He answered again, " Nay, whatsoever you do with me, it shall be my will." Yet if nature, a little raised and refined, will enable a man to do this, will not grace, will not union and communion with Christ, enable a man to do as much, yea, infinitely more?

(3) As that obedience that accompanies salvation is free and willing obedience, so it is *cheerful and delightful obedience.* It is a believer's meat and drink, it is his joy and crown, it is a pleasure, a paradise to his soul always to be obeying his Father's will, always to be found about his Father's business: Ps. 40. 8, " I delight to do thy will, O my God; yea, thy law is in my heart." As the sun rejoiceth to run his race, so do the saints rejoice to run the race of obedience. God's work is wages, yea, it is better than wages; therefore they cannot but delight in it. Not only *for* keeping, but also *in* keeping of his commands, there is great reward: Ps. 112. 1, " Blessed is the man that feareth the Lord, that delighteth greatly in his commandments": that is, in the studying and obeying of his commandments. Ps. 119. 16, " I will delight myself in thy statutes; I will not forget thy word." Ver. 35, " Make me to go in the path of thy commandments, for therein do I delight." Ver. 47, " And I will delight myself in thy commandments, which I have loved." Ver. 143, " Trouble and anguish have taken hold on me, yet thy commandments are my delight." Divine commands are not grievous to a lover of Christ; for *nihil difficile amanti,* nothing is difficult to him that loveth. The love of Christ, the growing knowledge of Christ, the embraces of Christ, make a gracious soul studious and indus-

trious to keep the commandments of Christ, in lip and life, in word and work, in head and heart, in book and breast.

Thus you see that that obedience that accompanies salvation is ready, free, and cheerful obedience.

5. IT IS RESOLUTE

[5] *Fifthly*, The obedience that accompanies salvation, is resolute obedience. Josh. 24. 15, "I and my household will serve the Lord." He is fully resolved upon it, come what may; in the face of all dangers, difficulties, impediments and discouragements, he will obey the Lord, he will follow the Lord. So those worthies, Heb. 11, "of whom the world was not worthy," obeyed divine commands resolutely, resolvedly, in the face of all manner of deaths and miseries. So Paul was "obedient to the heavenly vision," though bonds did attend him in every place, Acts 20. 23. He is better at obeying than at disputing; "I conferred not, says he, with flesh and blood," Gal. 1. 15. 16. So Peter and John, and the rest of the apostles, despite all threatenings and beatings, obey the Lord; they keep fast and close to their Master's work. "Whether it be right in the sight of God to hearken more unto you than unto God, judge ye. For we cannot but speak the things which we have seen and heard. And now, Lord, behold their threatenings: and grant unto thy servants, that with all boldness they may speak thy word. And when they had called the apostles, and beaten them, they commanded that they should not speak in the name of Jesus, and let them go. And they departed from the presence of the council, rejoicing that they were counted worthy to suffer shame for his name. And daily in the temple, and in every house, they ceased not to teach and preach Jesus Christ." (Acts 4. 19, 20, 29, and 5. 40-42, compared.)

Thus you see, no trials, no troubles, no terrors, no threats, no dangers, no deaths, could deter them from resolute obedience to divine precepts. It is not the fiery furnace, nor the lions' den, nor the killing sword, nor the torturing rack, that can frighten gracious souls from their obedience to their dearest Lord: Ps. 119. 106, "I have sworn, and I will perform it, that I will keep thy righteous judgments."

6. ITS AIM IS THE DIVINE GLORY

[6] *Sixthly,* The end of that obedience that accompanies salvation is, *divine glory.* The aim of the obedient soul, in prayer and praises, in talking and walking, in giving and receiving, in living and doing, is divine glory: Rom. 14. 7, 8, "For none of us liveth to himself, and no man dieth to himself. For whether we live, we live unto the Lord; and whether we die, we die unto the Lord: whether we live therefore, or die, we are the Lord's." In all actions, the obedient soul intends to promote the divine glory. If Satan, the world, or the " old man " do at any time propound other ends to the soul, this great end, divine glory, cancels out all those ends; for this is most certain, that which a man makes his greatest and his highest end, will cancel out all other ends. Look, as the light of the sun doth extinguish and put out the light of the fire, so when a man makes the glory of God his end, that end will extinguish and put out all carnal, low, base ends; that man that makes himself the end of his actions, that makes honour, riches, applause, &c., the end of his actions, must at last lie down in eternal sorrow, he must dwell in everlasting burnings. The man is as his end is, and his work is as his end is; if that be naught, all is naught; if that be good, all is good, and the man is happy for ever, Isa. 30. 33, and 33. 14.

7. IT IS CONSTANT

[7] *Seventhly,* that obedience that accompanies salvation, that borders upon salvation, that comprehends salvation, is *a constant obedience.* Ps. 119. 112, "I have inclined my heart to do thy statutes alway, even to the end." The causes, springs, and motives of holy obedience are lasting and permanent, and therefore the obedience of a sound Christian is not like the morning dew, or a deceitful bow: Ps. 44. 17-19, "All this comes upon us; yet have we not forgotten thee, neither have we dealt falsely in thy covenant. Our heart is not turned back, neither have our steps declined from thy ways; though thou hast sore broken us in the place of dragons, and covered us with the shadow of death." The

love of Christ, the promises of Christ, the presence of Christ, the discoveries of Christ, the example of Christ, and the recompense of reward held forth by Christ, make a sound Christian hold on, and hold out, in ways of obedience, in the face of all dangers and deaths. Neither the hope of life, nor the fear of death, can make a sincere Christian either change his master or decline his work: Philip. 2. 12, "Wherefore, my beloved, as ye have always obeyed, not as in my presence only, but now much more in my absence, work out your own salvation with fear and trembling." This was the Philippians' glory, that they were constant in their obedience; whether Paul was present or absent, they constantly minded their work.

Ah! but hypocrites and time-servers are but passionate, transient, and inconstant in their obedience; they talk of obedience, they commend obedience, and now and then in a fit they step in the way of obedience, but they do not walk in a way of obedience, they are only constant in inconstancy: Job. 27. 10, "Will the hypocrite delight himself in the Almighty? Will he always call upon God?" Or, as the Hebrew hath it, will he in every time call upon God? Will he call upon God in time of prosperity and in time of adversity? in time of health and in time of sickness? in time of strength and in time of weakness? in time of honour and in time of disgrace? in time of liberty and in time of durance. The answer to be given is, he will not always, he will not in every time, call upon God. As a lame horse, when he is heated, will go well enough, but when he cools, he halts downright; even so an hypocrite, though for a time he may go on fairly in a religious way, yet when he hath attained his ends, he will halt downright, and be able to go no further.

The abbot in Melancthon lived strictly, and walked demurely, and looked humbly, so long as he was but a monk; but when, by his seeming extraordinary sanctity, he got to be made abbot, he grew intolerably proud and insolent, and being asked the reason of it, confessed that his former carriage and lowly looks was but to see if he could find the keys of the abbey. Ah! many unsound hearts there be, that will put on the cloak of religion, and speak like angels, and look like saints, to find the keys of preferment, and when they have found them, none prove more proud, base, and vain than they. Ah! but that obedience that accompanies salvation is constant and durable. A Christian in his course goes straight on heavenwards. "The two milch-kine," 1 Sam. 6. 12, "took the straight way to the way of Beth-shemesh, and went along the highway, lowing as they went, and turned not aside to the right hand or to the left." So gracious souls go straight along the highway to heaven, which is the way of obedience; though they go lowing and weeping, yet they still go on, and turn not aside to the right hand nor to the left. If by the violence of temptation or corruption they are thrust out of the way at any time, they quickly return into it again. They may sometimes step out of the way of obedience, but they cannot walk out of the way of obedience. This honest traveller may step out of his way, but he soon returns into it again, and so doth the honest soul, Ps. 119. 3, 4.

8. IT IS PASSIVE AS WELL AS ACTIVE

(8) *Eighthly, and lastly, Passive obedience accompanies salvation as well as active.* "Every one that will live godly in Christ Jesus must suffer persecution," 2 Tim. 3. 12; 2. 12, from tongue or pen, from hand or heart. "If we suffer with him, we shall reign with him," Rom. 8. 17, 18. There is no passing into paradise but under the flaming sword. "Through many afflictions we must enter into the kingdom of heaven," Acts 14. 22. A sincere heart is as willing to obey Christ passively as actively: Acts 21. 13. "I am ready, not to be bound only, but also to die at Jerusalem, for the name of the Lord Jesus." I am willing, says Paul, to lose my comforts for Christ, I am ready to endure any distresses for Christ, I am willing to lose the creature, and to leave the creature for Christ. Paul, Philip. 3. 8, speaks of himself as having been like one in a sea-tempest, that had cast out all his precious wares and goods for Christ's sake; "for whom," says he, "I have suffered the loss of all." So must we, in stormy times, cast all overboard for Christ, and swim to an immortal crown, through sorrows, blood, and death. But

because I have in this treatise spoken at large of the sufferings of the saints, I shall say no more of it in this place; and thus you see what that obedience is that accompanies salvation.

The things that accompany salvation: LOVE

The fifth thing that I am to shew you is, what love that is that accompanies salvation.

That love doth accompany salvation I have formerly shewed you; but now I shall shew you what that love is that doth accompany salvation; and that I shall do in these following particulars. I shall not speak of the firstness, freeness, fulness, sweetness, and greatness of Christ's love to us, but of that love of ours that accompanies salvation, concerning which I shall say thus:

The qualities of love

1. IT IS SUPERLATIVE

(1) *First,* The love that accompanies salvation is *a superlative love, a transcendent love.* True love to Christ doth wonderfully transcend and surpass the love of all relations; the love of father, mother, wife, child, brother, sister, yea, life itself, Mat. 10. 37, 38; Luke 14. 26, 27, 34. Ps. 73. 25, " Whom have I in heaven but thee? And there is none upon earth that I desire besides thee." Christ will be *Alexander* or *Nemo,* he will be all or nothing at all. There are the greatest causes of love, there are the highest causes of love, there are all the causes of love, to be found in Christ. In angels and men there are only some particular causes of love; all causes of love are eminently and only to be found in Christ. Col. 1. 19, " It pleased the Father that in him should all fulness dwell." There is not only fulness, but an overflowing of fulness in Jesus Christ. All wisdom, all knowledge, all light, all life, all love, all goodness, all sweetness, all blessedness, all joys, all delights, all pleasures, all beauties, all beatitudes, all excellencies, all glories are in Christ, Col. 2. 9. The true lovers of Christ know that Christ loves as a head, as a king, as a father, as a husband, as a brother, as a kinsman, as a friend. The love of all relations meets in the love of Christ; and this raises up a believer to love Christ

with a transcendent love. They know that Christ loves them more than they love themselves; yea, that he loves them above his very life, John 10. 17, 18. And *magnes amoris amor*, love is the magnet of love. Christ is amiable and lovely; he is famous and conspicuous; he is spotless and matchless in his names, in his natures, in his offices, in his graces, in his gifts, in his revelations, in his appearances, in his ordinances. He is full of gravity, majesty, mercy, and glory. "He is white and ruddy, the chiefest among ten thousand." His mouth is *sweetness*; yea, *all of him is desires*, or all of him is delights, Song of Solomon 5. 10-16. Christ is wholly delectable; he is altogether desirable from top to toe; he is amiable and lovely, he is glorious and excellent. Christ is lovely, Christ is very lovely, Christ is most lovely, Christ is always lovely, Christ is altogether lovely. He is "the express image of God"; he is "the brightness of his Father's glory." If the soul can but discover him, it shall find in him all high perfections and supereminent excellencies. And upon these and such like considerations the saints are led forth to love Jesus Christ with a most transcendent love.

2. IT IS OBEDIENT

(2) *Secondly*, That love that accompanies salvation is a love that obeys; *it is operative and working love.* The love of Christ makes a man subject to the commands of Christ: "If any man love me, he will keep my commandments"; and again, "He that hath my commandments, and keepeth them, he it is that loveth me," John 14. 21. Divine love is very operative: Ps. 116. 1, "I love the Lord," says David. Well, but how doth this love work? Why, says he, "I will walk in his ways, I will pay my vows, I will take the cup of salvation, I will offer the sacrifice of thanksgiving, and I will call upon the name of the Lord as long as I live," vers. 2, 9, 13, 14, 17. Divine love is not stinted nor limited to one sort of duty, but is free to all. He that loveth flieth, he that loveth runneth, he that loveth believeth, he that loveth rejoiceth, he that loveth mourneth, he that loveth giveth, he that loveth lendeth, he that loveth beareth, he that loveth

waiteth, he that loveth hopeth. Heb. 6. 10, "For God is not unrighteous, to forget your work and labour of love." Love makes the soul laborious. That love that accompanies salvation is very active and operative. It is like the virtuous woman in the Proverbs, that set all her maidens on work. It is never quiet, but in doing the will of God. It will not suffer any grace to sit idle in the soul. It will egg and set on all other graces to act and operate. Love sets faith upon drawing from Christ, and patience upon waiting on Christ, and humility upon submitting to Christ, and godly sorrow upon mourning over Christ, and self-denial upon forsaking of the nearest and dearest comforts for Christ. As the sun makes the earth fertile, so doth divine love make the soul fruitful in works of righteousness and holiness. He that loves cannot be idle nor barren. Loves makes the soul constant and abundant in well-doing: 2 Cor. 5. 14, "The love of Christ constraineth us." It doth urge us and put us forward; it carries us on as men possessed with a vehemency of spirit, or as a ship which is driven with strong winds towards the desired haven. Natural love makes the child, the servant, the wife, obedient; so doth divine love make the soul better at obeying than at disputing. A soul that loves Christ will never cease to obey till he ceases to be. That love that accompanies salvation is like the sun. The sun, you know, casteth his beams upward and downward, to the east and to the west, to the north and to the south; so the love of a saint ascends to God above, and descends to men on earth; to our friends on the right hand, to our enemies on the left hand; to them that are in a state of grace, and to them that are in a state of nature. Divine love will still be a-working one way or another.

3. IT IS SINCERE

(3) *Thirdly*, That love that accompanies salvation is *a sincere and incorrupt love*: Eph. 6. 24, "Grace be with all them that love our Lord Jesus Christ in sincerity. Amen." The true-bred Christian *amat Christum propter Christum*, loves Christ for Christ; he loves Christ for that internal and eternal worth that is in him; he loves him for his incompar-

able excellency and beauty, for that transcendent sweetness, loveliness, holiness, and goodness that is in him; he is none of those that loves Christ for loaves, neither will he with Judas kiss Christ and betray him; nor yet will he with those in the Gospel cry out, "Hosanna, Hosanna," one day, and "Crucify him, crucify him," the next, Mat. 21. 9, 15. They love Christ with a virgin love: Song of Solomon 1. 3, "The virgins love thee." They love thee in much sincerity, purity, and integrity; they love thee for that fragrant savour, for that natural sweetness, for that incomparable goodness that is in thee. So ver. 4, "The upright love thee," or as it is in the Hebrew, "Uprightnesses love thee," "uprightnesses" being put for "upright ones," the abstract for the concrete; or, "They love thee in uprightnesses," that is, most uprightly, most entirely, most sincerely, and not as hypocrites, who love thee for base, carnal respects; who love thee in compliment, but not in realities; who love thee in word and tongue, but despise thee in heart and life; who love the gift more than the giver. That love that accompanies salvation is real and cordial love, it is sincere and upright love, it makes the soul love Christ, the giver, more than the gift; it makes the soul love the gift for the giver's sake; it will make the soul to love the giver without his gifts. And verily, they shall not be long without good gifts from Christ, that love Christ more than his gifts.

The emperor Vespasian commanded that a liberal reward should be given to a woman that came and professed that she was in love with him; and when his steward asked him what *item* he should put to it in his book of accounts, the emperor answered, *Vespasiano adamato,* item to her that loved Vespasian. Ah, Christians, shall Vespasian, a heathen prince, reward her liberally that loved his person? and will not the Lord Jesus much more reward them with his choicest gifts that love him more than his gifts? Surely Christ will not be worse than a heathen, he will not act below a heathen! He shall never be a loser that loves Christ for that spiritual sweetness and loveliness that is in Christ; Christ will not live long in that man's debts.

4. IT IS VEHEMENT

(4) *Fourthly,* That love that accompanies salvation is *a vehement love, an ardent love.* It is a spark of heavenly fire, and it puts all the affections into a holy flame: Song of Solomon 1. 7, " Tell me, O thou whom my soul loveth, where thou feedest?" This amiable, amorous, pathetic style of address, " O thou whom my soul loveth," speaks the spouse's love to be hot and burning towards Christ. So in Isa. 26. 8, 9, " The desire of our souls is towards thee, and to the remembrance of thy name. With my soul have I desired thee in the night, yea, with my spirit within me, will I seek thee early." This affectionate, this passionate form of speech, " With my soul have I desired thee," and, " with my spirit within me will I seek thee," does elegantly set forth the vehement and ardent love of the church to Christ; so doth that pathetic exclamation of the church, " Stay me with flagons, comfort me with apples, for I am sick of love," Song of Solomon 2. 5. The betrothed virgin cannot shew more strong and vehement love to her beloved, than by being sick and surprised with love-qualms, when she meets him, when she enjoys him. It was so here with the spouse of Christ. The love of Christ to believers is a vehement love, an ardent love—witness his leaving his Father's bosom, his putting off for us his royal robes, his bleeding and his dying. And it doth naturally beget vehement and ardent love in all the beloved of God. Where Christ loves, he always begets somewhat like himself. That love that is flat, lukewarm, or cold, will leave a man to freeze this side heaven, but will fit him for the warmest place in hell. Dives' love was very cold, and he found the flames of hell to be very hot. That love that accompanies salvation is full of heat and fire.

5. IT IS PERMANENT

(5) *Fifthly,* That love that accompanies salvation is *lasting love, it is permanent love.* The objects of it are lasting, the springs and causes of it are lasting, the nature of it is lasting. The primitive Christians loved not their lives unto the death, Rev. 12. 11. Persecutors have taken away the mar-

tyrs' lives for Christ, but could never destroy their love to Christ: Eph. 6. 24, "Grace be with all that love the Lord Jesus in sincerity," or, "in incorruption," as the Greek word signifies; whereby the apostle gives us to understand, that true love to Christ is not liable to corruption, putrefaction, or decay, but is constant and permanent, lasting, yea, ever-lasting.

That love that accompanies salvation is like to the oil in the cruse and the meal in the barrel, that wasted not; it is like the apple-tree of Persia, that buddeth, blossometh, and beareth fruit every month; it is like the lamp in the story, that never went out; it is like the stone in Thracia, that neither burneth in the fire, nor sinketh in the water: Song of Solomon 8. 6, 7, "Love is strong as death; many waters cannot quench it, nor can the floods drown it. If a man would give all the substance of his house for love, it would be contemned." Love will outlive all enemies, temptations, oppositions, afflictions, persecutions, dangers, and deaths. Love's motto is *Nulli cedo,* I yield to none. Love is like the sun; the sun beginning to ascend in his circle, never goes back till he comes to the highest degree thereof.

True love abhors apostasy; it aspires to more perfection, and is contented not until, like Elijah's fiery chariot, it hath carried the soul to heaven. Many men's love to Christ is like the morning dew; it is like Jonah's gourd, that came up in a night and vanished in a night. But that love that accompanies salvation is like Ruth's love, a lasting and an abiding love. It is love that will bed and board with the soul, that will lie down and rise up with the soul, that will go to the fire, to the prison, to the grave, to heaven with the soul.

6. IT IS ABOUNDING

(6) *Sixthly,* that love that accompanies salvation, is *an abounding love, an increasing love.* Love in a saint is like the waters in Noah's time, that rose higher and higher. The very nature of true love is to abound and rise higher and higher. Philip. 1. 9, "This I pray, that your love may abound yet more and more."

The longer a believer lives, the more eminent and excellent causes of love he sees in Christ. Christ reveals himself gradually to the soul. Now, a believer's love to Christ rises answerable to the causes of love that he sees in Christ. The more light the more love. Knowledge and love, like the water and the ice, beget each other.

Man loves Christ by knowing, and knows Christ by loving. Man's love is answerable to his light. He cannot love much that knows but little; he cannot love little that knows much. As a man rises higher and higher in his apprehensions of Christ, so he cannot but rise higher and higher in his affections to Christ. Again, the daily mercies and experiences that they have of the love of Christ, of the care of Christ, of the kindnesses and compassions of Christ working more and more towards them, cannot but raise their affections more and more to him. As fire is increased by adding of fuel unto it, so is our love to Christ upon fresh and new manifestations of his great love towards us. As the husband abounds in his love to his wife, so the wife rises in her love to her husband. The more love the father manifests to the child, the more the ingenuous child rises in his affections to him. So the more love the Lord Jesus shews to us, the more he is beloved by us. Christ shewed much love to Mary Magdalene, and this raises in her much love to Christ. " She loved much, for much was forgiven her," Luke 7. 47, 48. As the Israelites, Num. 33. 29, removed their tents from Mithcah to Hashmonah, from *sweetness* to *swiftness,* as the words import, so the sweetness of divine love manifested to the soul makes the soul more sweet, swift, and high in the exercise and actings of love towards Christ. A soul under special manifestations of love, weeps that it can love Christ no more. Mr. Welch, a Suffolk minister, weeping at table, and being asked the reason of it, answered, it was because he could love Christ no more. The true lovers of Christ can never rise high enough in their love to Christ; they count a little love to be no love; great love to be but little; strong love to be but weak; and the highest love to be infinitely below the worth of Christ, the beauty and glory of Christ, the fulness, sweetness, and goodness of Christ. The top of their misery in this life is, that they love so little, though they are so much beloved.

7. IT CANNOT BE HID

(7) *Seventhly and lastly,* that love that accompanies salvation, *is open love, it is manifest love, it is love that cannot be hid, that cannot be covered and buried.* It is like the sun, it will shine forth, and shew itself to all the world. A man cannot love Christ, but he will shew it in these, and such like things as follow:

First, Divine love makes the soul even *ready to break, in longing after a further, clearer, and fuller enjoyment of Christ.* The voice of divine love is, "Come, Lord Jesus, come quickly," Rev. 22. 20. "Make haste, my beloved, and be thou like to a roe or to a young hart upon the mountains of spices," Song of Solomon 8. 14. "I desire to be dissolved, and to be with Christ, which for me is best of all," Philip. 1. 23. It is a mercy, says Paul, for Christ to be with me, but it is a greater mercy for me to be with Christ. I desire to die, that I may see my Saviour; I prefer not to live, that I may live with my Redeemer.

Love desires and endeavours for ever to be present, to converse with, to enjoy, to be closely and eternally united to its object, Christ. The longing of the espoused maid for the marriage day, of the traveller for his inn, of the mariner for his haven, and of the captive for his ransom, is not to be compared to the longings of the lovers of Christ after a further and fuller enjoyment of Christ.

The lovers of Christ do well know, that till they are taken up into glory, their chains will not fall off; till then their glorious robes shall not be put on; till then all sorrow and tears shall not be wiped from their eyes; till then their joy will not be full, their comforts pure, their peace lasting, their graces perfect, and this makes them look for and long after the enjoyment of the person of Christ.

It was a notable saying of one, "Let all the devils in hell," saith he, "beset me round; let fasting macerate my body; let sorrows oppress my mind; let pains consume my flesh; let watchings dry me, or heat scorch me, or cold freeze me, let all these, and what can come more, happen unto me, so I may enjoy my Saviour."

Secondly, Love to Christ shews itself by *enabling the soul to abase itself that Christ may be exalted, to lessen itself to make Christ the greater, to cloud itself that Christ alone may shine.* Love cares not what it is, nor what it doth, so it may but advance the Lord Jesus; it makes the soul willing to be a footstool for Christ, to be anything, to be nothing, that Christ may be all in all. Rev. 4. 10, 11; John 3. 26-31; Philip. 3. 7, 8.

Thirdly, That love that accompanies salvation, sometimes shews itself by enabling the soul *to be cheerful and resolute, to be patient and constant in sufferings for Christ:* 1 Cor. 13. 7, "Love endureth all things." Love will not complain, love will not say the burden is too great, the prison is too dark, the furnace is too hot, the chains are too heavy, or the cup is too bitter. Acts 21. 13. A true lover of Christ can slight his life, out of love to Christ, as that blessed virgin in Basil, who, being condemned for Christianity to the fire, and having her estate and life offered her, if she would worship idols, cried, " Let money perish, and life vanish, Christ is better than all."

So Alice Driver said, " I drove my father's plough often, yet I can die for Christ as soon as any of you all." That love that accompanies salvation, makes a Christian free, and forward in suffering anything that makes for the glory of Christ.

Fourthly, that love that accompanies salvation, shews itself by enabling the soul *to be pleased or displeased, as Christ is pleased or displeased.* A soul that loves Christ hath his eye upon Christ, and that which makes Christ frown makes him frown, and what makes Christ smile makes him smile. Love is impatient of anything that may displease a beloved Christ.

Look what Harpalus once said, *Quod regi placet, mihi placet,* what pleaseth the king pleaseth me; and a true lover of Christ says, What pleaseth Christ pleaseth me. Holiness pleaseth Christ and holiness pleaseth me, says a lover of Christ. It pleaseth Christ to overcome evil with good, to overcome hatred with love, enmity with amity, pride with humility, and passion with meekness, and the same pleaseth me, says a lover of Christ. 1 John 4. 17, "As he is, so are we

245

in this world." Our love answers to Christ's love, and our hatred answers to Christ's hatred; he loves all righteousness and hates all wickedness; so do we, say the lovers of Christ, Ps. 119. 113, 128, 163.

It is said of Constantine's children, that they resembled their father to the life, and that they put him wholly on. The true lovers of Christ resemble Christ to the life, and they put him wholly on. Hence it is that they are called Christ, 1 Cor. 12. 12.

Fifthly, True love to Christ shews itself sometimes by enabling the lovers of Christ *to expose themselves to suffering, to save Christ from suffering in his glory;* to adventure the loss of their own crowns, to keep Christ's crown upon his head; to adventure drowning, to save Christ's honour from sinking. Thus did the three children, Daniel, Moses, and other worthies, Heb. 11.

I have read of a servant who dearly loved his master, and knowing that his master was looked for by his enemies he put on his master's clothes, and was taken for his master, and suffered death for him.

Divine love will make a man do as much for Christ; it will make a man hang for Christ and burn for Christ: Rev. 12. 11, "They loved not their lives unto the death." Christ and his truth were dearer to them than their lives. They slighted, contemned, yea, despised their very lives, when they stood in competition with Christ and his glory, and chose rather to suffer the greatest misery than that Christ should lose the least dram of his glory.

Sixthly, That love that accompanies salvation shews itself sometimes by enabling the lovers of Christ *to be affected and afflicted with the dishonours that are done to Christ:* Ps. 119. 136. "Mine eyes run down with rivers of tears, because men keep not thy law." Also Jer. 9. 1, 2. So Lot's soul was vexed, racked, and tortured with the filthy conversation of the wicked Sodomites, 2 Pet. 2. 7, 8. The turning of his own flesh, his wife, into a pillar of salt did not vex him, but their sins did rack his righteous soul: Ps. 69. 9, "The reproaches of them that reproached thee fell upon me." A woman is most wounded in her husband, so is a Christian in his Christ.

Though Moses was as a dumb child in his own cause, yet when the Israelites, by making and dancing about their golden calf, had wounded the honour and glory of God, he shews himself to be much affected and afflicted for the dishonour done to God. The statue of Apollo is said to shed tears for the afflictions of the Grecians, though he could not help them; so a true lover of Christ will shed tears for those dishonours that are done to Christ, though he knows not how to prevent them. It is between Christ and his lovers as it is between two lute strings that are tuned one to another; no sooner is one struck, but the other trembles; so no sooner is Christ struck, but a Christian trembles, and no sooner is a Christian struck, but Christ trembles: " Saul, Saul, why persecutest thou me?" Acts 9. 4.

Seventhly, That love that accompanies salvation doth shew itself by enabling the soul *to observe with a curious critical eye Christ's countenance and carriage, and by causing the soul to be sad or cheerful, as Christ's carriage and countenance is towards the soul.* When Christ looks sad, and carries it sadly, then to be sad, as Peter was: Christ cast a sad look upon him, and that made his heart sad; he went forth and wept bitterly. And when Christ looks sweetly, and speaks kindly, and carries it lovingly, then to be cheerful and joyful, as the church was in Song of Solomon 3. 4, " It was but a little that I passed from them, but I found him whom my soul loveth: I held him, and would not let him go, until I had brought him into my mother's house, and into the chamber of her that conceived me." So the church in Isa. 61. 10, " I will greatly rejoice in the Lord, my soul shall be joyful in my God; for he hath clothed me with the garments of salvation, he hath covered me with the robe of righteousness, as a bridegroom decketh himself with ornaments, and as a bride adorneth herself with her jewels." A true lover of Christ hath his eye always upon Christ, and as his countenance stands, so is he glad or sad, cheerful or sorrowful. Tigranes in Xenophon's History, coming to redeem his father and friends, with his wife, that were taken prisoners by king Cyrus, was asked among other questions this, viz., what ransom he would give for his wife? he answered he would redeem her liberty with his own life. But having prevailed for all their liberties, as they returned together, every one commended Cyrus for a goodly man, and Tigranes would needs know of his wife what she thought of him. "Truly," said she, "I cannot tell, for I did not so much as look on him or see him." "Whom then," said he, wondering, "did you look upon?" "Whom should I look upon," said she, "but him that would have redeemed my liberty with the loss of his own life." So a Christian, a true lover of Christ, esteems nothing worth a looking upon but Christ, who hath redeemed him with his own blood.

8. IT DELIGHTS TO SEE THE DIVINE IMAGE IN FELLOW-BELIEVERS

Eighthly, That love that accompanies salvation, *reaches forth a hand of kindness to those that bear the image of Christ.* 1 John 5. 1, 2, "Every one that loveth him that begat, loveth him also that is begotten of him. By this we know that we love the children of God, when we love God, and keep his commandments. He that loveth not his brother whom he hath seen, how can he love God whom he hath not seen?"

Now, because many mistake in their love to the saints, and the consequences that follow that mistake are very dangerous and pernicious to the souls of men, I shall therefore briefly hint to you the properties of that love to the saints that accompanies salvation. And,

(1) *The first property.* The first is this, true love to the saints is *spiritual*; it is a love for the image of God that is stamped upon the soul. Col. 1. 8, "Epaphras hath declared to us your love in the Spirit." A soul that truly loves, loves the Father for his own sake, and the children for the Father's sake. Many there are that love Christians for their goods. not for their good; they love them for the money that is in their purse, but not for the grace that is in their hearts. Many, like the Bohemian cur, fawn upon a good suit of clothes. Love to the saints, for the image of God stamped upon them, is a flower that grows not in nature's garden. No man can love grace in another man's heart but he that

248

hath grace in his own. Men do not more naturally love their parents, and love their children, and love themselves, than they do naturally hate the image of God upon his people and ways. True love is for what of the divine nature, for what of Christ and grace, shines in a man. It is one thing to love a godly man, and another thing to love him for godliness. Many love godly men as they are politicians, or powerful, or learned, or of a sweet nature, but all this is but natural love; but to love them because they are spiritually lovely, because they are "all glorious within, and their raiment is of embroidered gold," Ps. 45. 13, is to love them as becometh saints; it is to love them at so high and noble a rate that no hypocrite in the world can reach to it. The wasps fly about the tradesman's shop, not out of love to him, but because of the honey and the fruit that is there. This age is full of such wasps.

(2) *The second property.* Secondly, True love to the saints is *universal, to one Christian as well as another, to all as well as any*; to poor Lazarus as well as to rich Abraham, to a despised Job as well as to an admired David, to an afflicted Joseph as well as to a raised Jacob, to a despised disciple as well as to an exalted apostle. Philip. 4. 21, "Salute every saint," the meanest as well as the richest, the weakest as well as the strongest, the lowest as well as the highest. They have all the same Spirit, the same Jesus, the same faith; they are all fellow-members, fellow-travellers, fellow-soldiers, fellow-citizens, fellow-heirs, and therefore must they all be loved with a sincere and cordial love. The apostle James doth roundly condemn that partial love that was seen among professors in his days, James 2. 1, 2. Not that the apostle doth absolutely prohibit a civil differencing of men in place from others, but when the rich man's wealth is more regarded than the poor man's godliness, and when men behave so to the rich, as to cast scorn, contempt, disgrace, and discouragement upon the godly poor; this is a sin for which God will visit the sons of pride.

Pompey told his Cornelia, "It is no praise for thee to have loved *Pompeium Magnum,* Pompey the Great, but if thou lovest *Pompeium Miserum,* Pompey the Miserable, thou shalt be a pattern for imitation to all posterity." I will leave you to apply it.

Romanus the martyr, who was born of noble parentage, entreated his persecutors that they would not favour him for his nobility: "For it is not," said he, "the blood of my ancestors, but my Christian faith, that makes me noble."

Verily, he that loves one saint for the grace that is in him, for that holiness, that image of God, that is upon him, he cannot but fall in love with every saint that bears the lovely image of the Father upon him; he cannot but love a saint in rags, as well as a saint in robes; a saint upon the dunghill, as well as a saint upon the throne. Usually the most ragged Christians are the richest Christians; they usually have most of heaven that have least of earth, James 2. 5. The true diamond shines best in the dark.

(3) *The third property.* Thirdly, Our love to the saints is right, *when we love them and delight in them, answerable to the spiritual causes of love that shine in them,* as the more holy and gracious they are, the more we love them: Ps. 16. 2, 3, "My goodness extendeth not to thee, but to the saints that are in the earth, and to the excellent, in whom is all my delight." This is most certain, if godliness be the reason why we love any, then the more any excel others in the love, spirit, power, and practice of godliness, the more we should love them. There are those that seem to love such godly men as are weak in their judgments, low in their principles, and dull in their practices, and yet look with a squint eye upon those that are more sound in their judgment, more high in their principles, and more holy in their practices. This doubtless bespeaks more hypocrisy than sincerity. Verily, he hath either no grace, or but a little grace, that doth not love most where the spiritual causes of love do most shine and appear. Surely those Christians that envy those gifts and graces of God in others that outshine their own, are under a very great distemper of spirit. John's disciples muttered and murmured, because Christ had more followers and admirers than John; and John's disciples are not all dead, yea, they seem to have a new resurrection in these days. Well, as the fairest day hath its clouds, the finest linen its spots, the

richest jewels their flaws, the sweetest fruits their worms, so when precious Christians are under temptations, they may, and too often do envy and repine at those graces, abilities, and other excellencies that cloud, darken, and outshine their own. The best of men are too full of pride and self-love, and that makes them sometimes cast dirt and disgrace upon that excellency that they themselves lack, as did that great man that could not write his own name, and yet called the liberal arts a public poison and pestilence. There is no greater argument that our grace is true, and that we do love others for grace's sake, than our loving them best that have most grace, though they have least of worldly goods. A pearl is rich, if found on a dunghill, though it may glitter more when set in a ring of gold; so, many a poor believer is rich and glorious in the eye of Christ, and should be so in ours, though, like Job, he sits upon a dunghill, and though to the world he may seem to glister most when adorned with riches, honour, and outward pomp.

(4) *The fourth property*. Fourthly, True love to saints is *constant*: 1 Cor. 13. 8, "Love never faileth." It continues for ever in heaven. That love was never true that is not constant. Heb. 13. 1, "Let brotherly love continue." True love is constant in prosperity and adversity, in storms and calms, in health and sickness, in presence and in absence. "Thy own friend, and thy father's friend, forsake not." "A friend," says the wise man, "loves at all times and a brother is born for adversity," Prov. 17. 17. Prosperity makes friends, and adversity will try friends. A true friend is neither known in prosperity, nor hid in adversity.

True love is like to that of Ruth's to Naomi, and that of Jonathan's to David, permanent and constant. Many there be whose love to the saints is like Job's brooks, Job 6. 15, 16, which in winter when we have no need, overflow with tenders of service and shews of love; but when the season is hot and dry, and the poor thirsty traveller stands in most need of water to refresh him, then the brooks are quite dried up. They are like the swallow that will stay by you in the summer, but fly from you in the winter.

It is observed by Josephus of the Samaritans, that whenever the Jews' affairs prospered, they would be their friends, and profess much love to them; but if the Jews were in trouble, and wanted their assistance, then they would not own them, nor have anything to do with them. This age is full of such Samaritans, yet, such as truly love will always love. In the primitive times it was very much taken notice of by the very heathen, that in the depth of misery, when fathers and mothers forsook their children, Christians, otherwise strangers, stuck close to one another; their love of religion, and one of another, proved firmer than that of nature. "They seem to take away the sun out of the world," said Cicero the orator, "who take away friendship from the life of men," and we do not more need fire and water than constant friendship.

9. IT ENABLES THE SOUL TO RECEIVE CHRIST'S REBUKES

Ninthly, That love that accompanies salvation, doth manifest and shew itself by enabling the soul *to be quiet and still under Christ's rebukes.* Peter sits down quiet under a threefold reproof, "Lord, thou knowest all things, thou knowest that I love thee," John 21. 16-18. So Eli, "It is the Lord, let him do what seems good in his own eyes," 1 Sam. 3. 18. And Aaron "held his peace," when he saw the flames about his sons' ears, Lev. 10. 3. So David, "I was dumb, I opened not my mouth, because thou didst it," Ps. 39. 9. The lovers of Christ are like the Scythian, that went naked in the snow; and when Alexander wondered how he could endure it, he answered, "I am all forehead." Oh, the lovers of Christ are all forehead, to bear the rebukes of the Lord Jesus.

The lovers of Christ know that all his rebukes are from love; "whom he loves, he rebukes," Rev. 3. 19; they can see smiles through Christ's frowns; they know, that to argue that Christ hates them because he rebukes them, is the devil's logic; they know, that all the rebukes of Christ are in order to their internal and eternal good, and that quiets them; they know that all the rebukes of Christ are but forerunners of some glorious manifestations of greater love to their souls. Ps. 71. 20, 21, "Thou, which hast shewed me great and sore troubles, shalt quicken me again, and shalt bring me up

252

again from the depths of the earth. Thou shalt increase my greatness, and comfort me on every side." They know that it is the sorest judgment in the world, to go on freely in a way of sin without rebukes. "Ephraim is joined to idols, let him alone," Hosea 4. 17. And therefore they keep silence before the Lord, they lay one hand upon their mouths, and the other upon their hearts, and so sit mute before the holy one.

10. IT LAMENTS OVER DISHONOURS DONE TO CHRIST

Tenthly, That love that accompanies salvation, shews itself by working the heart *to be affected and afflicted with the least dishonours that are done to Christ*. Love is curious of little things; it is as much afflicted with an idle word or with an impure dream, as lovers of Christ are with adultery or blasphemy. David did but cut off the lap of Saul's garment, and his heart smote him, 1 Sam. 24. 5; though he did it to convince Saul of his false jealousy, and his own innocency. Love will not allow of the least infirmity. Rom. 7. 15, "That which I do, I allow not." Love will make a man aim at angelical purity and perfect innocency; love will be getting up to the top of Jacob's ladder; love can rest in nothing below perfection; love makes a man look more at what he should be than at what he is; it makes a man strive as for life to imitate the highest examples, and to write after the choicest copies. Love fears every image of offence, it trembles at the appearance of one; it doth not, it cannot, allow itself to do anything that looks like sin; it hates "the garment spotted with the flesh"; it shuns the occasions of sin as it shuns hell itself. This is the divine glory of a Christian's love. It is better to die with hunger than to eat that which is offered to idols, saith Augustine.

I have read of a holy man, who, out of his love to Christ and hatred of idolatry, would not give one halfpenny toward the building of an idol's temple, though he was provoked thereunto by intolerable torments. Love knows that the least evils are contrary to the greatest good; they are contrary to the nature of Christ, the commands of Christ, the spirit of Christ, the grace of Christ, the glory of Christ, the blood of Christ. Love knows that little dishonours, if I may call any sin little, make way for greater, as little thieves unlock the door and make way for greater. Love knows that little sins multiplied become great. As love knows that there is nothing less than a grain of sand; so love knows that there is nothing heavier than the sand of the sea, when multiplied.

11. IT KEEPS THE HEART FOR CHRIST ALONE

Eleventhly, That love that accompanies salvation, will shew itself by *keeping the doors of the heart shut against those treacherous lovers that would draw the heart from Christ.* Love is a golden key to let in Christ, and a strong lock to keep out others. Though many may knock at love's door, yet love will open to none but Christ: Song of Solomon 5. 6, "I opened to my beloved"; and 8. 7, "Many waters cannot quench love, neither can the floods drown it: if a man would give all the substance of his house for love, it would utterly be contemned"; or, as the Hebrew reads, "contemning, it would be contemned." When the world would buy his love, the Christian cries out with Peter, "Thy money perish with thee," Acts 8. 20. Love makes a man look with a holy scorn and disdain upon all persons and things, that attempt either to force or flatter him out of his love and loyalty to his beloved." It is neither force nor fraud, it is neither promises nor threatenings, it is neither the cross nor the crown, the palace nor the prison, the rod nor the robe, the hempen halter nor the golden chain, that will make love embrace a stranger in the room of Christ. Go, says divine love, offer your gold and empty glories to others; your pleasures and your treasures to others; put on your lion's skin and frighten others; as for my part, I scorn and contemn your golden offers, and I disdain and deride your rage and threats. Love makes a man too noble, too high, too gallant, and too faithful, to open to any lover but Christ, to let any lie between the breasts but Christ: Song of Solomon 1. 13, "A bundle of myrrh is my beloved unto me; he shall lie all night betwixt my breasts." When Basil was tempted with money and preferment, he answers "Give money that may last for ever, and glory that may eternally flourish." Love makes a man cry out when tempted, "Let not any man think that I will embrace other men's goods to forsake Christ." Love makes a man cry out when tempted, as that worthy convert did, "I am not the man that I was; when my heart was void of divine love, I was as easily conquered as I was tempted. Oh, but now he hath shed abroad his love in my soul, I am not the man that I was, I had rather die than fly, or fall before a temptation."

12. IT DELIGHTS IN SECRET COMMUNION WITH CHRIST

Twelfthly, That love that accompanies salvation shews itself by *secret visits, by secret expressions of love.* A soul that truly loves Christ, loves to meet him in a corner, to meet him behind the door, Song of Solomon 2. 14, to meet him in the clefts of the rock, where no eye sees, where no ear hears, where no heart observes, Mat. 6. 6. Feigned love is much in commending and kissing Christ in public; but unfeigned love is much in embracing and weeping over Christ in the secret place. The Pharisee loved to stand praying in the market-place and in the temple, Mat. 6. 2; but Nathanael was with Christ under the fig-tree, John 1. 48; and Cornelius was in prayer in the corner of his house, Acts 10; Peter on the housetop; the spouse was busy in the villages, Song of Solomon 7. 11. Souls that truly love Christ are much engaged in secret visits, in secret prayer, in secret sighing, in secret groaning, and in secret mourning. True love is good at bolting the door, and is always best when it is most with Christ in a corner. The secret revelations of himself that Christ makes to souls do much oblige them to the private seeking of him.

Arcesilaus in Plutarch's History, visiting his sick friend, and perceiving that he was in need, and yet through modesty was ashamed to ask, that he might satisfy the need and yet salve the modesty, secretly conveyed money under his pillow. His friend, finding it after he was gone, was wont to say, "Arcesilaus stole this." So Christ steals secret kindnesses upon his people, and that draws them out to be much in secret with him.

13. IT LONGS FOR THE FULL ASSURANCE OF
CHRIST'S LOVE

Thirteenthly, That love that accompanies salvation shews itself *by breathing after more clear evidence and full assurance of Christ's love to the soul.* Divine love would fain have her drop turned into an ocean, her spark into a flame, her penny into a pound, her mite into a million. Souls that truly love can never see enough, and never taste enough, and never feel enough, and never enjoy enough of the love of Christ; when once they have found his love to be better than wine, then nothing will satisfy them but the kisses of his mouth: Song of Solomon 1. 2, "Let him kiss me with the kisses of his mouth." Not with a kiss, but with the kisses of his mouth. A soul once kissed by Christ, can never have enough of the kisses of Christ; his lips drop myrrh and mercy; no kisses can be compared with the kisses of Christ. The more any soul loves Christ, the more serious, studious, and industrious will that soul be to have the love of Christ revealed, confirmed, witnessed, and sealed to it. That is a sweet word of the spouse: Song of Solomon, 8. 6, "Set me as a seal upon thine heart, as a seal upon thine arm; for love is strong as death." "Set me as a seal upon thine heart"; that is, let me be deeply engraven as a seal into thine heart and affections; let the love and remembrance of me make a deep impression in thee, and set me as a seal or signet on thine arm.

[1] The seal, you know, is for ratifying, confirming, and making sure of things. Oh, says the spouse, establish and confirm me in thy love, and in the outward expressions and manifestations of it.

[2] Seals among the Jews were used not as ornaments only, but as monuments of love that were continually in sight and remembrance. Oh! says the church, let me be always in thy sight and remembrance as a monument of thy love. In the old law, you know, the high priest did bear the name of Israel engraven on stones upon his heart and shoulder for a memorial, Exod. 28. 11, 12, 21, 29. Ah! says the church, let my name be deeply engraven upon thy heart, let me be always

in thy eye, let me be always a memorial upon thy shoulder.

[3] Great men have their signets upon their hands as tokens of precious esteem: Jer. 22. 24, "As I live, saith the Lord, though Coniah the son of Jehoiakim king of Judah were the signet upon my right hand, yet would I pluck thee thence." Ah! says the spouse, Oh highly prize me, Lord Jesus! highly esteem of me; oh let me be as dear and precious unto thee as the signet that thou carriest about with thee, or as signets are to great men that wear them!

14. IT ENABLES THE BELIEVER TO COMMIT HIS ALL
TO CHRIST

Fourteenthly and lastly, That love that accompanies salvation, shews itself by enabling a true lover of Christ *to commit his richest treasures, his choicest jewels, to the care and custody of Christ.* Where we love we will trust, and as we love we will trust. Little trust bespeaks little love, great trust bespeaks great love. The lovers of Christ commend to Christ's care their pearls of greatest price, their names, their lives, their souls, their crowns, their innocency, their all. It was a notable saying of Luther, "Let him that died for my soul see to the salvation of it." Cæsar received not his wounds from the swords of enemies, but from the hands of friends, that is, from trusting in them. Oh, but the lovers of Christ shall never receive any wounds by trusting in Christ, by committing their choicest jewels to his care; for he hath a powerful hand and a wise and loving heart! Christ will hold fast whatever the Father or the saints put into his hand.

And thus I have shewed you what that love is that doth accompany salvation.

The things that accompany salvation: PRAYER

I come now, in the sixth place, to shew you what prayer that is that doth accompany salvation. But I see that I must contract what remains into a narrow room, lest I should tire out both the reader and myself, which, that I may not, I shall endeavour by divine assistance to mind brevity in what remains.

Now, that prayer doth accompany salvation, I have formerly shewed. Now I am briefly to shew you what prayer that is that doth accompany salvation, and that I shall do in these following particulars.

(1) *The requisites of prayer as a form of divine worship*

(1) *First, Prayer is a divine worship wherein we speak to God in faith, humility, sincerity, and fervency of spirit, through the medium of Christ, begging those good things that we and others want, deprecating what we and others fear, and giving thanks for what we and others have received.* Prayer is a speaking to God face to face; it is Jacob's ladder by which the soul climbs up to heaven; it is Noah's dove that goes and returns not till it brings assurance of peace.

But not to please you with notions, you must remember that that prayer that accompanies salvation is such prayer as hath in it all the requisites of prayer. Now there are four requisites in prayer.

[1] *The first requisite.* First, *The person must be righteous*: James 5. 16, "The fervent prayer of a righteous man availeth much"; John 9. 31, "God heareth not sinners." The Jews urge it as a proverb, An unclean person polluteth his own prayers. Good motions from a bad heart make no music in heaven; the sweet words that drop from deceitful lips are but lies in the account of God, Hosea 11. 12.

I have read of a jewel, that, being put in a dead man's mouth, it loseth all its virtue. Prayer in the mouth of a wicked man that is dead God-wards, Christ-wards, heaven-wards, and holiness-wards, is a jewel that loseth all its virtue: Ps. 50. 16, 17, "But unto the wicked God saith, What hast thou to do to declare my statutes, or that thou shouldest take my covenant into thy mouth? seeing that thou hatest instruction, and castest my words behind thee." Bias, an heathen, being at sea in a great storm, and perceiving many wicked wretches with him in the ship calling upon the gods, "Oh," saith he, "forbear prayer, hold your tongues; I would not have the gods take notice that you are here; they will sure drown us all, if they should." You are wise, and know how to apply it.

[2] *The second requisite.* The second requisite in prayer
258

is this, *The matter of your prayer must be good*: 1 John 5. 14, "And this is the confidence that we have in him, That if we ask anything according to his will, he heareth us." The favourites of heaven have no further the ear of the King of kings in prayer, than the matter of their prayer is good, and "agreeable to his will," Rom. 8. 27. The matter of your prayer must fall under some particular or general precept or promise, or else God will never own it nor honour it with acceptance. You must not pray as Augustine prayed before his conversion; he prayed for continency, with a proviso: "Lord, give me continency," saith he, "but not yet." Such hypocrisy is double iniquity, and God will deal with such sinners accordingly.

[3] *The third requisite.* Thirdly, as the matter of your prayer must be good, so *the manner of your prayer must be right*. God regards not so much the matter as the manner of our prayer. God loves not only that a man should pray, but that he should pray well; not only that he should do good, but that he should do it well.

Now for the better and further clearing of this truth, I shall shew you, by divine assistance, what it is to pray in the right manner, and this I shall do in the following particulars:

First, To pray in a right manner, is *to pray understandingly, to pray knowingly*: 1 Cor. 14. 15, "I will pray with understanding." He that doth not pray understandingly, doth not pray but prate; as that parrot in Rome that could distinctly say over the whole creed: John 4. 22, "Ye worship ye know not what," says Christ. So many pray they know not what. "Without knowledge the mind cannot be good," Prov. 19. 2. And can the prayer be good when the mind is bad? A blind mind, a blind sacrifice, a blind priest, are abominable to God. It was a good saying of one, "God heareth not the words of one that prayeth," saith he, "unless he that prayeth heareth them first himself." And, verily, God will never understand that prayer that we do not understand ourselves.

Secondly, To pray in a right manner, is *to pray believingly*: Heb. 11. 6, "He that cometh unto God, must believe that he is"; that is, that he is really as good, as gracious, as glorious, as excellent, and as constant, as his Word reports him to be; and that he is "a rewarder of them that diligently seek him." Mark 11. 24, "Therefore I say unto you, What things soever ye desire, when ye pray, believe that ye receive them, and ye shall have them." In the Greek the word is in the present tense, "ye do receive them," to shew the certainty of receiving them. You shall as certainly receive the good things that believingly you ask in prayer, as if you had them already in your hand. God will never let the hand of faith go empty away in prayer. Faith is God's darling, and he never fails to give it a worthy portion, a Benjamin's portion, a Hannah's portion, a double portion: James 1. 5-7, "If any of you lack wisdom, let him ask of God, that giveth to all men liberally, and upbraideth not; and it shall be given him. But let him ask in faith, nothing wavering: for he that wavereth is like a wave of the sea, driven with the wind, and tossed. For let not that man think that he shall receive anything of the Lord." He that prayeth doubtingly, shuts the gates of heaven against his own prayers.

It is reported in the life of Luther, that when he prayed it was *tanta reverentia ut si Deo, et tanta fiducia ut si amico,* with so much reverence, as if he were praying to God; and with so much boldness, as if he had been speaking to his friend. Faith in prayer makes a man divinely familiar and bold with God in prayer. That prayer that hath not the image and stamp of faith upon it, is no prayer in divine account. The sweetest flowers of paradise are only acceptable to God as they are tendered to him by the hand of faith.

When a poor man came to present a petition to the emperor Augustus with his hand shaking and trembling for fear, the emperor was much displeased, and said, "It is not fit that any should come with a petition to a king as if a man were giving meat to an elephant"; that is, afraid to be destroyed by him. Verily Jehovah loves to see every one of his petitioners come to him with a steadfast faith, and not with a trembling hand. Christ gets most glory, and the soul gets most good, by those prayers that are accompanied with the actings of faith.

Thirdly, To pray in a right manner, is *to pray intensely, fervently, earnestly.* So James 5. 16, "The effectual fervent prayer of a righteous man availeth much"; or, as the Greek hath it, "the working prayer," that is, such prayer as sets the whole man a-work. The word signifies such a working as denotes the liveliest activity that can be. As physic kills the body if it work not, so doth prayer the soul, if it be not working-prayer. As a painted fire is no fire, a dead man no man, so a cold prayer is no prayer. In a painted fire there is no heat; in a dead man there is no life; so in a cold prayer there is no omnipotency, no devotion, no blessing. It is not cold but working prayer that can lock up heaven three years, and open heaven's gate at pleasure, and bring down the sweetest blessings upon our heads, and the choicest favours into our hearts. Cold prayers are as arrows without heads, as swords without edges, as birds without wings: they pierce not, they cut not, they fly not up to heaven. Cold prayers do always freeze before they reach to heaven. So Jacob was earnest in his wrestling with God: "Let me alone," says God. "I will not let thee go except thou bless me," says Jacob, Gen. 32. 24-27. Jacob, though lamed and hard laid at, will not let the Lord go without a blessing. Jacob holds with his hands when his joints were out of joint, and so, as a prince, prevails with God. Jacob prays and weeps, and weeps and prays, and so prevails with God: Hosea 12. 4, "Yea, he had power over the angel, and prevailed: he wept and made supplication unto him." It is not the labour of the lips, but the travail of the heart; it is not the pouring forth of a flood of words, but the pouring out of the soul, that makes a man a prince, a prevailer with God. A man that would gain victory over God in prayer must strain every string of his heart; he must, in beseeching God, besiege him, and so get the better of him; he must strive in prayer even to an agony; he must be like importunate beggars, that will not be put off with frowns, or silence, or sad answers. Those that would be masters of their requests must with the importunate widow press God so far as to put him to the blush; they must with a holy impudence, as Basil speaks, make God ashamed to look them in the face, if he should deny the importunity of their souls. An importunate soul will never cease till he speed; he will devour all discouragements; yea, he will turn discouragements into encouragements, as the woman of Canaan did, till Christ says, "Be it unto thee, O soul, as thou wilt." As a body without a soul, much wood without fire, a bullet in a gun without powder, so are words in prayer without fervency of spirit. The hottest springs send forth their waters by boiling up.

I have read of one who, being sensible of his own dulness and coldness in prayer, chid himself thus: "What! dost thou think that Jonah prayed thus when he was in the belly of hell? or Daniel, when he was in the lions' den? or the thief, when he was upon the cross?" and I may add, or the three children, when they were in the fiery furnace? or the apostles, when they were in bonds and prisons? Oh! that Christians would chide themselves out of their cold prayers, and chide themselves into a better and a warmer frame of spirit when they make their supplications before the Lord. An importunate soul in prayer is like the poor beggar that prays and knocks, that prays and waits, that prays and works, that knocks and knits, that begs and patches, and will not stir from the door till he hath an alms. And verily he that is good at this will not be long a beggar in grace. God will make his heart and his cup to overflow.

Fourthly, To pray in a right manner, is, *to pray assiduously, constantly, as well as fervently.* Luke 18. 1, "And·he spake a parable unto them, to this end, that men ought always to pray, and not to faint"; or as it is in the Greek, not to "shrink back," as sluggards in work or cowards in war. Now men pray always, first, when their hearts are always prepared to pray, or in a praying frame; secondly, when they do not omit the duty when it is to be performed, or when they take hold on every opportunity to pour out their souls before the Lord. 1 Thes. 5. 17, "Pray without ceasing." A man must always pray habitually, though not actually; he must have his heart in a praying disposition in all estates and conditions, in prosperity and adversity, in health and sickness, in strength and weakness, in wealth and wants, in life and death. So in Eph. 6. 18, "Praying always with all prayer and supplication in the spirit, and watching thereunto with all perseverance, and supplication for all saints." Our daily weaknesses, our daily wants, our daily fears, our daily dangers, and our daily temptations, bespeak our daily prayers. Rom. 12. 12, "Rejoicing in hope, patient in tribulations, continuing instant in prayer"; this contains a metaphor taken from dogs that hunt, that will not give over the game till they have got it. A dog, of all creatures, is best able to endure hunger; he will run from place to place, and never leave off till he hath got his prey. So a child of God in his hunting after God, Christ, grace, peace, mercy, glory, never gives over till he hath found his heavenly prey. Song of Solomon, 3. 4, "At length I found him whom my soul loved; I held him, and would not let him go." The spouse never left hunting after her beloved till she had found him. Gracious souls reckon that they have nothing till they speed in the things they sue for; they pray as if they had never prayed, and think that they have done nothing till they have done the deed. It is observed by some of Proteus, the heathen sea-god, that he was wont to give certain oracles; but it was hard to make him speak and deliver them without his turning of himself into several shapes and forms; yet if they would hold out and press him hard without fear, into whatsoever form or shape he appeared, they were sure to have satisfactory oracles. So if we will continue constant in our wrestling with God for blessings, though God should appear unto us in the form or shape of a judge, an enemy, a stranger, &c., yet if we continue to press him hard for mercy, verily mercy will come in the long run, and we shall say, that it is not in vain for men to hold on praying, even though God for a time delays giving the particular favours they sue for. As that emperor said, *Oportet imperatorem stantem mori,* "it behoves an emperor to die standing," so may I say, *Oportet Christianum mori precantem,* it behoves a Christian to die praying.

Fifthly, To pray in a right manner, is *to pray sincerely*: Ps. 17. 1, "Give ear unto my prayer, that goeth not out of feigned lips"; or, as it is in the Hebrew, out of "lips of deceit." Ps. 145. 18, "The Lord is nigh unto all them that call upon him: to all that call upon him in truth." Your heart and tongue must go together; word and work, lip and life, prayer and practice must echo one to another, or all will be lost, heaven lost, and the soul lost for ever. It is not the greatness of the voice, nor the multitude of words, nor the sweetness of the tone, nor studied notions, nor eloquent expressions, that pleases Jehovah, but truth in the inward parts, Ps. 51. 6. When the Athenians inquired of the oracle the cause of their often unprosperous successes in battle against the Spartans, seeing they offered in sacrifice to the gods the choicest things they could get, which their enemies did not, the oracle gave them this answer, That the gods were better pleased with their inward supplication without ambition, than with all their outward pomp in costly sacrifices. Ah, souls! the reason why you are so unsuccessful in your religious duties and services is, that you are no more sincere and upright in them. Were there more singleness and sincerity of heart in your duties, you would have surer and sweeter returns from heaven.

It is reported of Joachim, the father of the Virgin Mary, that he would often say, *Cibus et potus mihi erit oratio,* "prayer is my meat and drink." Ah, Christians! the more sincere you are, the more will prayer be your meat and drink; and the more prayer is a delight and pleasure to you, the more will you be the pleasure and delight of God, who delights in those that delight in his service, and that count his work better than wages. It was more troublesome to Severus the emperor to be asked nothing, than to give much; when any one of his courtiers had not made bold with him, he would call him and say, *Quid est cur nihil petis?* "what meanest thou to ask me nothing?" So says Christ to upright souls: "Hitherto have ye asked nothing in my name; ask, and ye shall receive, that your joy may be full," John 16. 24. Christ hath a full purse, a noble heart, and a liberal hand.

[4] *The fourth requisite* in prayer is this, viz., your prayer must be directed *to a good end*; it must be to the glory of God, and to the internal and eternal advantage of your own and others' souls. The chiefest end, the target, the mark, at which the soul must aim in prayer, is God's glory: "What-

soever ye do, do all to the glory of God," 1 Cor. 10. 31.
When God crowns us, he doth but crown his own gifts in us;
and when we give God the glory of all we do, we do but give
him the glory that is due unto his name; for he works all
our works in us and for us. God measures all men's actions
by their ends: if their end be good, all is good; if the end be
naught, all is naught. The end determineth the action. All
actions of worship are good or bad, as the mark is at which
the soul aims. He that makes God the object of prayer, but
not the end of prayer, doth but lose his prayer, and take
pains to undo himself. God will be all in all, or he will be
nothing at all; he will be *Alexander* or *Nemo* (chief or
nothing). He will be both the object and the end of prayer,
or else he will abhor your prayer. Those prayers never reach
his ear, they are never lodged in his bosom, that are not
directed to his glory. The end must always be as noble as
the means, or else a Christian acts below himself, yea, below
his very reason.

Ah, Christians! it is not a flood of words, nor high strains
of wit, nor vehemency of affections in prayer, but holy and
gracious ends, that will render prayer acceptable and
honourable to God, comfortable and profitable to yourselves
and others; yea, the directing of one prayer to divine glory
doth more torture and torment Satan than all the prayers in
the world that are directed to ends below divine glory. It is
not simply prayer, but the soul's aiming at divine glory in
prayer, that adds to Christ's crown and Satan's hell.

And thus I have shewed you all the requisites of prayer,
even of such prayer as accompanies salvation. I shall now
proceed to some other particulars for the further and fuller
opening of this truth.

(2) *Prayer betters the whole man*

(2) *Secondly,* That prayer that accompanies salvation
betters the whole man. By it faith is increased, hope
strengthened, the spirit exhilarated, the heart pacified, the
conscience purified, temptations vanquished, corruptions
weakened, the affections inflamed, the will more renewed,
and the whole man more advantaged. Prayer is a spiritual

chair, wherein the soul sitteth down at the feet of the Lord, to receive the influences of his grace. Prayer is the regal gate by which the Lord entereth into the heart, comforting, quieting, strengthening, quickening, and raising of it. The Scripture affords us a cloud of witnesses to prove this truth, but I appeal to praying saints. Ah, tell me, tell me, praying souls, do not you find it so? I know you have done so, and do, and that is it that makes prayer a pleasure, a paradise unto you.

(3) *Eight differences between the prayers of the godly and those of the ungodly*

(3) *Thirdly,* You may judge what prayer that is that accompanies salvation *by considering the difference that is betwixt the prayers of the godly and those of the wicked.* Now the difference between the prayers of the one and the other I shall shew you in the following particulars.

The first difference. Gracious souls do trade and deal with God in prayer, only upon the account and credit of Christ. They beg mercy to pardon them, and grace to purge them, and balm to heal them, and divine favour to comfort them, and power to support them, and wisdom to counsel them, and goodness to satisfy them, but all upon the account of Christ's blood, of Christ's righteousness, of Christ's satisfaction, and of Christ's intercession at the right hand of the Father, Rev. 4. 10, 11. They seek the Father through the Son, they present their suits always in Christ's name, for so is the will of Christ: John 14. 13, 14, "And whatsoever ye shall ask in my name, that will I do, that the Father may be glorified in the Son. If ye shall ask anything in my name, I will do it." John 15. 16, "Whatsover ye shall ask of the Father in my name, he will give it you." Chap. 16. 23, "Verily I say unto you, whatsover ye shall ask the Father in my name, he will give it you." The Greek is pregnant, and may be read not only "Whatsover," but also "How many things soever ye shall ask or beg of the Father in my name, he will give them to you." There is no admission into heaven, except we bring Christ in our arms: Eph. 2. 18, "For through him we both have access by one Spirit

266

unto the Father." The Greek word signifies "a leading by the hand." It is an allusion to the custom of princes, into whose presence there is no admission, unless we be brought in by one of the favourites.

Plutarch reports that "It was wont to be the way of some of the heathens, the Molossians, when they would seek the favour of their prince, to take up the king's son in their arms, and to go and kneel before the king."

Ah, Christians! Christ is near and dear unto the Father; the Father hath determined to give out all his loves and favours through his Son; if you bring Christ in the arms of your faith, you gain the Father's heart, and in gaining his heart you gain all. The Father's mercies melt, his heart turns, his compassions are kindled, upon the sight of his Son's merits and mediation. As Joseph said to his brethren, "Ye shall not see my face unless you bring your brother Benjamin," so says God, You shall not see my face unless you bring the Lord Jesus with you.

Now, gracious souls, in all their prayers, present Jesus Christ before the Father, and upon his account they desire those things that make for their external, internal, and eternal good. Ah! but vain men treat and trade with God in prayer upon the account of their own worth, righteousness, worthiness and services: Isa. 58. 2, 3, "Yet they seek me daily, and delight to know my ways, as a nation that did righteousness, and forsook not the ordinance of their God. They ask of me the ordinances of justice, they take delight in approaching to God: Wherefore have we fasted, say they, and thou seest not? Wherefore have we afflicted our souls, and thou takest no knowledge?" Here you see they stand upon their own practices and services, and expostulate the case with God in an angry manner, because God did not answer their hypocritical performances. So the proud Pharisee stands in prayer upon his own worthiness and righteousness: Luke 18. 11, 12, "The Pharisee stood and prayed thus with himself: God, I thank thee, that I am not as other men are, extortioners, unjust, adulterers, or even as this publican. I fast twice in the week, I give tithes of all that I possess." So did those hypocrites in Mat. 6. 23 stand very much upon their outward services and performances, though they were but shining sins, but filthy rags.

The second difference. Souls truly gracious pray more *to get off their sins than they do to get off their chains.* Though bonds did attend Paul in every place, as he himself says, Acts 20. 23, yet he never cries out, O wretched man that I am, who shall deliver me from my bonds, but, " O wretched man that I am, who shall deliver me from my sins, from this body of death?" Rom. 7. 23. But wicked men strive in prayer more to get off their chains than to get off their sins; more to be delivered from enemies without than lusts within; more to get out of the furnace than to be delivered from their spiritual bondage, Ps. 78. 34; Zech. 7. 5-7; Isa. 26. 16, 17.

The third difference. The stream and cream of a gracious man's spirit runs most out in prayer after spiritual and heavenly things, as is abundantly evident by those prayers of the saints that are upon record throughout the Scripture, Ps. 4. 6, 7, and 27. 4; but the stream and cream of vain men's spirits in prayer runs most out after poor, low, carnal things, as you may see in comparing the following scriptures together, Hosea 7. 14; Zech. 7. 5-7; James 4. 3.

The fourth difference. A gracious soul *looks and lives more upon God in prayer than upon his prayer.* He knows, though prayer be his chariot, yet Christ is his food. Prayer may be a staff to support him, but Christ is that manna that must nourish him, and upon him he looks, and lives: Ps. 5. 3, " In the morning will I direct my prayer upon thee " (or " marshal and set in order my prayer," as it is in the Hebrew), " and will look up " (or "look out," as it is in the Hebrew) " as a watchman looks out to discover the approaches of an enemy." But vain men live and look more upon their prayers than they do upon God; nay, usually they never observe what returns they have from heaven. They are like those that shoot arrows, but do not mind where they fall. Wicked men think it is religion enough for them to pray; and to look after their prayers, to see how their prayers speed, is no article of their faith. But a gracious soul is of a more noble spirit; when he hath prayed he will stand upon his watch-tower, and observe what God will speak: Ps. 85. 8,

" I will hear what God the Lord will speak; I will listen, and lay my obedient ear to what the Lord shall speak; for he will speak peace unto his people, and to his saints: but let them not return to folly"; or, as the Hebrew may be read, "And they shall not return to folly." Wicked men would have God to be all ear to hear what they desire, when themselves have never an ear to hear what he speaks. But deaf ears shall always be attended with dumb answers. Justice always makes mercy dumb, when sin hath made the sinner deaf.

The fifth difference. No discouragements can take gracious souls off from prayer, but the least discouragement will take off carnal hearts from prayer, as you may see in the following scriptures compared together: Ps. 40. 1, 2, and 44. 10-23; Mat. 15. 21-29; Mal. 3. 14; Isa. 58. 1-3; Amos 8. 3-5.

When one of the ancient martyrs was terrified with the threatenings of his persecutors, he replied, " There is nothing," saith he, " of things visible, nothing of things invisible that I fear; I will stand to my profession of the name of Christ, and contend earnestly for the faith once delivered to the saints, come what will." It is neither the hope of life, nor the fear of death, that can take a real Christian off from prayer. He is rather raised than dejected, he is rather quickened than discouraged, by delays or denials; he will hold up and hold on in a way and course of prayer, though men should rage and lions roar, and the furnace be heated seven times hotter. But it is not so with carnal hearts, Job 27. 9, 10.

The sixth difference. When a gracious man prays, he hath his heart in his prayer; when he falls to prayer, he makes heartwork of it. So David, Ps. 42. 4, " When I remember these things, I pour out my heart." So Hannah, 1 Sam. 1. 15, " I am a woman of a sorrowful spirit," said she, " and have poured out my soul before the Lord." So the Israelites in 1 Sam. 7. 6, " pour out their souls like water before the Lord." So the church in Isa. 26. 8, 9, " The desire of our soul is to thy name, and to the remembrance of thee. With my soul have I desired thee in the night; yea, with my spirit within me will I seek thee early." Gracious souls know that no prayer is acknowledged, accepted, and rewarded by

269

God, but that wherein the heart is engaged sincerely and wholly. It is not a piece, it is not a corner of the heart, that will satisfy the maker of the heart. The true mother would not have the child divided. As God loves a broken and a contrite heart, so he loathes a divided heart. God neither loves halting nor halving; he wills to be served truly and totally. The royal law is, "Thou shalt love and serve the Lord thy God with all thy heart, and with all thy soul," Deut. 10. 12. Among the heathen, when the beasts were cut up for sacrifice, the first thing the priest looked upon was the heart, and if the heart was naught the sacrifice was rejected. Verily, God rejects all those sacrifices wherein the heart is not.

Now, wicked men are heartless in all their services, in all their prayers, as you may see in comparing the following scriptures together; I shall not transcribe the words, because I must cut short the work: Isa. 29. 13; Mat. 15. 7-9; Ezek. 33. 30-32; Zech. 7. 4-6; 2 Chron. 25. 1, 2. As the body without the soul is dead, so prayer, unless the heart be in it, is but dead prayer in the eye and account of God. Prayer is only lovely and weighty as the heart is in it, and no otherwise. It is not the lifting up of the voice, nor the wringing of the hands, nor the beating of the breasts, but the stirrings of the heart, that God looks at in prayer. God hears no more than the heart speaks; if the heart be dumb, God will certainly be deaf. No prayer takes with God but that which is the travail of the heart.

The seventh difference. Gracious souls usually come off from prayer with hearts more disengaged from sin, and more vehemently set against it. The precious communion that they have with God in prayer, the sweet breathings of God into their hearts, whilst they are a-breathing out their requests in his ears, and the secret assistance, stirrings, and movings of the Spirit upon their souls in prayer, arm them more against sin, and make them stand upon the highest terms of defiance with sin. How shall I do this or that wickedness against God? says the praying soul; Oh I cannot, I will not do anything unworthy of him that hath caused his glory to pass before me in prayer.

Ah! but wicked men come off from prayer with hearts more encouraged to sin, and more resolved to walk in ways of sin: Prov. 7. 14-24, "I have peace-offerings with me," saith the harlot; " this day have I paid my vows: therefore came I forth to meet thee, diligently to seek thy face, and I have found thee. Come, let us take our fill of love until the morning; let us solace ourselves with loves." So in Jer. 7. 9, 10, " Will ye steal, murder, and commit adultery, and swear falsely, and burn incense unto Baal, and walk after other gods whom ye know not; and come and stand before me in this house, which is called by my name, and say, We are delivered to do all these abominations?" Wicked men are like Louis, king of France, that would swear and then kiss the cross, and then swear more bitterly and then kiss the cross. So they sin and pray, and pray and sin; and the more they pray, the more easily, resolutely, impudently do they sin. They make use of prayer to charm their consciences, that so they may sin with more pleasure and less regret. Ah! what pains do such sinners take to go to hell, and to arm their consciences against themselves in that day, wherein they shall say, There is no help, there is no hope!

The eighth difference. Lastly, *Gracious souls do more eye and observe how their own hearts are wrought upon in prayer, than how others' hearts are wrought upon.* When they pray, they look with a curious eye upon their own spirits, they look with a narrow eye upon their own hearts, and observe how they are affected, melted, humbled, quickened, raised, spiritualised, and bettered by prayer. But vain men, as they pray to " be seen of men," so they eye most how others like their prayers, and are affected and taken with their prayers. They are most critical in observing what operations their prayers have upon others' hearts, but never mind, to any purpose, how they operate upon their own hearts; a worse plague cannot befall them, Mat. 6. 23.

And thus I have endeavoured to shew you what a wide difference there is betwixt the prayers of the godly and the ungodly; and by this, as by the former particulars laid down, you may see what prayer that is that accompanies salvation.

Now in the seventh place, I shall shew you what perseverance that is that accompanies salvation, and that I shall do
in these following particulars.

The properties of perseverance

1. PERSEVERANCE APPERTAINS TO A HOLY PROFESSION

(1) *First,* That perseverance that accompanies salvation, is
Perseverance in a holy profession. Heb. 4. 14, " Seeing then
that we have a great high priest, that is passed into the
heavens, Jesus the Son of God, let us hold fast our profession
by a strong hand," or " by a hand of holy violence." So in
chap. 10. 23, " Let us hold fast the profession of our faith
without wavering " (or as it is in the Greek, " without tilting, or tossing to one side or other "), " for he is faithful that
promised." The Greek signifies a forcible holding, a holding with both hands. Therefore let no temptation, affliction, opposition, or persecution, take us off from our holy
profession, but let us hold our profession with a forcible
hand, yea, with both hands, in the face of all difficulties,
dangers, and deaths, as Cynægirus, the Athenian captain,
did the ship that was laden with the rich spoil of his country.

2. IT APPERTAINS TO HOLY AND SPIRITUAL PRINCIPLES

(2) *Secondly,* That perseverance that accompanies salvation, is *a perseverance in holy and spiritual principles.* It is
an abiding in love, John 15. 9, 10; and an abiding in faith and
hope, 1 Cor. 13. 13. Perseverance is not a particular distinct
grace of itself; but such a virtue as crowns all virtue; it is
such a grace as casts a general glory and beauty upon every
grace; it is a grace that leads every grace on to perfection.

To persevere in holy and heavenly principles, is to persevere in believing, in repenting, in mourning, in hoping; it
is to persevere in love, in fear, in humility, in patience, in
self-denial. Now it is this perseverance in holy and gracious
principles that accompanies salvation, that leads to salvation. No grace, no, not the most sparkling and shining
grace, can bring a man to heaven of itself, without perse-

verance; not faith, which is the champion of grace, if it faint and fail; not love, which is the nurse of grace, if it decline and wax cold; not humility, which is the adorner and beautifier of grace, if it continue not to the end; not obedience, not repentance, not patience, nor any other grace, except they have their perfect work. It is perseverance in grace that crowns every grace and every gracious soul with a crown of glory at last. Rev. 2. 10, " Be thou faithful unto death, and I will give thee a crown of life." Such as only believe for a time, and repent for a time, and love for a time, and rejoice for a time, and hope for a time, as all hypocrites only do, but do not persevere and hold out, will be doubly miserable in the day of vengeance. Perseverance is the accomplishment of every grace; without it, he that fights cannot hope to overcome; and he that for the present doth overcome, cannot look for the crown, unless he still perseveres and goes on conquering and to conquer, till he finds all his enemies slain before him.

3. IT IS AN ABIDING IN THE DOCTRINE OF CHRIST

(3) *Thirdly,* That perseverance that accompanies salvation is *an abiding or continuing in the word or doctrine of Christ.* John 15. 7, " If ye abide in me, and my words abide in you, ye shall ask what you will, and it shall be done unto you." 1 John 2. 14, " I have written unto you, young men, because ye are strong, and the word of God abideth in you." Ver. 24, " Let that therefore abide in you which ye have heard from the beginning. If that which ye have heard from the beginning shall remain in you, ye also shall continue in the Son, and in the Father." 2 John 9, " Whosoever transgresseth, and abideth not in the doctrine of Christ, hath not God; he that abideth in the doctrine of Christ, he hath both the Father and the Son." None shall receive the end of their faith, the salvation of their souls, but those that hold fast the doctrine of faith, soundly, sincerely, and entirely to the end: John 8. 31, " If ye continue in my word, then are ye my disciples indeed." It is the end that crowns the action, as the evening crowns the day, as the last act commends the whole scene. It is not enough to begin well

except we end well; the beginning of Christians is not so considerable as the end. Manasseh and Paul began ill, but ended well; Judas and Demas began well, but ended ill. It is not the knowledge of the doctrine of Christ, nor the commending of the word of Christ, but the abiding in Christ's word, the continuing in Christ's doctrine, that accompanies life and glory, and that will render a man happy at last. Those who, with Hymenæus and Alexander, put away, or make shipwreck of the doctrine of faith, of the word of faith, shall, by the Lord or his people, or by both, be delivered unto Satan, that they may learn not to blaspheme, 1 Tim. 1. 19, 20; 1 Cor. 5. 5. Usually the end of such is worse than the beginning. Double damnation attends those that begin in the spirit and end in the flesh, 2 Pet. 2. 20-22; 2 Tim. 3. 13.

4. IT IS A CONTINUANCE IN GRACIOUS ACTIONS

(4) *Fourthly, and lastly,* That perseverance that accompanies salvation is a perseverance *in holy and gracious actions and motions; it is a continuing in pious duties and religious services,* Philip. 3. 10-14; Isa. 40. 31. The life of a Christian consists in motion, not in sitting. A Christian's emblem should be an house moving towards heaven; he must never stand still, he must always be a-going on from faith to faith, and from strength to strength. When saints have done their work in this life, they shall sit upon thrones in a better life. Perseverance is a going on, a holding out in ways of piety and sanctity: Acts 1. 14, " These all continued with one accord in prayer and supplication. Chap. 2. 42, "And they continued steadfastly in the apostles' doctrine and fellowship, and in breaking of bread, and in prayers." Ver. 46, " And they continuing daily with one accord in the temple, and breaking bread from house to house, did eat their meat with gladness and singleness of heart." 1 Tim. 5. 5, " Now she that is a widow indeed, and desolate, trusteth in God, and continueth in supplications and prayers night and day." Rom. 12. 12, " Continuing instant in prayer." Christians must work hard in a wilderness before they sit down in paradise. They must make a constant progress in holiness before they enter into happiness. It is the excel-

lency of perseverance, that it keeps a Christian still in motion God-wards, heaven-wards, holiness-wards. It is a grace that quickens a man to motion, to action; it keeps a man always going, always doing. And motion is the excellency of the creature; and the more excellent any creature is, the more excellent is that creature in its motions, as you may see in the motions of the celestial bodies, the sun, moon, and stars. Perseverance is a perpetual motion in ways of grace and holiness, Ps. 44. 16-20. Perseverance will make a man hold up and hold on in the work and ways of the Lord, in the face of all impediments, discouragements, temptations, tribulations, and persecutions. As the moon holds on her motion though the dogs bark, so perseverance will make a Christian hold on in his holy and heavenly motions though vain men bark and bite.

And thus I have shewed you what perseverance that is that accompanies salvation.

The things that accompany salvation: HOPE

Now in the eighth place I shall shew very briefly,
(1) That hope doth accompany salvation.
(2) What that hope is that doth accompany salvation.
(3) What are the properties of hope.

The nature of hope

1. *That hope doth accompany salvation, these scriptures plainly shew:* Rom. 8. 24, "For we are saved by hope"; Gal. 5. 5, "For we through the Spirit wait for the hope of righteousness by faith"; Eph. 1. 18, "The eyes of your understanding being enlightened; that ye may know what is the hope of his calling, and what the riches of the glory of his inheritance in the saints"; 1 Thes. 5. 8, "But let us, who are of the day, be sober, putting on the breastplate of faith and love, and for an helmet the hope of salvation"; Titus 3. 7, "That, being justified by his grace, we should be made heirs according to the hope of eternal life"; Chap. 1. 2, "In hope of eternal life, which God, that cannot lie, promised before the world began."

By all these scriptures it doth fully appear, that hope doth accompany salvation; it doth border upon eternal life.

Hope expects and waits patiently for promised good

2. The second thing that I am to shew you is, *what hope that is that doth accompany salvation,* that comprehends salvation; and that I shall do with as much brevity and perspicuity as I can, in the following particulars:

First, That hope that accompanies salvation *is a grace of God whereby we expect good to come, waiting patiently till it come.*

(1) I call it a grace of God, because he is the *donor of it*; and therefore he is called the God of hope: Rom. 15. 13, "Now the God of hope fill you with all joy and peace in believing." God is called the God of hope, because he is the only object of our hope, and the only author and worker of hope in the soul. Hope is no natural affection in men. Men are not born with hope in their hearts, as they are born with tongues in their mouths. Hope is nobly descended; it is from above; it is a heavenly babe that is formed in the soul of man by the power of the Holy Ghost. And as hope is not a natural affection, so hope is not a moral virtue, which men may attain by their frequent actions; but hope is the theological virtue that none can give but God.

(2) I say it is a grace of God, whereby we expect *good* to come; I say good, not evil, for evil is rather feared than hoped for by any.

The object of this hope hath four qualities: it must be a good hope, it must be a thing of the future, it must be possible, and it must be difficult to obtain.

(3) I say hope is a grace of God, whereby we expect good *to come,* patiently waiting till it come. Hope makes the soul quiet and patient till it comes to possess the good desired and hoped for: Rom. 8. 25, "But if we hope for that we see not, then do we with patience wait for it." The Hebrew word that is often translated "hope," signifies a very vehement intention, both of body and mind, a stretching forth of the spirit or mind, in waiting for a desired good.

2. Secondly, That hope that accompanies salvation *is*

always conversant about holy and heavenly objects, as about God and Christ: 1 Tim. 1. 1, "Paul an apostle of Jesus Christ, by the commandment of God our Saviour, and Lord Jesus Christ, which is our hope." In these words, Christ is set forth as the chief object of our hope, because by his merits and mercy, we hope to obtain the remission of our sins, and the eternal salvation of our souls. Sometimes hope is exercised about the righteousness of Christ: Gal. 5. 5, "For we through the Spirit wait for the hope of righteousness by faith." Sometimes hope is exercised about God the Father: 1 Pet. 1. 21, "Who by him do believe in God, that raised him up from the dead, and gave him glory; that your faith and hope might be in God"; Jer. 14. 8, "Oh, the hope of Israel, the Saviour thereof in the time of trouble"; Chap. 17. 13, "O Lord, the hope of Israel, all that forsake thee shall be ashamed"; ver. 17, "Thou art my hope in the day of evil." Sometimes hope is exercised and busied about the Word and promises: Ps. 119. 49, "Remember the word unto thy servant, upon which thou hast caused me to hope"; ver. 81, "My soul fainteth for thy salvation; but I hope in thy word"; ver. 114, "Thou art my hiding-place, and my shield: I hope in thy word"; Ps. 130. 5, "I wait for the Lord, my soul doth wait, and in his word do I hope"; Ps. 119. 74, "They that fear thee will be glad when they see me; because I have hoped in thy word"; ver. 147, "I prevented the dawning of the morning, and cried: I hoped in thy word." Hope in the promise will keep the head from aching, and the heart from breaking; it will keep both head and heart from sinking and drowning. Hope exercised upon the promise brings heaven down to the heart. The promises are the ladder by which hope gets up to heaven. Hope in the promise will not only keep life and soul together, but will also keep the soul and glory together; hope in the promise will support distressed souls; hope in the promise will settle perplexed souls; hope in the promise will comfort dejected souls; hope in the promise will restore wandering souls; hope in the promise will confirm staggering souls; hope in the promise will save undone souls. The promise is to hope as hope is to the soul; the promise is the anchor of hope, as hope is the anchor of the soul. Look, what the breasts are to the child, and oil is to the lamp, that the promises are to hope, Rom. 8. 24. Hope lives and thrives, as it feeds upon the promises, as it embraces the promises. The promises are the sweetmeats of heaven, upon which hope lives. And every degree of hope brings a degree of joy into the soul, which makes it cry out, Heaven, heaven, Heb. 11. 13; Ps. 16. 11; Titus 3. 7.

Again, hope is exercised about the glory and felicity, the happiness and blessedness, that is at God's right hand. Titus 2. 13, " Looking for that blessed hope, and the glorious appearing of the great God, and our Saviour Jesus Christ. Hope makes a man stretch out his neck and put forth his hand, and look as earnestly for the glorious appearing of Christ as Sisera's mother did for the happy return of her son. The hoping soul is often a-sighing out, " Why are his chariot wheels so long a-coming?" Col. 1. 5, " For the hope which is laid up for you in heaven." Hope in this place is taken, by a metonymy, for the things hoped for, viz., all that glory and felicity, that blessedness and happiness, that is laid up for us in heaven. So in Rom. 8. 24, 25; Col. 1. 27; Rom. 5. 2. So too, in Heb. 6. 18, " Who have fled for refuge to lay hold upon the hope set before us." Hope here is put for the object of hope, viz., heaven and happiness. Hope lays such fast hold, as the Greek word here signifies, upon heaven and happiness, that none shall ever be able to take those precious things out of hope's hand. So hope is put for the glorious things hoped for, Eph. 1. 18. And thus you see those precious and glorious objects, about which that hope that accompanies salvation is exercised.

3. Thirdly, The hope that accompanies salvation, that comprehends salvation, that borders upon salvation, *is grounded upon the firmest foundations, to wit, the promises of God*, Prov. 10. 28, as hath been fully shewed before; and it is built upon the free grace of God, 1 Peter 1. 13. It is built upon the infinite and glorious power of God, Rom. 4. 21. It is built upon the truth and faithfulness of God, 2 Tim. 2. 13. These precious and glorious foundations do bear up the hopes of the saints, as the pillars bore up the

hangings in the tabernacle. A believer's hope is founded upon the love of Christ, the blood of Christ, the righteousness of Christ, the satisfaction of Christ, and the intercession of Christ; but the hopes of hypocrites and wicked men, are always built upon weak, slender, and sandy foundations. Sometimes they build their hopes upon their outward profession, upon their having lamps, though they are empty lamps, Mat. 25. 3; and sometimes upon their duties and services, as the Jews, scribes, and Pharisees did, Isa. 58. 1-3; Mat. 6. 1, 2; and sometimes upon their outward privileges, crying out, "The temple of the Lord, the temple of the Lord are we"; and sometimes they build their hopes upon others' good opinion of them and sometimes upon flashes of joy, and sometimes upon enlargements in duties, and sometimes upon the heat and vigour of their spirits in religious services, &c. All these are but sandy foundations, and they that build their hope upon them will certainly fall, and great will be their fall. The hopes of the saints are built upon the surest and the strongest foundations. It was a good saying of one of the ancients; "I consider," said he, "three things in which all my hope consisteth, to wit, 1, God's love in my adoption; 2, the truth of his promise; and 3, his power of performance. Therefore, let my foolish cogitation murmur as long as it list, saying, Who art thou? or, What is that glory? or, By what merits dost thou hope to attain it? For I can answer with sure confidence, I know whom I have believed, 2 Tim. 1. 12. And I am certain, first, that in his love he adopted me; secondly, that he is true in his promise; and thirdly, that he is able to perform it. This is the threefold cord which is not easily broken." (Bernard.)

The properties of hope

3. The third thing I am to shew is what are the properties of hope. That hope that accompanies salvation, that borders upon salvation, that comprehends salvation, that brings salvation, may be known from all false hopes, *by the excellent properties of it,* and they are these that follow.

1. IT RAISES THE HEART TO LIVE ABOVE

[1] *The first property* of that hope that accompanies salvation is this: *it elevates and raises the heart to live above, where its treasure is.* This hope is from above, and it makes the heart to live above: it is a spark of glory, and it leads the heart to live in glory. Divine hope carries a man to heaven, for life to quicken him, and for wisdom to direct him, and for power to uphold him, and for righteousness to justify him, and for holiness to sanctify him, and for mercy to forgive him, and for assurance to rejoice him, and for happiness to crown him. Divine hope takes in the pleasures of heaven beforehand; it lives in the joyful expectation of them. It fancies to itself, as I may say, the pleasures and joys of eternity, and lives in a sweet anticipation of what it possesseth by faith. Hope's richest treasures, and choicest friends, and chiefest delights, and sweetest contents, are in the country above; and therefore hope loves best to live there most.

2. IT STRENGTHENS THE SOUL AGAINST AFFLICTIONS AND TEMPTATIONS

[2] *The second property* of that hope that accompanies salvation is this: *it will strengthen the soul against all afflictions, oppositions, and temptations*: 1 Thes. 5. 8, "But let us, who are of the day, be sober, putting on the breastplate of faith and love, and for an helmet, the hope of salvation." Look, as the helmet defends and secures the head, so doth hope defend and secure the heart. Hope is a helmet that keeps off all darts that Satan or the world casts at the soul. The hopes of heavenly riches made those worthies in Heb. 11 to despise the riches of this world. The hopes they had of a heavenly country made them willing to leave their own country, and to live in the very land of promise as in a strange country. The hopes they had of possessing at last a house not made with hands, but eternal in the heavens, made them willingly and cheerfully to live in deserts, and in mountains, and in dens, and caves of the earth. The hopes they had of a glorious resurrection made them courageously

to withstand the strongest temptations, Rom. 5. 2-5. A saint's hope will outlive all fears and cares, all trials and troubles, all afflictions and temptations. Saints have much in hope, though little in hand; they have much in reversion, though but little in possession; they have much in promise, though but little in the purse. A saint can truly say, *Spero meliora,* "I hope for better things"; "my hopes are better than my possessions." Hope can see heaven through the thickest clouds; hope can see light through darkness, life through death, smiles through frowns, and glory through misery. Hope holds life and soul together; it holds Christ and the soul together; it holds the soul and the promises together; it holds the soul and heaven together; and so it makes a Christian to stand and triumph over all afflictions, oppositions, and temptations.

3. IT MAKES THE SOUL LIVELY AND ACTIVE

[3] *The third property* of that hope that accompanies salvation is this: *it makes the soul lively and active*: Ps. 119. 166, "Lord, I have hoped for thy salvation, and done thy commandments." Hope puts the soul upon doing, upon obeying: 1 Pet. 1. 3, "Blessed be the God and Father of our Lord Jesus Christ, which, according to his abundant mercy, hath begotten us again unto a lively hope, by the resurrection of Jesus Christ from the dead." It is called a lively hope, because it brings life and comfort into the soul; it is called a lively hope in opposition to the withering and dying hopes of hypocrites and wicked men; it is called a lively hope, because it flows from lively causes, viz. the Spirit of Christ, and the soul's union and communion with Christ; but mainly it is called a lively hope because it puts the soul upon lively endeavours. Hope will make a man pray as for life, hear as for life, mourn as for life, obey as for life, and work and walk as for life. Hope will not say this work is too hard, and that work is too hot; this work is too high, and the other work is too low. Hope will make a man put his hand to every work. Hope makes a man more motion than notion; it makes a man better at doing than at saying. Hope gives life and strength to all religious duties and ser-

vices: 1 Cor. 9. 10, "He that plougheth should plough in hope; and he that thresheth in hope shall be partaker of his hope." Hope will put a Christian upon ploughing and threshing, that is, upon the hardest and most difficult services for God and his glory. If fleshly hopes of gaining the honours, riches, and favours of this world made Absalom, Ahithophel, Jehu, Haman, and many heathens, full of life and activity, full of motion and action, verily holy and heavenly hopes will make men much more lively and active, by how much heavenly hopes are more excellent than earthly. A man full of hope will be full of action. A lively hope and a diligent hand are inseparable companions. Hope will make a man do though he dies for doing.

4. IT GIVES THE BELIEVER GREAT QUIETNESS

[4] *The fourth property* of that hope that accompanies salvation is this: *It will make a man sit, Noah-like, quiet and still in the midst of all storms and tempests, in the midst of all commotions, concussions, and mutations.* When others are at their wits' end, then hope will house the soul, and lodge it fair and quiet in the bosom of God: Job 11. 18, "And thou shalt be secure, because there is hope: yea, thou shalt dig about thee, and thou shalt take thy rest in safety." The Hebrew word that is here rendered *rest*, is from a root that signifies to rest and sleep quietly, as in one's bed. Hope will bring the soul to bed safely and sweetly, in the darkest night, in the longest storm, and in the greatest tempest: Heb. 6. 19, "Which hope we have as an anchor of the soul, both sure and stedfast, and which entereth into that within the veil." Hope is that anchor of the soul, that keeps it quiet and still in all storms and tempests; it keeps the soul from dashing upon the rocks, and from being swallowed up in the sands. Hope is an anchor that is fastened above, not below; in heaven, not in earth; within the veil, not without; therefore the ship, the soul of a believer, must needs be safe and secure. That ship will never be split upon the rocks, whose anchor is in heaven. Hope enters within the veil, and takes fast anchor-hold on God himself; and therefore blow high, blow low, rain or shine,

7. IT NEVER DIES

[7] *The seventh property* of that hope that accompanies salvation, and that comprehends salvation, is this: *it is permanent and lasting; it will never leave the soul till it hath lodged it in the bosom of Christ.* Prov. 14. 32, " The righteous hath hope in his death." The righteous man's hope will bed and board with him; it will lie down with him, and rise up with him; it will go to the grave, and to heaven with him: his motto is, *Cum expiro spero,* when I breathe my last, I hope.

The Jews' ancient custom was, as they went by the way with a corpse to burial, to pluck up every one the grass, as though they would say they were not sorrowing as men without hope, for their brother was but so cropped off, and should spring up again in the morning of the resurrection. And the Jews to this very day do not hesitate to call their sepulchres the houses or places of the living.

That hope that accompanies salvation is a long-lived hope; it is a living hope. 1 Pet. 1. 3, " Blessed be the God and Father of our Lord Jesus Christ, which, according to his abundant mercy, hath begotten us again unto a lively hope," or a living hope: a hope that will not die, a hope that will not leave a man in life nor death. Ps. 71. 14, " But I will hope continually, and will yet praise thee more and more." No trials, no troubles, no afflictions, no oppositions, shall keep down my hope, says David. I am resolutely resolved, in the face of all dangers, difficulties, and deaths, to keep up my hopes; come what will, I will rather let my life go than my hope go: I will hope continually. A hopeless condition is a very sad condition; it is the worst condition in the world; it makes a man's life a very hell. If " hope deferred maketh the heart sick," as the wise man speaks, Prov. 13. 12, then the loss of hope will make the soul languish, it will make it choose strangling rather than life; it will make a man's life a continual death. A soul without hope is like a ship without anchors. Lord, where will a soul stay that stays not upon thee by hope? A man had better part with anything than his hope.

When Alexander went upon a hopeful expedition, he gave away his gold; and when he was asked what he kept for himself, he answered, *Spem majorum et meliorum,* the hope of greater and better things. A believer's hope is not like that of Pandora, which may fly out of the box, and bid the soul an everlasting farewell. No; it is like the morning light; the least beam of it shall shortly yield to a complete sunshine. It is *aurora gaudii,* the dawn of joy, and it shall shine forth brighter and brighter till it hath given the believer full possession of his Christ and crown. This will be the hypocrite's hell and horror when he comes to die, that his hope will be like the morning dew, like the spider's web, like the crackling of thorns under a pot, and like the giving up of the ghost, Job. 8. 13, 14, and 11. 20, and 27. 8; Prov. 14. 32, and 11. 7. And this is now the upright man's joy, that whoever and whatever leaves him, yet his hope will not leave him, till he hath put on his crown and is set down in paradise. And thus you see what hope that is that doth accompany salvation. Before I close this chapter, take these two cautions with you; they will make for your comfort and settlement.

[1] *The first caution* is this: *that all saints have not these things that accompany salvation in the same degree.* If thou hast the least measure or degree of that knowledge that accompanies salvation, or of that faith that accompanies salvation, or of that repentance, or of that obedience, or of that love, that accompanies salvation, thou mayest be as assuredly confident of thy salvation, as if thou wast already in heaven. The least degree, O Christian, of those things that accompany salvation, will certainly yield thee a heaven hereafter, and why then should it not yield thee a heaven here? It will undoubtedly yield thee a crown at last; and why should it not yield thee comfort and assurance now? I judge it may, if thou art not an enemy to thine own soul, and to thy own peace and comfort.

[2] *The second caution* is this: *Though thou dost not find every one of those things in thee that do accompany salvation, yet if thou dost find some of those things, aye, though but a few of those things, yea, though but one of*

those things that accompanies salvation, that comprehends salvation, that borders upon salvation, thy estate is safe, and happiness will be thy portion at last. Thy sense and feeling of one of those precious things that accompanies salvation, should be of more power to enable thee to conclude that thy estate is good, than any other thing should enable thee to conclude that all is naught, and that thou shalt miscarry at last. Do not always side with sin and Satan against thine own precious soul.

Having thus opened up to you the way and means of attaining to a well-grounded assurance, I shall now hasten to a close.

CHAPTER VI

The differences between a true and a counterfeit assurance, between sound assurance and presumption.

A well-grounded assurance bears these following marks

1. IT IS ATTENDED BY A DEEP ADMIRATION OF GOD'S LOVE
AND FAVOUR IN CHRIST

(1) *The first difference.* A sound and well-grounded assurance *is attended with a deep admiration of God's transcendent love and favour to the soul in the Lord Jesus.* The assured soul is often a-breathing it out thus: Ah, Lord! who am I, what am I, that thou shouldst give into my bosom the white stone of absolution, when the world hath given into their bosoms only the black stone of condemnation? Rev. 2. 17. Lord! what mercy is this, that thou shouldst give me assurance, give me water out of the rock, and feed me with manna from heaven, when many of thy dearest ones spend their days in sighing, mourning and complaining for want of assurance. Lord! what manner of love is this, that thou shouldst set me upon thy knee, embrace me in thy arms, lodge me in thy bosom, and kiss me with the sweet kisses of thy blessed mouth, with those kisses that are " better than wine," Song of Solomon 1. 2, yea, better than life, when many are even weary of their lives because they lack what I enjoy? Ps. 63. 3. Ah, Lord! by what name shall I call this mercy, this assurance that thou hast given me? it being a mercy that fits me to do duties, to bear crosses, and to make the best use of mercies; that fits me to speak sweetly, to judge righteously, to give liberally, to act seriously, to suffer cheerfully, and to walk humbly. I cannot, says the assured soul, but sing it out with Moses, " Who is like unto thee, O Lord, amongst the gods? Who is like thee, glorious in holiness, fearful in praises, doing wonders?" Exod. 15. 2. And with the apostle, " Oh, the height, the depth, the length and breadth of the love of Christ, which passeth knowledge,"

Eph. 3. 18, 19. If the queen of Sheba, says the assured soul, was so swallowed up in a deep admiration of Solomon's wisdom, greatness, goodness, excellency and glory, that she could not but admiringly breathe it thus out, " Happy are thy men, happy are these thy servants, which stand continually before thee, and that hear thy wisdom," 1 Kings 10. 8, Oh then, how should that blessed assurance that I have of the love of God, of my interest in God, of my union and communion with God, of my blessedness here and my happiness hereafter, work me to a deep and serious, to a real and perpetual, admiration of God.

2. IT CAUSES THE SOUL EVER TO SEEK A FULLER ENJOYMENT OF GOD AND CHRIST

(2) *The second difference.* Secondly, A well-grounded assurance doth always *beget in the soul an earnest and an impatient longing after a further, a clearer, and fuller enjoyment of God and Christ.* Ps. 63. 1, " O God, thou art my God "—here is assurance; well, what follows?—" early will I seek thee. My soul thirsteth for thee; my flesh longeth for thee in a dry and thirsty land, where no water is." The assured soul cries out, " I desire to be dissolved, and to be with Christ," Philip. 1. 23; and " Make haste, my beloved," Song of Solomon 8. 14; and, " Come, Lord Jesus, come quickly," Rev. 22. 17. O Lord Jesus, says the assured soul, thou art my light, thou art my life, thou art my love, thou art my joy, thou art my crown, thou art my heaven, thou art my all. I cannot but long to see that beautiful face that was spit upon for my sins, and that glorious head that was crowned with thorns for my transgressions. I long to take some turns with thee in paradise, to see the glory of thy Jerusalem above, to drink of those rivers of pleasures that be at thy right hand, to taste of all the delicacies of thy kingdom, to be acquainted with those secrets and mysteries that have been hid from all ages, and to be swallowed up in the full enjoyment of thy blessed self, Eph. 3. 5; Col. 1. 26.

3. IT IS USUALLY STRONGLY ASSAULTED BY SATAN

(3) *The third difference.* Thirdly, A well-grounded

assurance *is usually strongly assaulted by Satan on all sides.* Satan is such a grand enemy to the joy and peace, to the salvation and consolation, of the saints, that he cannot but make use of all his devices and stratagems to amaze and amuse, to disturb and disquiet, the peace and rest of their souls. No sooner had Jesus Christ heard that lovely voice from heaven, "This is my beloved Son, in whom I am well pleased," Mat. 3. 17 and 4. 1, 2, but he was desperately assaulted by Satan in the wilderness. No sooner was Paul dropped out of heaven, after he had seen visions of glory that were unutterable, but he was immediately assaulted and buffeted by Satan, 2 Cor. 12. 7. Stand up, stand up, assured Christians, and tell me whether you have not found the blast of the terrible one to be as a storm against the wall, Isa. 25. 4. Since the Lord said unto you, "Be of good cheer, your sins are forgiven you," have not you found Satan to play the part both of the lion and the wolf, both of the serpent and the fox? And all to weaken your assurance, and to cause you to question the truth of your assurance, and to cast water upon your assurance, and to take off the freshness and sweetness, the beauty and glory, of your assurance; I know you have. His malice, envy, and enmity is such against God's honour and glory, and your comfort and felicity, that he cannot but be very studious and industrious to make use of all traps, snares, methods, and ways whereby he may shake the pillars of your faith, and weaken and overthrow your assurance. Pirates, you know, do most fiercely assault those ships and vessels that are most richly laden; so doth Satan those precious souls that have attained to the riches of full assurance.

Assurance makes a paradise in believers' souls, and this makes Satan to roar and rage. Assurance fits a man to do God the greatest service and Satan the greatest dis-service, and this makes him mad against the soul. Assurance makes a saint to be too hard for Satan at all weapons, yea, to lead that "son of the morning" captive, to spoil him of all his hurting power, to bind him in chains, and to triumph over him; and this makes his hell a great deal hotter, Rom. 8. 32-39. And therefore never wonder at Satan's assaulting your assurance, but expect it and look for it. The jailor is quiet when his prisoner is behind bolts, but if he be escaped then he pursues him with hue and cry. So long as the soul is behind bolts and in bondage under Satan, Satan is quiet and is not so apt to molest and vex it; but when once a soul is made free, and assured of his freedom by Christ, John 8. 36, then says Satan, as once Pharaoh did, " I will arise, I will pursue, I will overtake, I will divide the spoil; my lust shall be satisfied upon them; I will draw my sword, my hand shall destroy them," Exod. 15. 9. The experience of all assured saints doth abundantly confirm this. Israel going into Egypt had no enemies, no opposition, but travelling to Canaan they were never free.

4. IT MAKES A BELIEVER BOLD

(4) *The fourth difference.* Fourthly, A well-grounded assurance *makes a man as bold as a lion; it makes him valiant and gallant for Christ and his cause, in the face of all dangers and deaths.* After the Holy Ghost was fallen upon the apostles, and had assured them of their internal and eternal happiness, oh! how bold, how undaunted, how resolute were they in the face of all oppositions, afflictions, and persecutions! as you may see from the second of the Acts of the Apostles to the end of the Acts. Assurance had this same operation upon David's heart: Ps. 23. 4, 6 compared, " Surely goodness and mercy shall follow me all the days of my life." Well, David, but how doth this assurance of yours operate? Why, saith he, " Though I walk through the valley of the shadow of death, I will fear no evil." So it was with Moses. Having an assurance of the " recompense of the reward," he fears not the wrath of the king, " for he endured, as seeing him who is invisible," Heb. 11. 26, 27. So in Heb. 10. 34, "And ye took joyfully the spoiling of your goods, knowing in yourselves that ye have in heaven a better and an enduring substance." The knowledge and assurance that they had in their own hearts of enjoying in heaven a better and a more enduring substance, made them bear cheerfully and gallantly the spoiling of their worldly goods. Though the archers—the world, the flesh, and the

devil—do shoot sore at a soul under assurance, yet his bow will still abide in strength. Assurance will make a man to break a bow of steel, to trample down strength, and to triumph over all oppositions and afflictions.

Colonus the Dutch martyr called to the judge that had sentenced him to death, and desired him to lay his hand upon his heart, and asked him whose heart did most beat, his or the judge's. Assurance will make a man do this, and much more for Christ and his cause.

5. IT MAKES A BELIEVER SEEK THE HAPPINESS OF OTHER MEN

(5) *The fifth difference.* Fifthly, A well-grounded assurance of a man's own eternal happiness and blessedness will *make him very studious and laborious to make others happy*: Ps. 66. 16, "Come and hear, all ye that fear God, and I will tell you what he hath done for my soul." I will acquaint you with the soul blessings, with the soul favours, that God hath crowned me with. I was darkness, but he hath made me light; I was unrighteousness, but he hath made me righteous; I was deformed, but he hath made me complete; I was full of sores, and spots, and blemishes, but he hath washed me, and made me all fair, without spot or wrinkle. I have found my lack of assurance, I now see the worth of assurance; I have long sought assurance, and now I find the sweetness of assurance. Ah! it is such a pearl of price, it is such a beam of God, it is such a spark of glory, that makes my soul a rich amends for all its waiting, weeping, and wrestling.

So, when it pleased God to call Paul by his grace, and to reveal Christ in him and to him, ah! how doth he labour, as for life, to bring others to an acquaintance with Christ, and to an acceptance of Christ, and to an assurance of everlasting happiness and blessedness by Christ! After Paul had been in paradise, he makes it his all to bring others to paradise, 2 Cor. 12. So the spouse in the Song of Solomon, having assurance of her interest in Christ, how doth she labour, by all holy and heavenly rhetoric and logic, by all the strains of love and sweetness, to draw the daughters of Jerusalem to a sight of Christ! Song of Solomon 5. 10-16, and 6. 1, &c. When a beam of divine light and love had shone upon Andrew, he labours to draw his brother Simon to the fountain of all light and love, John 1. 40-42. And when Philip had but a glance of Christ's countenance, his pulse beats, and his heart calls upon Nathanael to come and share with him in that loving-kindness that was better than life, John 1. 43-47.

The constant cry of souls under the power of assurance is, "Come, taste and see how good the Lord is," Ps. 34. 8. Ah, sinners, sinners! " his ways are ways of pleasantness, and all his paths are peace," Prov. 3. 17; his "commands are not grievous," 1 John 5. 3, but joyous; "his yoke is easy, and his burden is light," Mat. 11. 30; not only *for* keeping, but also *"in* keeping of his commands there is great reward," Ps. 19. 11. Assurance will strongly put men upon the winning of others by counsel, by example, by prayer. and by communicating their spiritual experiences to them. Assurance will furnish a man with will, skill, and experience to confute all those false reports that vain men frequently cast upon the Lord and his ways. It will make a man proclaim to the world "that one day in the Lord's courts is better than a thousand years elsewhere," Ps. 84. 10; that there are more glorious joys, more pure comforts, more abiding peace, more royal contents, more celestial delights, in one day's walking with God, in one hour's communion with God, than is to be found in all things below God. And by these and such like ways, souls under the power of a well-grounded assurance endeavour to make others happy with themselves. A soul under assurance is unwilling to go to heaven without company. He is often a-crying out, Father, bless this soul too, and crown that soul too: let us to heaven together, let us be made happy together.

6. IT STRENGTHENS A BELIEVER AGAINST ALL SIN

(6) *The sixth difference.* Sixthly, A well-grounded assurance of God's love, and of a man's everlasting happiness and blessedness, *will exceedingly arm and strengthen him against all wickedness and baseness,* Ezek. 16. 60-63. No man loathes sin, and himself for sin, as such a man; no man wars and

watches against sin more than such a man; no man sighs and mourns, bleeds and complains, under the sense of sinful motions and sinful operations more than such a man, Luke 7. 44, 50. Every stirring of sin makes a man that is under the power of assurance to cry out, " O wretched man that I am, who shall deliver me from this body of death?" Rom. 7. 22-25 : Ps. 85. 8, " I will hear what God the Lord will speak; for he will speak peace unto his people, and to his saints : and let them not turn again to folly," or, as the Hebrew will bear, " And they shall not return to folly." God's speaking peace to his people fences and fortifies them against folly and vanity.

The assurance that Joseph had of his master's love armed him against the lascivious assaults of his lustful mistress; and will not divine love, that is stronger than death, do this and more? Song of Solomon 8. 6, 7. Assurance makes a man say to his sins, as he to his idols, " Get you hence, for what have I any more to do with idols?" Hosea 14. 8, compared with verses 2-6. So says the assured soul, Away pride, away passion, away worldly-mindedness, away uncleanness, away uncharitableness, for what have I any more to do with you? Assurance makes the soul speak to sin as David speaks to sinners : Ps. 119. 115, " Depart from me, ye workers of iniquity; for I will keep the commandments of my God " : so says the assured soul, Depart from me, O my lusts, for I have tasted of the love of God, and I have given up myself wholly and only to God, and I cannot but keep the commandments of my God. The Jewish Rabbins report, that the same night that Israel departed out of Egypt towards Canaan, all the idols and idolatrous temples in Egypt were broken down by lightning and earthquakes. So when Christ and assurance come to be set up in the soul, all the idols of Satan and a man's own heart are cast down, and cast out as an abomination. Sound assurance puts a man upon " purifying himself, even as Christ is pure," 1 John 3. 2, 3. The assured Christian knows, that it is dangerous to sin against light, that it is more dangerous to sin against love, that it is most dangerous to sin against love revealed and manifested. God may well say to such a Christian, " Is this thy kindness to thy friend?" To sin under assurance, is to sin against great mercy, it is to sin against the highest hopes of glory; and this will certainly provoke God to be angry. 1 Kings 11. 9, "And the Lord was angry with Solomon, because his heart was turned from the Lord God of Israel, that had appeared to him twice." To sin under assurance, is to sin in paradise; it is to sin under the flaming sword, it is to sin in the suburbs of heaven, it is to run the hazard of losing that favour " that is better than life," of that " joy that is unspeakable and full of glory," and of that "peace that passes understanding." To sin under assurance, is to cast reproach upon Christ, to grieve the Spirit, to wound conscience, to weaken your graces, to blur your evidences, to usher in calamities, to embitter your mercies, and to provoke the tempter to triumph over your Saviour. Verily, that assurance is but presumption that works men to play with sin, to be bold with sin, to make light of sin, to walk on in ways of sin. Such assurance will never bring a man to heaven, it will never keep him from dropping into hell, yea, it will double his damnation, and make him the most miserable among all damned, miserable, forlorn spirits. Ah, Lord! from such an assurance deliver my soul; and give me more and more of that divine assurance that makes sin to be more hateful than hell, and that makes the soul to be more careful to avoid the one, than it is fearful of falling into the other.

7. IT IS ATTENDED BY LOVE, HUMILITY, AND JOY

(7) *The seventh difference.* Seventhly, A well-grounded assurance *is always attended with three fair handmaids, or with three sweet companions,*

(1) *The first handmaid.* The first is *love*. Oh! the assurance of divine favour doth mightily inflame a man's love to Christ. Mary Magdalene loved much; Christ's love to her drew out her love very much to Christ, Luke 7. Assurance makes the soul sing it out with that sweet singer of Israel, "I will dearly love thee, O Lord, my strength," Ps. 18. 2. Lovers know not how to keep silence; lovers of Christ are full of gracious expressions. *Magnes amoris est amor;* the

magnet of love is love. It is impossible for a soul not to love Christ, that knows he is beloved of Christ. Christ's love constrains the soul to love, not by forcible but loving necessity. Praxiteles, the Greek sculptor, exquisitely drew love, taking the pattern from that passion which he felt in his own heart. When a believer finds the heart of Christ to be beating towards him, his heart will strongly beat towards Christ. Divine love is like a rod of myrtle, which, as Pliny reports, makes the traveller that carries it in his hand, that he shall never be faint, or weary of walking or loving. Love alone overpowereth all power. Love is the diadem; none but the queen must wear it. Love is the wedding garment; none but the spouse can fit it. Love is a magnet to draw, as well as a fire to warm. He that doth not love Christ was never assured of the love of Christ.

(2) *The second handmaid,* or companion that attends a well-grounded assurance, is *humility.* David, under assurance, cries out, "I am a worm and no man," Ps. 22. 6; Abraham, under assurance, cries out, that he is but "dust and ashes"; Jacob, under assurance, cries out, that he was "not worthy of the least of all mercies"; Job, under assurance, "abhors himself in dust and ashes"; Moses had the honour and the happiness to speak with God "face to face"; he was very much in God's books, in God's favour; and yet a more humble soul the earth did never bear. The great apostle Paul, under all the revelations and glorious manifestations of God to him, counts himself "less than the least of all saints," Eph. 3. 8. That is presumption, that is a delusion of the devil, and no sound assurance, that puffs and swells the souls of men, that makes men prize themselves above the market, above the value that God hath put upon them.

(3) *The third handmaid,* or companion that attends assurance, is *holy joy.* Ah! this assurance causes the strong waters of consolation to overflow the soul. Assurance raises the strongest joy in the soul: Luke 1. 46, 47, and Mary said, "My soul doth magnify the Lord, and my spirit hath rejoiced in God my Saviour." When a man comes to be assured that God is his Saviour, at once his spirit rejoices in God. This truth is set forth by three parables in Luke 15.

It is found, too, in 1 Pet. 1. 8, 9, "Whom having not seen, ye love; in whom, though now ye see him not, yet believing, ye rejoice with joy unspeakable, and full of glory: receiving the end of your faith, even the salvation of your souls." Oh the joy, the joy, the inexpressible joy that attends a well-grounded assurance! Assurance raises a paradise of delight in the soul. Tertullian saith, *In quibus operamur, in illis et gaudemus,* in what things or persons we act, in those things or persons we rejoice. A Christian, under the power of assurance, works all his works in Christ; in him, therefore, and in him alone, he rejoiceth.

8. IT SPRINGS FROM THE WITNESS OF THE HOLY SPIRIT

(8) *The eighth difference.* Eighthly, and lastly, A well-grounded assurance *sometimes springs from the testimony and witness of the Spirit of God.* The Spirit sometimes witnesses to a believer's spirit that he is born of God, that he is beloved of God, that he hath union and communion with God, and that he shall reign for ever with God: Rom. 8. 26, "The Spirit itself beareth witness with our spirits, that we are the children of God." The Spirit itself witnesseth not only the gifts and graces of the Spirit, but the Spirit itself witnesseth together with our own spirit, that we are the children of God. Sometimes the saints have two witnesses joining their testimonies together to confirm and establish them in these blessed and glorious truths, that they are the sons of God and heirs of glory; and this is their honour as well as their comfort, that the blessed Spirit should bear witness at the bar of their consciences that they are the sons of God: 1 Cor. 2. 12, "Now we have received, not the spirit of the world, but the Spirit which is of God; that we might know the things that are freely given to us of God"; that is, that we may know our election, vocation, justification, sanctification, and glorification. A man may receive many things that are freely given of God, and yet not know them till the Spirit comes and makes them known to the soul.

The characteristics of the Holy Spirit's witness

Quest. But you may say to me, How shall we know the

whispering of the Holy Spirit from the hissing of the old serpent? How shall we know the report, the witness, and testimony of the Spirit of Christ, from that report, witness, and testimony that the old serpent deludes and deceives many by, in these days wherein he mostly appears in his angelical robes?

Ans. I answer, you may know the whispering of the Spirit from the hissing of the old serpent by these following things, which I desire that you would seriously consider, as you value the peace and settlement, the satisfaction, consolation, and salvation of your own souls.

1. IT IS INWARD AND SECRET

(1) *The first difference.* First, The Spirit of Christ *doth not witness by any outward voice, as God did from heaven of Christ, Mat. 3. 17; nor by an angel, as to the Virgin Mary, Luke 1. 30-34; but in an inward, secret, glorious, and unspeakable way he bids believers be of good cheer, their sins are forgiven them, as Christ said to the palsied man in the Gospel, Mat. 9. 2.* And this truth is to be solemnly observed against those poor deceived and deluded souls in these days that would make the world believe that they have had such and such glorious things made known by an outward, audible voice from heaven. It is much to be feared that they never found the inward, the sweet, the secret, the powerful testimony and report of the Spirit of Christ, that boast, and brag, and rest so much upon an outward testimony. In 1 Kings 19. 11-13, you read of "a great strong wind that rent the mountains, and brake in pieces the rocks: but the Lord was not in the wind: and after the wind there was an earthquake; but the Lord was not in the earthquake: and after the earthquake a fire; but the Lord was not in the fire: and after the fire there was a still small voice," and the Lord spake to Elijah in that still small voice. Ah, Christians! the Spirit of the Lord makes not a noise, but he comes in a still small voice, as I may say, and makes a soft and secret report to the soul, that it is beloved, that it is pardoned, and that it shall be for ever glorified.

2. IT IS GAINED IN HOLY WAYS

(2) *The second difference.* Secondly, The testimony and witness of the Spirit of Christ *is only gained and enjoyed in holy and heavenly ways,* as you may clearly see by comparing the following Scriptures together: Acts 10. 4; Dan. 9. 20-22; Isa. 64. 5; Acts 10. 44. The Spirit of the Lord is a Holy Spirit, and he cannot, he will not, make any report of the love of the Father to the soul out of a way of holiness. Verily, all those glorious reports that many boast they have met with in sinful ways, in wretched and ungodly ways, are from the hissing of the old serpent, and not from the whisperings of the Spirit of grace. I think it is little less than blasphemy for any to affirm, that the blessed Spirit of Christ doth make reports of the love and favour of God to persons walking in ways of wickedness and baseness.

3. IT IS CLEAR, FULL, AND SATISFYING

(3) *The third difference.* Thirdly, The testimony and witness of the Spirit of Christ, *is a clear, a full, a satisfying testimony and witness,* John 14. 17; 1 John 3. 24. The soul sits down under the home-reports of the Spirit, and saith, Lord, it is enough; the soul being full, sits down and sweetly sings it out: " My beloved is mine, and I am his. I am my well-beloved's, and his desire is towards me," Song of Solomon 2. 16, and 7. 10. " The Lord is my portion and the lot of mine inheritance," Ps. 16. 5. " I have none in heaven but thee, neither is there any on earth that I desire in comparison of thee," Ps. 73, 25. " Henceforth is laid up for me a crown of righteousness," 2 Tim 4. 8. " Make haste, my beloved," &c., Song of Solomon, 8. 14. Such power, majesty, and glory, attends the glorious testimony of the Spirit of Christ, as scatters all clouds, as resolves all doubts, as answers all objections, and as silences the wrangling soul. If the testimony of the Spirit of Christ were not a full, satisfying testimony, it could never fill the soul with such joy as is " unspeakable and full of glory," and with " such peace as passes understanding "; if the testimony were not satisfactory, the soul would still be under fears and doubts, the

heart would still be a-wrangling and complaining that it might be left to perish and to find the door of mercy shut against it. If you bring news to a condemned person that the king hath pardoned him, and that he will receive him to favour, and confer such and such dignity upon him, yet this doth not quiet him nor satisfy him, till he knows it is the king's act. Till he is satisfied in that, he cannot say it is enough, he cannot be cheerful, he cannot be full of delight. But when he is satisfied that it is the king's act, that the king hath certainly done this and that for him, then he is satisfied, and then sighing and mourning flies away, and then he rejoices with joy unspeakable. So it is with a believing soul under the testimony and witness of the spirit of Christ.

4. IT IS NOT OPERATIVE IN ALL BELIEVERS

(4) *The fourth difference.* Fourthly, Though the Spirit be a witnessing Spirit, *yet he doth not always witness to believers their adoption, and their interest in Christ.* There is a mighty difference between the working of the Spirit and the witness of the Spirit. There are oftentimes many glorious and efficacious works of the Spirit, as faith, love, repentance, and holiness, where there is not the witness of the Spirit, Isa. 50. 10. David at that very time had the Spirit, and many sweet workings of the Spirit in him and upon him, when he had by sin lost the witness and testimony of the Spirit, Ps. 51. 10-12. Though the Spirit of the Lord be a witnessing and a sealing Spirit, yet he doth not always witness and seal up the love and favour of the Father to believers' souls, as you may see by the following scriptures, and as the experience of many precious Christians can abundantly evidence: Job 23. 8, 9; 1 John 5. 13; Ps. 88 and Ps. 77; Micah 7. 8, 9; Isa. 8. 17. All believers do not see a like need of this testimony, they do not all alike prize this testimony, they do not all alike observe it and make good use of it; and, therefore, it is no wonder if the Spirit be a witnessing Spirit to some and not to others. You do but gratify Satan and wrong your own souls, when you argue that certainly you have not the Spirit, because he is

not a witnessing and a sealing Spirit to your souls. Though it be the office of the Spirit to witness, yet it is not his office always to witness to believers their happiness and blessedness. The Spirit may act one way and in one room of the soul, when he doth not act in another. Sometimes the Spirit works upon the understanding, sometimes upon the will, sometimes upon the affections, sometimes upon faith, sometimes upon fear, sometimes upon love, sometimes upon humility. Our hearts are the Spirit's harps. If a man should always touch one string in an instrument, he would never play various tunes, he would never make pleasant music; no more would the Spirit, if he should be always a-doing one thing in the soul. Therefore he acts variously. Sometimes he will shew himself a quickening Spirit, sometimes an enlightening Spirit, sometimes a rejoicing Spirit, sometimes a sealing Spirit, and always a supporting Spirit.

5. IT IS A SURE TESTIMONY

(5) *The fifth difference.* Fifthly, The testimony and witness of the Spirit *is a sure testimony, a sure witness.* The Spirit is truth itself; he is the great searcher of the deep things of God. The Spirit of the Lord is the discoverer, the confuter, and destroyer of all false spirits. The Spirit is above all possibility of being deceived; he is omnipotent, he is omniscient, he is omnipresent; he is one of the cabinet-council of heaven; he lies and lives in the bosom of the Father, and can call them all by name upon whom the Father hath set his heart, and therefore his testimony must needs be true. It is a surer testimony than if a man should hear a voice from heaven pronouncing him to be happy and blessed. You may safely and securely lay the weight of your souls upon this testimony; it never hath deceived, it never will deceive any that hath leaned upon it. This testimony will be a rock that will bear up a soul, when other false testimonies will be but "a reed of Egypt" that will deceive the soul, that will undo the soul; as I am afraid many in this age of delusion have found by sad experience.

6. IT IS ALWAYS ACCOMPANIED BY THE TESTIMONY OF OUR OWN SPIRIT

(6) *The sixth difference.* Sixthly, The testimony of God's Spirit *is always accompanied with the testimony of our own spirit.* These may be distinguished, but they can never be separated. When the Spirit of God bears his witness for a man, the man's own spirit doth not witness against him. Look, as face answers to face, so doth the witness of a believer's spirit answer to the witness of the Spirit of Christ. Rom. 8. 16, "The Spirit witnesseth together with our spirits that we be the sons of God." Now, if our own consciences do not testify first that we are sons and heirs, the Spirit doth not testify; for the Spirit bears witness together with our spirits. The Word is very express in 1 John 3. 21, "But if our hearts condemn us not, then have we confidence toward God. But if our hearts condemn us, God is greater than our hearts, and knoweth all things." 1 John 5. 8-12, and "There are three that bear witness in earth, the Spirit, and the water, and the blood, and these three agree in one." The Spirit doth witness eminently and efficiently; water and blood witness materially; and our spirits and reason instrumentally. By the Spirit we may understand the Holy Ghost, by whose strength we lay hold on Christ and all his benefits. By water we may understand our regeneration, our sanctification; and by blood we may understand the blood and righteousness of Christ, that is imputed and applied by faith to us. "And these three agree in one," that is, they do all three of one accord testify the same thing.

7. IT IS ALWAYS ACCORDING TO SCRIPTURE

(7) *The seventh difference.* Seventhly, The witness of the Spirit *is ever according to the Word.* There is a sweet harmony between the inward and the outward testimony, between the Spirit of God and the Word of God. The scriptures were all indited by the Spirit, 2 Pet. 1. 20, 21; and therefore the Spirit cannot contradict himself, which he would do, if he should give any testimony contrary to the testimony of the Word. It is blasphemy to make the testi-

mony of the Spirit to contradict the testimony of the Word. The Spirit hath revealed his whole mind in the Word, and he will not give a contrary testimony to what he hath given in the Word. The Word saith, They that are born again, that are new creatures, that believe and repent, shall be saved. But thou art born again, thou art a new creature, thou believest and repentest; therefore thou shalt be saved, saith the Spirit. The Spirit never looseth where the Word bindeth, the Spirit never justifies where the Word condemns, the Spirit never approves where the Word disapproves, the Spirit never blesses where the Word curses. In the Old Testament all revelations were to be examined by the Word, Deut. 13. 1-4. Isa. 8. 20, " To the law and to the testimony: if they speak not according to this word, it is because there is no light (or no morning) in them." So in that of John 16. 13, " The Spirit shall lead you into all truth: for he shall not speak of himself; but what he shall hear, that shall he speak." Here the Holy Ghost is brought in as some messenger or ambassador who only relates things faithfully according to that he hath in charge. Such as look and lean upon the hissing of the old serpent, may have a testimony that they are blessed, against the testimony of the Word; but wherever the Spirit of Christ gives his testimony, it is always according to the Word. Look, as indenture answers to indenture, or as the counterpart exactly answers to the principal conveyance—there is article for article, clause for clause, covenant for covenant, word for word—so doth the testimony of the Spirit exactly answer to the testimony of the Word.

8. IT IS HOLY

(8) *The eighth difference.* Eighthly, *It is a holy witness, a holy testimony.* It is formally, it is originally holy, it is effectually holy. Nothing makes the heart delight more in the love, study, practice, and growth of holiness, than the glorious testimony of the Holy Spirit; and the more clear and full the testimony is, the more holy and gracious it will make the soul. Nothing puts upon the soul such golden engagements to holiness, as the Spirit sealing a man up to the

day of redemption, as the Spirit speaking and sealing peace, love, and pardon to the soul, Ps. 85. 8; 1 Cor. 15. 31; 2 Cor. 5. 14. Nothing makes a man more careful to please Christ, more fearful to offend Christ, more studious to exalt Christ, and more circumspect to walk with Christ, than this testimony of the Spirit of Christ. Verily, that is not the blessed whispering of Christ's Spirit, but the hissing of the old serpent, that makes men bold with sin, that makes men dally with sin, that makes man a servant to sin, that breeds a contempt of ordinances, a neglect of holy duties, a carelessness in walking with God. And from those hissings of the old serpent, O Lord, deliver my soul, and the souls of all thy servants that put their trust in thee!

9. IT IS ONLY BESTOWED ON RENEWED HEARTS

(9) *The ninth difference.* Ninthly and lastly, *Assurance is a jewel, a pearl of such price, that God only bestows it upon renewed hearts.* The Spirit never sets his seal upon any, but upon those that Christ hath first printed his image upon. God gives the white stone, Rev. 2. 17, but only to those from whom he hath taken the heart of stone; Ezek. 36. 25, 26, 27 compared. Christ never tells a man that his name is written in the book of life, till he hath breathed into him spiritual life, Luke 10. 20. Christ never says, "Son, be of good cheer, thy sin is pardoned," till he hath first said, " Be thou healed, be thou cleansed," Luke 5. 18-20. Christ never gives a man a new name that is better than the names of sons and daughters, till he hath made him a new creature, Isa. 56. 5; 2 Cor. 5. 17. Of slaves Christ first makes us sons, before we cry Abba, Father, Rom. 8. 15. Of enemies, he first makes us friends, before he will make us of his court and household, Eph. 2. 13-20. Christ will never hang a pearl in a swine's snout, nor put new wine into old bottles, nor his royal robes upon a leprous back, nor his golden chain about a dead man's neck, nor his glistering crown upon a traitor's head. The Spirit never sets his seal upon any but those that Christ hath first set as a seal upon his heart, Eph. 1. 13; Song of Solomon 8. 6. The Spirit only bears witness to such as hate sin as Christ hates it, and that

love righteousness as Christ loves it, that hate sin more than hell, and that love truth more than life, Ps. 45. 7. A soul sealed by the Spirit will pull out right eyes, and cut off right hands, for Christ; such souls will part with a Benjamin, and offer up an Isaac, for Christ. And this is to be seriously minded against those deceived and deluded souls that remain yet in their blood, and that wallow in their sins, and yet boast and brag of the seal and of the witness and testimony of the Spirit.

And thus I have shewed you the difference between the whisperings of the Spirit and the hissing of the old serpent, between a true testimony and a false.

CHAPTER VII

Answers to several special questions about assurance.

Nine methods whereby assurance may be strengthened and maintained

[1] *The first question.* But methinks I hear some precious souls saying, Sirs! we have, after much praying, weeping, and waiting, gained this pearl of price, assurance; but oh, how shall we do to strengthen it, how shall we do to keep it? Satan will labour to weaken our assurance, and to rob us of this jewel that is more worth than a world; what means must we use to strengthen our assurance and to secure it?

Now to this question I shall give these following answers:

First, If you would have your assurance strengthened and maintained, then *keep close to soul-strengthening ways, be serious and sincere, be diligent and constant in the use of those means and ways wherein you first gained assurance,* as prayer, reading and hearing the Word, breaking of bread, and the communion of saints. A conscientious and warm-hearted use of holy and heavenly means is blessed, not only with a preservation of assurance, but likewise with an addition and increase of it. The ways of God, and his goings in the sanctuary, wrought wonders upon thee when thou wast dead, how much more will they work upon thee and for thee now thou art by grace made alive? He that will not apply himself to God's strengthening methods will quickly find his assurance weakened, if not wholly decayed. He that thinks himself too good for ordinances, will quickly grow weak in his assurance. The choicest prophets, and highest apostles, if I may so speak, that had attained to the fullest assurance, kept close to the ways and precious institutions of Christ. Verily, those that pretend to live above ordinances, and yet live below them, never knew by experience what a mercy it was to have a well-grounded assurance, or else they have lost that blessed assurance that once they had.

Secondly, If you would strengthen and maintain your assurance, then *dwell much upon your spiritual and eternal privileges,* viz., your adoption, justification, reconciliation, &c., 1 Pet. 2. 9. This you shall find by experience will mightily tend to the strengthening and maintaining of your assurance. He that neglects this rule will quickly find his sun to set in a cloud, his harp to be turned into mourning, and his organ into the voice of them that weep, Job 30. 31.

Thirdly, If you would strengthen and maintain your assurance, then *see to it that your hearts run more out to Christ than to assurance;* to the sun than to the beams, to the fountain than to the stream, to the root than to the branch, to the cause than to the effect, Song of Solomon 1. 13. Assurance is sweet, but Christ is more sweet. Assurance is lovely, but Christ is altogether lovely, Song of Solomon 5. 16. Assurance is precious, but Christ is most precious, Prov. 3. 15. Though assurance be a flower that yields much comfort and delight, yet it is but a flower. Though assurance be a precious box, yet it is but a box. Though assurance be a ring of gold, yet it is but a ring of gold. And what is the flower to the root, what is the box to the ointment, what is the ring to the pearl? No more is assurance as compared with Christ. Therefore let thy eye and heart, first, most, and last, be fixed upon Christ, then will assurance bed and board with thee; otherwise thou wilt quickly find thy summer to be turned into winter.

Fourthly, If you would strengthen and maintain your assurance, then see to it *that your hearts are more taken up with Christ than with your graces.* Though grace be a glorious creature, yet it is but a creature; therefore let grace have your eye, but be sure that Christ has your heart. Christ must have your heart. Christ will not allow your very graces to be co-rivals with him. He that minds his graces more than Christ, or that sets his graces upon the throne with Christ, will quickly find what it is to lose the face and favour of Christ. Your graces are but Christ's servants and hand-maids; you may look upon them, but you must not make a match with them. It is a reproach to Christ, that those who have married the master should at the same time match with the servant. The queen may look upon her glistering courtiers, but she must live upon the king; the wife may take pleasure in her lovely babes, but she must live upon her husband, and be most observant of her husband. So gracious souls may look upon their graces, but they must live upon king Jesus; they may take pleasure in their graces, but they must live upon Christ, and be most observant of Christ. This is the way to keep Christ and assurance, and he that walks contrary to this rule will soon find the loss of both. Christ will be *Alexander* or *Nemo*; that is, he will be all in all, or he will be nothing at all. Though his coat was once divided, yet he will never suffer his crown to be divided, John 19. 23; Isa. 42. 8.

Fifthly, If you would have your assurance strengthened and maintained, then *labour to use it for the strengthening of your soul against temptations, to the fencing of your soul against corruptions, to the raising of your resolutions, to the inflaming of your affections, to the bettering of your Christian walk.* Assurance is a pearl of price; he that will keep it must make good use of it. The ready way to maintain our natural strength, and to increase it, is to use it well. Assurance is one of the choicest and chiefest talents that ever God entrusted man with, and he that doth not put it to good use and employ it, will quickly lose it. God will not suffer so golden a talent to gather rust, Mat. 25. 28. Win gold and wear gold, make use of gold and keep gold; win assurance and wear assurance, make use of assurance and keep assurance. Dionysius the elder, being informed of one that had hidden great store of money, commanded him upon pain of death to bring it to him, which he did, but not all; but with the remainder he went and dwelt in another country, where he bought an inheritance, and fell upon some employment, which, when Dionysius heard, he sent him his money again which he had taken from him, saying, "Now thou knowest how to use riches, take that I had from thee." I shall leave you to make the application.

Sixthly, If you would have your assurance strengthened

and maintained, then *walk humbly with your God,* Micah 6. 8. God makes the humble man's heart his house to dwell in: Isa. 57. 15, " Thus saith the high and lofty One that inhabiteth eternity, whose name is Holy; I dwell in the high and holy place, with him also that is of a contrite and humble spirit, to revive the spirit of the humble, and to revive the heart of the contrite ones." The highest heavens and the lowest hearts are the habitations wherein the Holy One delights to dwell. Now this phrase, " I will dwell with the humble," takes in several things: 1. It includes God's care of the humble. 2. It takes in God's assisting and strengthening of the humble. 3. It takes in God's protection; " I will dwell with the humble," that is, I will protect him and secure him, Job 22. 29. 4. It takes in God's sympathising with the humble. 5. It takes in God's applying all suitable good to the humble, Isa. 57. 18, and 63. 9. 6. It takes in God's ruling and overruling the heart and the affections of the humble. 7. It takes in God's teaching of the humble. But, 8, and lastly, It includes and takes in a clearer, a fuller, and a larger manifestation and communication of God to humble souls, Ps. 10. 17, and 25. 9. Ah! saith God, I will dwell with the humble; that is, I will more richly, more abundantly, and more gloriously manifest and make known my grace and glory, my goodness and sweetness, my loving-kindness and tenderness, to humble souls. Now tell me, humble souls, will not God's dwelling thus with you contribute very much to the strengthening and maintaining of your assurance? James 4. 6, " But he giveth more grace: wherefore he saith, God resisteth the proud " (or as the Greek word emphatically signifies, " he sets himself in battle array against the proud "), " but giveth grace to the humble." Humility is both a grace, and a vessel to receive grace. God pours in grace into humble souls, as men pour liquor into an empty vessel. And verily, the more grace you have, the more will your assurance be strengthened and maintained. Well! remember this, the humble man's mercies are the sweetest mercies, the greatest mercies, the most growing and thriving mercies, the most blessed and sanctified mercies, and the most lasting and abiding mercies. Therefore, as you would have your assurance strengthened and maintained, walk humbly with your God; I say again, walk humbly, walk humbly with your God, and you shall wear the crown of assurance to your grave.

Seventhly, If you would keep and maintain you assurance, then *take heed and watch against those particular sins by which other saints have lost their assurance.* Take heed of carnal confidence and security. David lost his assurance by not guarding his heart against those evils, Ps. 30. 6, 7. Again, take heed of a light, careless, and negligent spirit in holy and spiritual things. The spouse in the song of Solomon lost her assurance, and her sweet communion with Christ, by her careless spirit, Song of Solomon 5. 2, 3, 6, compared. Again, take heed of a stout and unyielding spirit under the afflicting hand of God; this made God hide his face from them, Isa. 57. 17. In a word, take heed of tasting of forbidden fruit, remembering what Adam lost by a taste.

Eighthly, If you would maintain and keep your assurance, then *frequently and seriously consider the wonderful difficulty of recovering assurance when it is lost.* Oh! the sighs, the groans, the complaints, the prayers, the tears, the heart-rending, and the soul-bleeding that the recovery of thy lost assurance will cost. The gaining of assurance at first cost thee dear, but the regaining of it, if thou shouldst be so unhappy as to lose it, will put thee to more pains and charge. Of the two, it is easier to keep assurance now thou hast it, than to recover it when thou hast lost it. It is easier to keep the house in repair, than when it is fallen to build it up.

Ninthly, and lastly, *Consider solemnly the sad and woeful evils and inconveniences that will certainly follow upon the loss of your assurance.* I will only touch upon a few.

(1) None of the precious things of Christ will be so sweet to thee as formerly they have been.

(2) You will neither be so fervent in duty, nor so frequent in duty, nor so abundant in duty, nor so spiritual in duty, nor so lively in duty, nor so cheerful in duty, as formerly you have been.

(3) Afflictions will sooner sink you, temptations will

sooner overcome you, oppositions will sooner discourage you.

(4) Your mercies will be bitter, your life a burden, and death a terror to you; you will be weary of living, and yet afraid of dying.

Six methods whereby souls which have lost assurance may be kept from fainting

Now, the second question is this: Suppose souls have not been so careful to keep and maintain their assurance as they should have been, but upon one account or another have left that blessed assurance that once they had; how may such sad souls be supported and kept from fainting, sinking, and languishing under the loss of assurance?

To this question I shall give these following answers:

First, Souls that have lost that sweet assurance that once they had, may be supported and kept from fainting and sinking *by considering, that though they have lost their assurance, yet they have not lost their sonship*; for once sons, always sons! You are sons, though dejected sons; you are sons, though comfortless sons; you are sons, though mourning sons, Rom. 8. 15-17. Once children, always children; once heirs, always heirs; once beloved, always beloved; once happy, always happy: 2 Sam. 23. 5, " Although my house be not so with God; yet he hath made with me an everlasting covenant, ordered in all things, and sure: for this is all my salvation, and all my desire, although he make it not to grow." Well, says David, though neither myself nor my house have been so exact and perfect in our walkings before God as we should, for we have broken our covenants with him, and dealt unworthily by him, and turned our backs upon him, yet he hath made with me an everlasting covenant, he hath engaged himself to an everlasting covenant, that he will be my Father, and that I shall be his son. And this is my salvation and the everlasting ground of consolation and support to my soul.

The *second* support is this, Consider, *that though your comfort, joy, and peace, doth depend much upon your assurance, yet your eternal happiness and blessedness doth not depend upon your assurance.* If it did, you might be happy and miserable in a day, aye, in an hour. Your happiness lies in your union with God, in your communion with God, in your interest in God, and not in your seeing and knowing your interest; your joy and comfort lies in your seeing and knowing your interest in God, but your everlasting happiness lies in your being interested in God. The welfare and happiness of the child lies in the interest that he hath in his father, but the joy and comfort of the child lies in his seeing, in his knowing, of his interest in his father. It is so between the Lord and believers: Ps. 144. 15, "Happy is the people that is in such a case; yea, happy is that people whose God is the Lord." Among the philosophers there were two hundred and eighty opinions concerning happiness, some affirming happiness to lie in one thing, some in another. Ah! but by the Spirit and Word we are taught that happiness lies in our oneness with God, in our nearness and dearness to God, and in our conformity to God. Mark, the Scripture pronounces him happy whose hope is in God, though he lack assurance: Ps. 146. 5, "Happy is he that hath the God of Jacob for his help, whose hope is in the Lord his God." Again, he is happy that trusteth in the Lord, though for the present he lack assurance: Prov. 16. 20, "And whoso trusteth in the Lord, happy is he." Again, he is happy that feareth the Lord, that hath set up God as the object of his fear, though he lack assurance of the love of God: Prov. 28. 14, "Happy is the man that feareth always": that fears to offend, that fears to disobey, that fears to rebel. Again, he is happy that believes in Christ, that rests and stays upon Christ, as the Scriptures everywhere testify, though he may lack assurance.

Happiness lies not in any transient act of the Spirit, as assurance is, but in the more permanent and lasting acts of the Spirit. The philosopher could say that, "he was never a happy man that might afterwards become miserable." If a man's eternal happiness did lie in the assurance of his happiness, then might a man be crowned with Xerxes' steersman in the morning, and beheaded with him in the evening of the same day.

But this is the believer's blessedness, that his condition is always good, though he doth not always see it to be good; that his state is always safe, though it be not always comfortable.

The *third* support to keep those precious souls from fainting and sinking that have lost the sweet assurance that once they had, is to consider that *though their loss be the greatest and saddest loss that could befall them, yet it is a recoverable loss, it is a loss that may be recovered, as the following scriptures do clearly evidence.* Ps. 71. 20, 21, and 42. 5, 7, 8; Isa. 54. 7, 8; Micah 7. 18, 19; Song of Solomon 3. 4; Ps. 84. 11, &c. And doth not this age, as well as former ages, furnish us with many instances of this kind? Doubtless many there are among the precious sons and daughters of Zion that have lost this pearl of price, and after waiting, weeping, and wrestling, have found it again; therefore be not discouraged, O sighing, losing souls! In the loss of temporals, it is a great support to men's spirits that their loss may be made up, and why should it not be so in spirituals also?

The *fourth* support to keep their hearts from sinking, and breaking that have lost the sweet assurance that once they had, is, seriously to consider *that your loss is no greater, and no sadder, than what the noblest and the choicest saints have sustained, as you may see by comparing the following scriptures together.* Ps. 30. 6, 7, and 51. 12; Job 23. 8, 9; Isa. 8. 17. Those who were once the worthies of this world, and who are now triumphing in that other world among the princes of glory, sometimes lost the sweet assurance and sense of divine love and favour that they usually enjoyed; therefore let not your spirits faint and fail. In temporal trials it is a comfort and a support to have companions with us; and why should it not much more be so in spirituals? Acts 16.

The *fifth* support to bear up their spirits that have lost the sweet assurance that once they had, is for them *to remember, and seriously mind, that though they have lost assurance, yet they have not lost the blessed breathings and sweet influences of the Spirit upon them.* Witness their love to Christ, their longing after Christ, their fear of offending

313

Christ, their care to please Christ, their high esteem of Christ, and their mourning for the dishonours that by themselves or others are done to Christ. A man may enjoy the warmth, heat, and influence of the sun, when he hath lost the sight of the sun. David had lost his assurance, he had lost the sight of the sun; and yet he enjoyed the warmth and influences of it upon his heart, as is evident in Psalm 51.

Though thy sun, O Christian, be set in a cloud, yet it will rise again, and in the interim thou hast and dost enjoy the warmth and influences of the sun; therefore sorrow not, mourn not, as one without hope. Those warm influences that the Sun of righteousness hath now upon thy heart, are infallible evidences that he will shine forth and smile upon thee as in the days of old; therefore let thy bow still abide in strength, Ps. 42. 5, 7, 8, 11.

The *sixth* support to keep their hearts from fainting and sinking that have lost that sweet assurance that once they had, is seriously to consider, *that it will be but as a day, but as a short day, before the loss of their assurance shall be made up with a more clear, full, perfect, and complete enjoyment of God.* Ere long, O mourning soul, thy sun shall rise and never set, thy joy and comfort shall be always fresh and green; God shall comfort thee on every side, it shall be night with thee no more, thou shalt be always in the bosom of God, Isa. 57. 18-20. Ps. 71. 20, 21, "Thou which hast shewed me great and sore troubles shalt quicken me again, and shalt bring me up again from the depth of the earth. Thou shalt increase my greatness, and comfort me on every side." The day is at hand, O perplexed soul, when thou shalt have smiles without frowns, light without darkness, day without night, wine without water, sweet without bitter, and joy without sorrow.

The year of jubilee is at hand. Thou now sowest in tears, thou shalt shortly reap in joy; yea, "everlasting joy shall be upon thy head," and "sorrow and sighing shall flee away"; therefore faint not.

*Five methods whereby souls which have lost assurance
may recover it*

The third question is this; What means must souls use to
recover assurance when it is lost?

I shall give a few short answers to this question, and so
draw to a close.

First, If thou wouldst recover assurance, then thou must
*labour diligently to find out that sin, that Achan, that hath
robbed thee of thy assurance.* Surely it is not for infirmities,
but enormities, that God hath put out thy candle, and
caused thy sun to set at noon. Surely thou hast been feeding
on, I say not tasting of, forbidden fruit, that God hath
stripped thee of thy robes, and taken the crown from off
thy head, and turned thee out of paradise. But this is not
all.

Therefore, in the *second* place, *weep much, mourn much,
over the Achan, over those wickednesses that have turned
thy day into night, thy rejoicing into sighing.* David doth
thus in Psalm 51, and God takes him up from his knees, and
restores to him " the joy of his salvation." Though God be
displeased with your sins, yet he is well-pleased with your
tears. The promise is, that he will "revive the spirit of the
contrite," Isa. 57. 15. It is said of Adam that he turned his
face towards the garden of Eden, and from his heart lamented his fall. Ah! losing souls, turn your face towards
heaven, and from your hearts lament your fall, lament your
loss. Nothing moves God like penitent tears. No sooner
doth Ephraim weep over his sins, but the compassions of
God are stirring towards him, and God cannot hold but he
must proclaim to the world that mourning Ephraim, be-
moaning Ephraim, is his dear son, his pleasant child, and
that he will " surely have mercy on him "; or, as the Hebrew
hath it, " I will have mercy, have mercy on him," or " I will
abundantly have mercy on him," Jer. 31. 18-20. When our
hearts are set to weep over our sins, God will so act in ways
of love towards us, that it shall not be long night with our
souls. God will never suffer them to be drowned in sorrow
that are set upon drowning their sins in penitential tears.

The Jews have a saying, that since the destruction of Jerusalem, the door of prayers hath been shut; but the door of tears was never shut, saith one. God hath by promise engaged himself that those that "sow in tears shall reap in joy," Ps. 126. 5. The tears of the saints have such a kind of omnipotency in them, that God himself cannot withstand them: 2 Kings 20. 5, "I have seen thy tears, behold, I will heal thee; on the third day thou shalt go up unto the house of the Lord."

Thirdly, If you would recover assurance, then *sit not down discouraged, but be up and doing.* Remember what a pearl of price thou hast lost, and "repent and do thy first works," Rev. 2. 4, 5. Fall close to the good old work of believing, meditating, examining, praying, hearing, and mourning. Begin life again, and set afresh upon those very ways by which at first thou didst get assurance; fall upon family duties, apply thyself to public ordinances, be much in secret services; stir up every gift that is in thee, stir up every grace that is in thee, stir up all the life that is in thee, and never leave blowing till thou hast blowed thy little spark into a flame; never leave turning thy penny, till thou hast turned thy penny into a pound; never leave improving thy mite, till thy mite be turned into a million. God will be found in the use of means, and he will restore our lost mercies in the use of means, Ps. 22. 26. But this is not all.

Therefore, in the *fourth* place, *wait patiently upon the Lord.* David did so, and at length, the Lord brought him out of a horrible pit, or out of a pit of noise and confusion, and set his feet upon a rock, and established his goings, and put a new song of praise into his mouth, Ps. 40. 1-3. God never hath failed, and never will fail the waiting soul. Though God loves to try the patience of his children, yet he doth not love to tire out the patience of his children; therefore he will not contend for ever, neither will he be always wroth, lest the spirits of his people should fail, Isa. 57. 16-19. Assurance is a jewel worth waiting for. It is a pearl that God gives to none but such as have waited long at mercy's door. It is a crown that every one must win by patient waiting before he can wear it. God doth not think the greatest mercies too good for waiting souls, though he knows the least mercy is too good for impatient souls. The breasts of the promises lie fair and open to waiting souls, Isa. 30. 18, and 64. 4, and 49. 23. The waiting soul shall have anything of God, but the froward and impatient soul gets nothing from God but frowns, and blows, and wounds, and broken bones. Sad souls would do well to make that text their bosom companion, John 14. 18, "I will not leave you comfortless," or orphans, "I will come to you." And also Heb. 10. 36, 37, "For ye have need of patience, that after ye have done the will of God, ye might receive the promise. For yet a little while" (as it is in the Greek), "and he that shall come will come, and will not tarry."

Fifthly and lastly, If you would recover assurance, then *take heed of refusing comforts when God brings them to your door; take heed of throwing away gospel cordials.* This was Asaph's sin: "My soul refused to be comforted." God comes and offers love to the soul, and the soul refuses it; God comes and spreads the promises of consolation before the soul, and the soul refuses to look upon them; God comes and makes tenders of the riches of grace, and the soul refuses to accept of them. Sometimes the hand, the man that brings the cordial, is not liked, and therefore men refuse it. Well! remember this: when gold is offered, men care not how great or how base he is that offers it. Neither should we care by whom the cordials and consolations of the gospel are offered to us, whether they are offered by the hand of Isaiah, a prophet of the blood-royal, as some think, or by Amos, from amongst the herdsmen of Tekoa. If the sweetmeats of heaven are set before thee, it is thy wisdom and thy duty to taste of them, and to feed upon them, without stumbling at the hand that presents them.

Conclusion

I shall now make a few short uses of what hath been said, and so conclude.

[1] *The first use.* You that have assurance, *be thankful for it.* It is a jewel worth more than heaven and earth; therefore be thankful. Assurance is a mercy nobly-descen-

ded; it is from above. Man is not born with it in his heart, as he is with a tongue in his mouth, James 1. 17. Assurance is a peculiar mercy; it is a flower of paradise that God sticks only in his children's bosoms. Assurance is a mercy-sweetening mercy; it is a mercy that puts the garland upon all our mercies. Assurance makes every bitter sweet, and every sweet more sweet. He enjoys little that lacks it, he lacks nothing that enjoys it; therefore be you thankful that have and do find the sweetness of it.

If Philip, king of Macedonia, rejoiced that Alexander, his son, was born in the days of Aristotle, how much more cause have you to rejoice, upon whose heads the Lord hath put the crown of assurance, a crown of more worth and weight than all princes' crowns in the world.

[2] *The second use.* If God hath given you assurance, then *do not envy the outward felicity and happiness of the men of the world*, Ps. 37. 17, 18; Prov. 23. 17. Indeed what are mountains of dust to mountains of gold? what are the stones of the street to rocks of pearl? what are crowns of thorns to crowns of gold? No more are all the treasures, honours, pleasures, and favours of this world to assurance. The envious man hath so many tortures as the envied hath praisers. Envy justly kills and torments the envious. The men of the world are real objects of pity, but not of envy. Who envies the prisoner at the bar? Who envies the malefactor that is going to execution? Who envies the dead man that is going to his grave? God hath done more for thee by giving thee assurance than if he had given thee all the world, yea, ten thousand worlds.

When the Spanish ambassador boasted that his master was king of such a place, and of such a place, and of such a place, the French ambassador answered, " My master is king of France, king of France, king of France "; signifying thereby that France was of as much worth as all the kingdoms under the power of the king of Spain. Ah, Christians! when the men of the world shall cry out, Oh, their riches! oh, their honours! oh, their preferments! you may well cry out, Oh, assurance, assurance, assurance! there being more real worth and glory in that than is to be found in all the wealth and glory of the world; therefore do not envy the outward prosperity and felicity of worldly men.

[3] *The third use.* If God hath given you assurance, then *give not way to slavish fears.* Fear not the scorn and reproaches of men, fear not that you will suffer want. God will not deny him a crust to whom he hath given a Christ; he will not deny him a crumb upon whom he hath bestowed a crown; he will not deny him lesser mercies upon whom he hath bestowed assurance, which is the prince of mercies. Fear not death, for why shouldst thou fear death, that hast assurance of a better life?

[4] *The fourth use.* If God hath given you a well-grounded assurance of your everlasting happiness and blessedness, then question *his love no more.* God doth not love to have his love at every turn called in question by those that he hath once assured of his love; he doth expect, that as no sin of ours doth make any substantial alteration in his affections to us, so not even his sharpest dispensations should make any alteration in our thoughts and affections towards him, Ps. 89. 30-35; Jer. 31. 3; Eccles. 9. 8.

[5] *The fifth use.* If God hath given you assurance, then *live holily, live angelically, keep your garments pure and white, walk with an even step, be shining lights,* Rev. 3. 4; Mat. 5. 16. Your happiness here is your holiness, and in heaven your highest happiness will be your perfect holiness. Holiness differs nothing from happiness, but in name. Holiness is happiness in the bud, and happiness is holiness at the full. Happiness is nothing but the quintessence of holiness. The more holy any man is, the more the Lord loves him, John 14. 21-23.

Augustine doth excellently observe, in his tract on John 1. 14, "that God loved the humanity of Christ more than that of any other man, because he was fuller of grace and truth than any other man." The philosopher could say, "Without virtue, God is but an empty name." So are all our professions without holiness. Holiness is the very marrow and quintessence of all religion. Holiness is God stamped and printed upon the soul; it is Christ formed in the heart; it is our light, our life, our beauty, our glory, our joy, our crown, our heaven, our all. The holy soul is happy in life, and blessed in death, and shall be transcendently glorious in the morning of the resurrection, when Christ shall say, Lo, here am I, and my holy ones, who are my joy; Lo, here am I, and my holy ones, who are my crown; and therefore, upon the heads of these holy ones will I set an immortal crown. Even so, Amen! Lord Jesus.